Philosophy in the Aristotelian-Thomist Tradition

Philosophy in the Aristotelian-Thomist Tradition

A Primer

DANIEL LOWERY

RESOURCE *Publications* • Eugene, Oregon

PHILOSOPHY IN THE ARISTOTELIAN-THOMIST TRADITION
A Primer

Copyright © 2024 Daniel Lowery. All rights reserved. Except for brief quotations in critical publications or reviews, no part of this book may be reproduced in any manner without prior written permission from the publisher. Write: Permissions, Wipf and Stock Publishers, 199 W. 8th Ave., Suite 3, Eugene, OR 97401.

Resource Publications
An Imprint of Wipf and Stock Publishers
199 W. 8th Ave., Suite 3
Eugene, OR 97401

www.wipfandstock.com

PAPERBACK ISBN: 979-8-3852-1223-1
HARDCOVER ISBN: 979-8-3852-1224-8
EBOOK ISBN: 979-8-3852-1225-5

01/30/24

Except where indicated, Scripture texts in this work are taken from the New American Bible, revised edition © 2010, 1991, 1986, 1970 Confraternity of Christian Doctrine, Washington, D.C. and are used by permission of the copyright owner. All Rights Reserved. No part of the New American Bible may be reproduced in any form without permission in writing from the copyright owner.

Contents

List of Figures | ix

Preface | xi

1   Introduction to the Aristotelean-Thomist Tradition | 1
    101. Philosophy | 1
    102. Philosophy and the Catholic Church | 2
    103. Realism | 4
    104. The Aristotelian-Thomist Tradition | 6
    105. Historical and Cultural Contexts | 9
    106. The Age of Mythology | 10
    107. The History of Philosophy | 11
    108. The Presocratic Era | 13
    109. The "Golden Age" of Greek Philosophy | 14
    110. Medieval Philosophy | 17
    111. Renaissance Philosophy | 20
    112. Enlightenment Philosophy | 20
    113. Nineteenth Century Philosophy | 22
    114. Twentieth Century Philosophy | 25

2   Metaphysics | 32
    201. Metaphysics | 32
    202. Key Concerns of Metaphysics | 33
    203. Metaphysical Realism | 33
    204. The Catholic Church and Metaphysical Realism | 35
    205. Alternative Views | 35
    206. A Graphical Display of Metaphysical Realism | 39
    207. Existence | 40
    208. Being | 41
    209. Actual vs. Potential Being | 43

  210. Mind-dependent Being | 47
  211. Substance | 49
  212. Form and Matter | 52
  213. Nature | 56
  214. Essence | 56
  215. Accidents, Properties, and Attributes | 58
  216. Transcendental Properties | 61
  217. Causation and Change | 63

3 Epistemology | 67
  301. Epistemology | 67
  302. Key Concerns of Epistemological Realism | 68
  303. Epistemological Realism | 68
  304. The Catholic Church and Epistemology | 70
  305. Alternative Views | 72
  306. A Chart Comparing Aspects of Epistemological Realism to Certain Alternative Epistemologies | 74
  307. Epistemological Realism and That Which Can Be Known | 75
  308. Other Perspectives Pertaining to That Which Can Be Known | 76
  309. The Nature of Knowledge | 77
  310. Types of Knowledge | 77
  311. Epistemological Realism and Knowledge Justification | 79
  312. Enlightenment Epistemologies and Knowledge Justification | 82
  313. Epistemological Realism and Evidence | 86
  314. Other Perspectives and Evidence | 90
  315. Epistemological Realism and Method(s) | 91
  316. Other Perspectives and Method(s) | 93
  317. Propositions | 94

4 Ethics, Morality, and Justice | 98
  401. The Good, the Moral, and the Just | 98
  402. Ethical Frameworks | 98
  403. Key Concerns of Ethical Realists | 99
  404. Ethical Realism | 100
  405. The Catholic Church and Ethical Realism | 101
  406. Alternative Views | 102
  407. Human Nature in the Aristotelian-Thomist Tradition | 106
  408. Alternative Views of Human Nature | 106
  409. The Good in the Aristotelian-Thomist Tradition | 108
  410. Alternative Views of the Good | 110
  411. A Disjunction in Ethical and Moral Thinking | 112

412. The Moral in the Aristotelian-Thomist Tradition | 114
413. Alternative Views of the Moral | 118
414. The Just in the Aristotelian-Thomist Tradition | 120
415. Alternative Views of the Just | 122

5 More Recent Expressions of Thomism | 133
501. New Directions | 133
502. Neo-Thomism | 135
503. Transcendental Thomism | 136
504. Existential Thomism | 138
505. Analytic Thomism | 143
506. Personalism | 146
507. Virtue Ethics | 150
508. Catholic Social Teaching | 150

Appendix 1: Reflection Questions | 153
Chapter 1: Introduction to Philosophy in the Aristotelian-Thomist Tradition | 153
Chapter 2: Metaphysics | 154
Chapter 3: Epistemology | 155
Chapter 4: Ethics, Morality, and Justice | 157
Chapter 5: More Recent Expressions of Thomism | 158

Appendix 2: Methods | 160

Appendix 3: Syllabus | 175

Appendix 4: Critical Thinking Questions | 181

Bibliography | 183

Name Index | 191

Subject Index | 195

List of Figures

Figure 1: Metaphysical Realism in the Aristotelian-Thomist Tradition | 39

Figure 2: Chart Comparing Aspects of Epistemological Realism to Certain Alternative Epistemologies | 75

Figure 3: Traditional Ethical Frameworks | 99

Figure 4: Post-Enlightenment Ethical Frameworks | 113

Preface

This text was written for a particular audience: men in formation for the diaconate in the Roman Catholic Church. As part of their formation, inquirers and candidates are introduced to philosophy. This is to be expected given the fruitful dialogue in which theology and philosophy have long engaged in the Catholic Church.

That said, an introductory course of this kind presents a number of pedagogical challenges. Few inquirers and candidates are likely to have had a college-level course in philosophy beyond, perhaps, a single survey course embedded in a general education program; and, if they had a course of this kind, many years have likely passed since then. Further, formation courses are often presented in condensed formats. It is simply not practical to assign separate texts addressing such key topics as the history of philosophy, metaphysics, epistemology, ethics and morality, and contemporary philosophy, too, let alone an accompanying text on logic and methods. Still further, the Catholic Church has long privileged a particular philosophical perspective: the Aristotelian-Thomist Tradition. The church does not endorse any particular philosophy as such. Nevertheless, the realism of the Aristotelian-Thomist Tradition has long complemented the church's core teachings and intellectual commitments. A generic or secular text would hardly serve the formation purposes to which this text is directed, especially when the content to be addressed is presented in a condensed format.

What then to do? One option is to use a text that simply poses philosophical questions for consideration. This strategy is now employed in some undergraduate courses in philosophy to good effect, in fact. The students walk away—hopefully—with a greater appreciation for the philosophical assumptions that undergird their deepest commitments and, perhaps, an enhanced capacity for introspection. This hardly seems appropriate for adults who are deeply committed to their faith, however, and who are now seeking to serve the church in new and challenging ways.

This text is designed to serve this particular audience, mature and highly accomplished men and women who are enrolled in structured formation programs in the Roman Catholic Tradition. This includes the diaconate, of course, but formation programs designed for aspiring lay ecclesial ministers as well.

The following design features will hopefully serve this purpose.

- This text is relatively short in length, comprising only 151 pages of text. That said, it does not shy away from some of the most challenging questions in philosophy. It is unlikely, in fact, that a student could walk away from an introductory course in philosophy with a true appreciation for the Aristotelian-Thomist Tradition unless he or she had wrestled with such core concepts as being, substance, essence, and nature. This material can, indeed, be difficult. Karol Wojtyla—later Pope John Paul II—reported that he struggled with metaphysics as a young man "from the first to the last page. I had to open a road through a dense forest of concepts, analyses, and axioms, without even being able to identify the terrain that I was treading on."[1] There is no getting around this level of difficulty. In John Paul II, however, we find ourselves in good company.

- The academic discipline of philosophy includes many sub-disciplines. The core content of this text is limited to the three most foundational of philosophy's sub-disciplines: metaphysics in chapter 2, epistemology in chapter 3, and ethics and morality in chapter 4. In order to establish some context, chapter 1 defines philosophy and realism, addresses the Roman Catholic Church's understanding of philosophy, and provides a brief synopsis of philosophy's development over the millennia. In contrast, chapter 5 looks ahead. It examines more recent developments in the Aristotelian-Thomist Tradition.

- A classic "primer design" is employed to clearly distinguish—to the extent possible—one concept from another. Further, these concepts are addressed in numbered sections with clear headings. This should facilitate the text's use in classroom settings and its subsequent use as a reference tool as well.

1. Acosta and Reimers, *Karol Wojtyla's Personalist Philosophy*, 18.

- The text is heavily footnoted in order to identify sources that can be further explored by those whose interest in philosophy may be stimulated. A bibliography is also provided.
- Every effort has been made to focus the narrative on essential topics and themes. Supplemental detail of some interest—but not essential as such—has been relegated to footnotes.
- The central focus of this text is philosophy rather than theology. That said, many who will read it will undoubtedly harbor deep faith commitments. Parallel and complementary ideas drawn from theology and church teachings are thus addressed in extended footnotes, all of which begin with the italicized heading: *Faith Connection*. Students are encouraged to make their own "connections" to the faith as well.
- To complement the narrative, illustrations are included in chapters 2, 3, and 4. Figure 2 on page 39 should prove particularly helpful in class discussions on the challenging topic of metaphysics. It is substantially based on a design developed by James M. Jacobs.
- Review questions for each chapter are included in appendix 1.
- Although the course associated with this text does not include a session on method *per se*, a glossary of methodological terms and concepts is provided in appendix 2. A number of these terms are typically introduced in class discussions.
- Both a name index and a subject index are provided for ease of reference. Both are extensive.
- Dates of birth and death—when applicable—are provided at the first mention of the many philosophers who are cited in this text. The designation BCE, i.e., before the common era, is indicated where applicable. All other dates refer to the common era.
- A sample syllabus for a course in which this text could be used is provided in appendix 3. The reading of original works is essential in a program offering of this kind. To this end, a supplemental text is recommended and suggested readings are identified in the "course outline" section of the syllabus. Further, a select set of questions are included in Appendix 4 to stimulate critical thinking.

My hope is that these design features will aid both instruction and learning.

That said, students—and instructors, too—should keep the limited focus of this text in mind. The history of philosophy is much more detailed than is indicated in chapter 1. The survey in chapter 1 pertains exclusively to the development of philosophy in the West; it does not address the rich patrimony of the East. Further, the broad stream of scholastic philosophy included many tributaries. Thomas Aquinas did not labor on his own. Although Peter Abelard, Bonaventure, and William of Ockham are mentioned in passing, virtually nothing is said of Anslem, Duns Scotus, and other notable "schoolmen." Still further, Thomist thought, in particular, is presented here in a rather streamlined fashion. Chapter 5 describes several contemporary "Thomisms," but those who inherited Thomist thought in the thirteenth through the sixteenth centuries also differed somewhat in their interpretations of the "Angelic Doctor's" teachings, including, most notably, Thomas of Vio (Cajetan) and Francisco Suarez.

Finally, I have written this text as a teacher and as a Roman Catholic deacon who has led formation programs rather than as a practicing philosopher. Although I have acquired some expertise pertaining to virtue ethics, political philosophy, and existentialism over the course of my career as a college instructor who has published widely on a broad range of topics, my academic endeavors have been devoted for the most part to—to use Ernest Boyer's conceptual framework—the threefold "scholarship of teaching, integration, and application" rather than to the "scholarship of discovery" typically pursued by practicing philosophers. Given this orientation and given the needs of students and instructors who will read this text, I have steered away from contested interpretations and interpretations of my own as well. The material included here is presented in a straightforward manner. That said, contemporary thinking pertaining to the good, the moral, and the just is developed in a bit more detail since these topics frequently come into play in pastoral settings. Finally, Aristotle and Thomas Aquinas are quoted extensively. It is important, I think, that we hear directly from these two pillars of the Aristotelian-Thomist Tradition.

Portions of chapter 4 were previously published in *Leadership: The Wisdom of the World and the Beatitudes*. These selections are referenced and/or repurposed here with the permission of the book's publisher, Wipf & Stock of Eugene, Oregon.

My hope is that students who read this text will benefit from it in their ministries, of course, but in their own intellectual and spiritual development as well. Socrates famously observed that "the unexamined life is not worth living." This is certainly true. To balance Socrates's view, however, Aristotle noted that "thinking itself is sometimes injurious to your health." Aristotle knew that balance is required, and so the fourfold focus that is reflected in all good formation programs: the intellectual, the human, the spiritual, and the pastoral. Balanced by sound human, spiritual, and pastoral formation, the kind of intellectual formation represented in our knowledge of and in our abiding appreciation for the Aristotelian-Thomist Tradition can benefit many of us—in my view—who serve the church.

In gratitude, this text is dedicated to my wife, Barbara, to our children, Katie and Christopher, and to our five grandchildren, Noah, Connor, Madeline, Weston, and Liam.

1

Introduction to the Aristotelean-Thomist Tradition

101. PHILOSOPHY

The etymology of the word "philosophy" is quite straight forward. Combining the Greek words for love, i.e., *philia*, and wisdom, i.e., *sophia*, a philosopher can be thought of as one who loves wisdom. Alternately, philosophy can be understood as "thinking about thinking." Anthony Quinton defines philosophy more formally as "rationally critical thinking of a more or less systematic kind about the general nature of the world (metaphysics or theory of existence), the justification of belief (epistemology or theory of knowledge), and the conduct of life (ethics or theory of value)."[1]

The boundaries between philosophy and other ways of knowing and talking about the world have shifted over time. The presocratic philosophers of sixth and fifth century BCE Greece sought to separate our understanding of the world from myth-making. In the early modern period, Francis Bacon (1561–1626) and the empiricists who followed him labored to distinguish science from the curricula of the schoolmen, i.e., the scholastics, who had taught in the universities founded across Europe in the high and late Middle Ages, i.e., 1100 to 1300. In the nineteenth and twentieth centuries, the social sciences and psychology, in particular, were effectively quartered off from the academic discipline of philosophy, and this calving process continues in the case of gender and culture studies. In our own time, academic philosophers are fighting a

---

1. Quinton, "Philosophy," 666.

kind of two-front war, in fact. On the one hand, they dismiss theological or spiritual "truths" as unknowable and hence irrelevant to philosophy. Any talk of God, the human soul, and revelation is beyond the pale for many academics and so, too, any larger consideration of human purpose or meaning. On the other hand, academic philosophers struggle to hold onto ground now being lost to certain emerging disciplines, including the neurosciences and artificial intelligence.

Given the fact that today's academic discipline of philosophy has conceded considerable ground in the sub-disciplines of metaphysics and ethics to the hard sciences and to the academic disciplines of political science and culture studies, too, little remains of philosophy's historical remit—it seems—except epistemology, and a rather narrow and technical kind of epistemology at that. Indeed, some contemporary writing in the academic discipline of philosophy seems quite narrow and tendential when compared to the contributions of the ancient Greeks and the scholastics. Much of today's philosophy resembles nothing so much as the counting of "angels who may or may not be dancing on the head of a pin," a witticism often used to disparage the schoolmen.[2]

102. PHILOSOPHY AND THE CATHOLIC CHURCH

Philosophy has had a somewhat mixed relationship with the church. Writing in the second century, Tertullian (155–220) famously asked: "What indeed has Athens to do with Jerusalem? What concord is there between the Academy and the church? What between heretics and Christians? Our instruction comes from 'the porch of Solomon,' who had himself taught that 'the Lord should be sought in simplicity of heart.' Away with all attempts to produce a mottled Christianity of Stoic, Platonic, and dialectic composition! We want no curious disputation after possessing Christ Jesus, no inquisition after enjoying the gospel! With our faith, we desire no further belief."[3] The Desert Fathers of the fourth, fifth, and sixth centuries eschewed philosophy in favor of asceticism and

---

2. *Faith Connection*: Some consider this a great loss, including, most notably, Pope John Paul II: "Abandoning the investigation of being, modern philosophical research has concentrated instead upon human knowing. Rather than make use of the human capacity to know the truth, modern philosophy has preferred to accentuate the ways in which this capacity is limited and conditioned. This has given rise to different forms of agnosticism and relativism." See John Paul II, *Fides et Ratio*, no. 49, no. 5.

3. Tertullian, "The Prescription Against Heretics," 3145–3146.

prayer. Writing at the end of the fourth century, Augustine (354–430) expressed a similar view: "What profit to me then was the ingenuity that nimbly picked its way amid those teachings, and the plethora of intricate books I had unraveled without human intuition to support me, if I was crippled and led astray by sacrilegious depravity where the teachings of true godliness were concerned? On the other hand, what disadvantage was it to your little ones that they were much more slow-minded than I? They did not forsake you, but stayed safely in the nest of your church to grow their plumage and strengthen the wings of their charity on the wholesome nourishment of the faith."[4] This disparaging view is reflected, too, in a fifteenth century spiritual classic written by Thomas à Kempis (1380–1471), *The Imitation of Christ*: "When the day of judgment comes, we shall not be asked what we have read but what we have done, not how well we have spoken but how devoutly we have lived. Tell me, where are those professors and teachers today whom you knew so well while they were living and flourishing in their learning?" Further, "how many people perish in a generation through empty learning, caring little for the service of God?"[5] And as we shall see in section 406, fideism, i.e., a perennial repudiation of philosophy and much of theology, too, persists in the church.

That said, Augustine journeyed to faith—by his own admission—through the way station of philosophy, most notably the works of Plato (425–347 BCE) and Plotinus (205–270).[6] They provided him with the concepts and the vocabulary he needed to think and speak about God, sin, grace, and so much more.[7] For his part, Thomas Aquinas (1225–1274) understood philosophy—and reasoning more generally—to be of service to sacred doctrine, which he thought of as a science: "This science can draw upon the philosophical sciences, not as though it stood in need of them, but only in order to make its teaching clearer. For it accepts its principles, not from the other sciences, as upon its superiors, but uses them as its inferiors and handmaidens: even so the master sciences make use of subordinate sciences . . ."[8] Further, "sacred doctrine also makes

---

4. Augustine, *The Confessions*, 73.
5. à Kempis, *The Imitation of Christ*, 33–34.
6. Augustine, *City of God*, 298.
7. *Faith Connection*: For the most part, the early church fathers embraced Plato's version of realism as a philosophical foundation for their work. Aristotle's realism and stoicism were employed to a lesser extent.
8. Aquinas, *The Summa Theologica and The Summa Contra Gentiles*, 9–10.

use of human reason, not, indeed, to prove faith (for thereby the merit of faith would come to an end), but to make clear other things that are set forth in this doctrine. Since, therefore, grace does not destroy nature, but perfects it, natural reason should minister to faith as the natural inclination of the will to charity."[9] The enduring value of philosophy—properly oriented to questions of truth and human purpose—are thus affirmed by these and other voices emanating from within the church, including, more recently, Pope John Paul II (1920–2005) in his encyclical letter *Fides et Ratio* (1998): "(The church) sees in philosophy the way to come to know fundamental truths about human life. At the same time, the church considers philosophy an indispensable help for a deeper understanding of faith and for communicating the truth of the Gospel to those who do not yet know it."[10]

The Catholic Church's particular views concerning metaphysical, epistemological, and ethical realism are addressed more specifically in sections 203, i.e., metaphysics; 304, i.e., epistemology; and 405, i.e., ethics, morality, and justice.[11]

103. REALISM

Philosophical realism holds that a wide variety of things, concepts, and standards of behavior exist quite independently of our encountering them or knowing anything about them. As affirmed by Clayton Littlejohn and

---

9. Aquinas, *The Summa Theologica and The Summa Contra Gentiles*, 15.

10. John Paul II, *Fides et Ratio*, no. 5.

11. *Faith Connection*: The Catechism of the Catholic Church affirms the twofold approach to truth espoused by Thomas Aquinas: "Human intelligence is surely already capable of finding a response to the question of origins. The existence of God the Creator can be known with certainty through his works, by the light of human reason, even if this knowledge is often obscured and disfigured by error. This is why faith comes to confirm and enlighten reason in the correct understanding of this truth: 'By faith we understand that the world was created by the word of God, so that what is seen was made out of things which do not appear.'" See *Catechism*, no. 286. Further, "by natural reason man can know God with certainty, on the basis of his works. But there is another order of knowledge, which man cannot possibly arrive at by his own powers: the order of divine Revelation." See *Catechism*, no. 50. Still further, "'faith seeks understanding' (St. Anselm). It is intrinsic to faith that a believer desires to know better the One in whom he has put his faith to understand better what he has revealed; a more penetrating knowledge will in turn call forth a greater faith, increasingly set afire by love. The grace of faith opens the 'eyes of your hearts' to a lively understanding of the contents of Revelation . . . " See *Catechism*, no. 158. Finally, "though faith is above reason, there can never be any real discrepancy between faith and reason." See *Catechism*, no. 159.

J. Adam Carter, "Realists believe that there is a mind-independent reality that includes things whose existence and character don't depend upon mental activity."[12]

Metaphysical realism asserts the independent existence, not just of sensible "things" in the world, but of certain universals, too. Consider, for instance, the words "mankind," "flowers," and "literature" and certain mind-dependent beings thought to exist, including numbers and abstract concepts of all sorts. In contrast, idealists assert the mind-dependence of all that we suppose to exist in the world. Although this might seem to imply solipsism, i.e., the view that only I exist and that everything else I think I encounter in the world are illusions, idealism more typically assumes a skeptical stance *vis-à-vis* the independent existence of things in the sensible world. For their part, logical positivists reject any talk of universals and mind-dependent beings out of hand. And conceptualists and nominalists reduce all such thinking to our typical way of talking about or coping with the panoply of things we encounter on a day-to-day basis. See section 205.

Epistemological realism argues that we can know the real world and that truth exists independently of us. Further, our knowledge of the world can be derived from both our senses, i.e., *a posteriori knowledge*, and reason, i.e., *a priori knowledge*. In contrast, some philosophers—both in ancient times and during the Enlightenment and beyond—have harbored skeptical views concerning our ability to know much if anything about the external world. See section 312.

Ethical realists assert the existence of objective standards of right and wrong. In doing so, they reject the ethical relativism and subjectivism endemic in various expressions of contemporary philosophy.

That said, a number of different positions fit uneasily under the rubric of philosophical realism. This includes Plato's metaphysics, for instance, which is sometimes described as a kind of idealism. Plato did not argue, however, that the Forms he postulated exist in our minds as such. According to Plato, the Forms we intuit from our encounters with things in the sensible world exist independently of our knowing anything about them or even our existence. This is a realist perspective.[13] As we shall see, however, this understanding is quite contrary to the version of realism espoused in the Aristotelian-Thomist Tradition.

---

12. Littlejohn and Carter, *Epistemology*, 57.
13. Hamlyn, "Idealism," 386.

104. THE ARISTOTELIAN-THOMIST TRADITION

In the fourth century BCE, Aristotle (384–322 BCE) rejected Plato's metaphysics and epistemology in favor of a comprehensive philosophical system firmly grounded in the world of sensible things and in fulsome relationships involving real people. In the thirteenth century, Thomas Aquinas embraced Aristotle's metaphysics, epistemology, and ethics to a considerable extent as he labored to reconcile the ancient philosopher's teachings to Christian theology. We thus speak today of an Aristotelian-Thomist Tradition. Indeed, we refer to these intellectual giants as the twin pillars of a "perennial tradition." It is important to note that the Aristotelian-Thomist Tradition is alive and well in our own time. As we shall see, contemporary work in the perennial tradition falls under the conceptual umbrellas of neo-Thomism, transcendental Thomism, existential Thomism, analytic Thomism, personalism, and virtue ethics.

Aristotle was born in northern Greece in 384 BCE. He was tutored under Plato and taught in his Academy for some 20 years, only to leave in 348 BCE following Plato's death. In Macedonia, Aristotle tutored King Philip's son Alexander (356–323 BCE) who would come to be known as Alexander the Great, the conqueror of much of the known world. In 335 BCE, Aristotle returned to Athens where he started his own school, the Lyceum. Near the end of his life, he was forced to flee Athens due to a trumped-up charge of impiety. Aristotle died in exile at the age of 62. As we shall see, Aristotle's philosophical interests—like Plato's—were quite broad. He produced foundational treatises on metaphysics, epistemology, ethics, and politics. Aristotle is credited, too, with having developed a formal system of logic.

Despite his prodigious output, Aristotle's lectures were nearly lost to the world on at least two occasions. The Lyceum had nearly collapsed by the third century BCE. As a consequence, Aristotle's lecture notes were bequeathed from one party to the next over an extended time period. Fortunately, Andronicus of Rhodes acquired them in the first century BCE and edited them, thereby preserving Aristotle's work for posterity. This legacy was threatened again by the fall of Rome in 476. For all intents and purposes, Aristotle's philosophy was lost to the West from that point forward through the advent of the high Middle Ages. The fall of Byzantium to the Ottomans in 1415 paved the way, however, for Aristotle's work to be examined by scholars across the Moslem world. Avicenna (Ibn Sina) (980–1037), Averroes (Ibn Rushd) (1126–1198), and Moses Maimonides (1135–1204), a Jew, wrote extensively about Aristotle and his teachings, and their manuscripts would gradually find their way into Europe.

Thomas Aquinas likely learned about Aristotle's works while a student at the University of Naples. In his own works—most notably his *Summa Contra Gentiles* (1259) and *Summa Theologica* (1265)—Aquinas referred to Aristotle simply as "the Philosopher." Aquinas was born in 1224 in the Kingdom of Naples. Much to his family's consternation, he joined the newly formed Dominican Order and promptly enrolled at the University of Paris under the tutelage of the Dominican scholar Albertus Magnus (1200–1280). Following a short stint at the University of Cologne, Aquinas returned to the University of Paris as an instructor. He served the Dominican community and the papacy in other capacities, too. Indeed, Aquinas was quite influential in his own day in the Dominican community and in the broader church as well. He died in 1274 at the age of 49. Thomas Aquinas was canonized by the Catholic Church in 1323.

As we shall see, Aquinas adopted Aristotle's realism as a foundation for his own work. (Key differences in emphasis are noted in sections 203, 210, 303, 412, and 414.) Like Aristotle, Aquinas affirmed the essential intelligibility of the sensible world. As noted by F. C. Copleston, "(Aquinas) does not construct a static world like that of Parmenides, nor does he present us with Heraclitan flux; fundamentally, he describes the world as it is known by us in daily experience. He presents us with a world which is shot through, as it were, by form, by intelligible structure, and which is therefore to that extent intelligible. On the other hand, he presents us with a changing and a developing world . . . Both Aquinas's metaphysics and modern science presuppose the familiar world of common experience."[14]

Thomas Aquinas's teachings engendered considerable controversy in his own day. A number of Franciscan scholars—including, most notably, Bonaventure (1221–1274)—questioned Aquinas's deferral to Aristotle rather than to Augustine. Shortly after his death, a number of realist propositions were condemned by church leaders in Paris and Oxford.[15] Despite these headwinds, Aquinas's teachings would prevail in the academy, and Thomist thought would go on to provide a philosophical foundation for the understanding of the faith endorsed by the Council of Trent in the sixteenth century.

14. Copleston, *Aquinas*, 109.
15. Kerr, *After Aquinas*, 12.

Thomas Aquinas's teachings—and scholasticism more generally—would go out of fashion during the Renaissance of the fifteenth and sixteenth centuries, the Reformation and Counter-Reformation of the sixteenth and seventeenth centuries, and the Enlightenment Period of the seventeenth and eighteenth centuries. During these eras, scholars would come to view philosophy as something entirely distinct from theology. For its part, the Catholic Church had entered into an extended period of intellectual dormancy. Apologetics and spirituality would assume pride of place over theology and philosophy.

In the nineteenth and early twentieth centuries, the church reversed course. It once again celebrated the philosophical realism of the Aristotelian-Thomist Tradition. In 1870, *Dei Filius* (*The Constitution of the Catholic Church*) was promulgated by Pope Pius IX (1792–1878) at the close of the First Vatican Council. It affirmed—*contra* Bonaventure—Thomas Aquinas's understanding of the relationship shared by faith and reason: "There is a twofold order of knowledge, distinct not only as regards its source, but also as regards its object. With regard to the source, we know at the one level by natural reason, at the other level by divine faith. With regard to the object, besides those things to which natural reason can attain, there are proposed for our belief mysteries hidden in God, which, unless they are divinely revealed, are incapable of being known . . . [Further], there can never be any real disagreement between faith and reason, since it is the same God who reveals the mysteries and infuses faith, and who has endowed the human mind with the light of reason."[16] And in 1879, Pope Leo XIII (1810—1903) formally invoked the name of Thomas Aquinas in his encyclical letter *Aeterni Patris* (*On the Restoration of Christian Philosophy*), referring to him as the "Angelic Doctor" and commending him to all who teach in Catholic schools and houses of formation: "We exhort you, venerable brethren, in all earnestness to restore the golden wisdom of St. Thomas, and to spread it far and wide for the defense and beauty of the Catholic faith, for the good of society, and for the advantages of all sciences."[17] In 1907, Pope Pius X (1835–1914) endorsed this exalted view in his encyclical letter *Pascendi Dominici Gregis* (*On the Doctrine of the Modernists*): "In the first place, with regard to studies, We will and ordain that scholastic philosophy be made the basis of the sacred sciences . . . And let it be clearly understood

---

16. Pius IX, "*Dei Filius*," 277.
17. Leo XIII, "The Revival of Thomism," 281.

INTRODUCTION TO THE ARISTOTELEAN-THOMIST TRADITION

above all things that the scholastic philosophy We prescribe is that which the Angelic Doctor has bequeathed to us . . . Further let Professors remember that they cannot set St. Thomas aside, especially in metaphysical questions, without grave detriment."[18] In 1914, Pius X went further, publishing 24 theses that together constituted—in his view—both "authentic Thomism" and "authentic Catholic Philosophy."[19] These several theses were primarily metaphysical in nature and enshrined Thomas Aquinas's understanding of existence, being, substance, essence, soul, and God.

In time, the Catholic Church would open itself to a broader stream of thinking. Indeed, the church has benefited from a number of very different philosophical perspectives over the course of the last 70 or so years, including phenomenalism, personalism, and existentialism. Language and culture studies have contributed to this renaissance as well. In his encyclical letter *Fides et Ratio* (*On the Relationship of Faith and Reason*), Pope John Paul II noted the seminal contributions of Thomas Aquinas, but affirmed that "the church has no philosophy of her own nor does she canonize any one particular philosophy in preference to others."[20] As F. C. Copleston has noted: "It is a mistake to speak of (Thomas Aquinas's) philosophy as a 'Christian philosophy' in any other sense than that it is compatible with Christianity. The fact that a philosophy is compatible with Christianity no more makes it a specifically Christian philosophy than the fact that a mathematical system is compatible with Christianity makes it a Christian mathematical system."[21] It is important to note, too, that John Paul II addressed a number of themes in his encyclical that were of secondary importance—at best—to scholastic philosophers, in general, and Thomas Aquinas, in particular, including the "crisis in meaning" now endemic in our culture and the central importance of the human person, too.

105. HISTORICAL AND CULTURAL CONTEXTS

We tend to think of philosophy as an endeavor that takes place in ivory towers. In this view, the academy is disconnected from the "real world" of everyday life, social movements, popular culture, and politics. This is

18. Pius X, *Pascendi Dominici Gregis*, no. 6.
19. Pius X, "Twenty-four Thomistic Theses."
20. John Paul II, *Fides et Ratio*, no. 49.
21. Copleston, *Aquinas*, 58.

a mistaken view, however. Philosophical perspectives tend to embody the spirit or ethos of the times in which they were formulated; and these perspectives, in turn, have impacted the broader culture, sometimes in profound ways. In his masterful text, *A Secular Age*, Charles Taylor (b. 1931) makes this clear. How is it possible, he asks, that we have moved—in a mere 500 years—"from a society in which it was virtually impossible not to believe in God to one in which faith, even for the staunchest believer, is one human possibility among others."[22] Taylor's answer is social imaginaries, "the ways in which (people) imagine their social existence, how they fit together with others, how things go on between them and their fellows, the expectations which are normally met, and the deeper normative notions and images which underlie these expectations."[23]

Indeed, it is hard to imagine Socrates (470–399 BCE), Plato, and Aristotle flourishing in any time other than the ascendency of Athens following the defeat of the Persians in 480 BCE. Similarly, stoicism seemed a perfect fit to many in the patrician class of imperial Rome. It is difficult, too, to imagine the work of the scholastics separate and apart from the founding of Europe's great universities in the latter stages of the Middle Ages. And the collapse of idealist philosophy—a remarkably optimistic brand of thinking—in the early twentieth century was due—in no small part—to the trauma of the First World War, which seemed to many to have sounded the death knell for cultural and political optimism in the West.

Conversely, the political realism of Niccolò Machiavelli (1469–1527) certainly led to the *realpolitik* of the modern era. Similarly, John Locke (1632–1704) profoundly influenced the thought of America's founding fathers, as did Fredrich Nietzsche (1844–1900) and Karl Marx (1818–1883), respectively, the nightmarish hopes of the Nazi regime in Germany and the aspirations of the Bolsheviks in Russia in the twentieth century. Again, philosophical perspectives both impact and are impacted by the "social imaginaries" of their times.

106. THE AGE OF MYTHOLOGY

As is noted below, the presocratics who were active in the sixth and fifth centuries BCE are considered the West's first philosophers. They are

---

22. Taylor, *A Secular Age*, 3.
23. Taylor, *A Secular Age*, 171.

recognized as such because they used reason and explanations drawn from nature to account for change and causation. Although this represented a dramatic innovation in thinking in the West, it had parallels in the East, most notably in India and China.[24] This is not to suggest, however, that mythmaking and story-telling in ancient times were devoid of truth. To assert this would be to dismiss much of the truth we believe to be contained, for instance, in the first eleven chapters of the Book of Genesis.

Lawrence Boadt described the sense-making capacity of myth as follows: "Myth allows us to speak of events of primal importance at the very beginning of time because it does not depend on knowing the scientific facts, but upon understanding the inner meaning of what happened and what purpose stands behind the event . . . The common themes and motifs used in myths are the symbols cherished by all ancient civilizations."[25] Walter Brueggemann prefers the term "memory": "The mode of the call"—the exegetical focus of Brueggemann's account of Genesis—"is story-telling . . . The faith that Israel transmits is not about a *structure* of reality (as in myth) not a *chronical* of events (as in history). Rather, it is about a memory that is transformed, criticized, and extended each time it is told. It is a tradition in which there are no objective controls but only the perception and passion, imagination, and discipline of those who care for the memory."[26]

Indeed, truth comes in many shapes and sizes.[27] That said, our focus in this text is philosophy, which began in the West with the presocratics.

107. THE HISTORY OF PHILOSOPHY

History is not the only lens through which to explore philosophy. Chapters 2, 3, and 4, for instance, investigate philosophy through the lenses of its three primary sub-disciplines: metaphysics, epistemology, and ethics. In foregrounding the evolution of philosophical thought over time,

---

24. Grayling, *The History of Philosophy*, 519–553.
25. Boadt, *Reading the Old Testament*, 130.
26. Brueggemann, *Genesis*, 4.

27. *Faith Connection*: For a full account of the interpretive methods endorsed by the Catholic Church, readers are referred to Pontifical Biblical Commission. See Pontifical Biblical Commission, *The Interpretation of the Bible in the Church*, 131–196. These methods include literary analyses and sociological and anthropological methods, too, all of which have proven particularly useful in exploring certain truth claims contained in the first 11 chapters of the Book of Genesis.

however, the history of philosophy can complement a topical approach of this kind. Indeed, the political, social, and cultural contexts in which particular philosophical positions emerged, developed, thrived, and declined over time are revealed more distinctly in a historical analysis than in a topical analysis.

That said, the evolution of philosophical thought has not followed the same pattern as the development of scientific thought. As affirmed by Thomas Kuhn, science tends to develop in a linear fashion. This is the sense in which science is thought to be "self-correcting." This pattern of linear development is only disrupted by significant "paradigm shifts," moments in time in which evidence contrary to a particular view accumulates to the point that an alternative explanation is required.[28] Think, for instance, of Nicholas Copernicus (1473–1543) and the replacement of a geocentric understanding of the solar system with a heliocentric model. Think, too, of the impact of Albert Einstein's theory of relativity on Newtonian physics. In contrast to science, the development of philosophical thought is marked by opposing views that often persist side-by-side over extended time periods. Examples include the very different metaphysics of Plato and Aristotle, Thomas Aquinas's realist understanding of universals and the nominalism of William of Ockham (1285–1347) in the high Middle Ages, and today's virtue ethics and the cultural relativism of postmodern thought. Further, certain philosophical views tend to come into vogue and pass out of fashion only to be recycled at later points in time. This includes such foundational concerns as our capacity to know anything at all about the sensible world and moral perspectives, too, including the concepts of duty, the nature of the good life, and justice.

Thumbnail sketches of various philosophies follow. They are the very briefest of descriptions, intended only to orient all that follows in space and time. The taxonomy employed is drawn from A. C. Grayling's excellent text, *The History of Philosophy*.[29] That said, perspectives asso-

28. Kuhn, *The Structures of Scientific Revolutions*.

29. As compelling as Grayling's work may be, it can be criticized on at least three counts. First, Grayling makes it clear that he is loath to countenance any philosophical view "tainted" by theology or spirituality. His treatment of Thomas Aquinas is thus cursory to say the least. There is also no mention whatsoever of religious existentialists, including Søren Kierkegaard. Second, Grayling inexplicably includes virtue ethics under the heading of analytic philosophy. He is not alone in this regard. As we shall see, today's resurgence in virtue ethics is better understood as a promising development in the Aristotelian-Thomist Tradition. And third, Grayling is clearly reluctant to include the culture critique that lies at the heart of the postmodern project under the disciplinary rubric of philosophy. Charles Taylor's remarkable work is excluded as

ciated with Aristotelian-Thomist realism and those directly opposed to realist metaphysics, epistemology, and ethics are examined more thoroughly in chapters 2, 3, 4, and 5.

108. THE PRESOCRATIC ERA

The first Greek philosophers are known collectively as the presocratics, even though a number of them were contemporaries of Socrates, Plato, and Aristotle and some even succeeded them. The presocratics can be divided into five groups or schools: the nature philosophers, the Pythagoreans, the "proto-metaphysicians,"[30] the sophists, and the skeptics.

The nature philosophers of ancient Greece tried to isolate the primary substance that underlies all things in the sensible world: air; water; fire; earth; the *apeiron*, a mysterious substance that was thought to underlie one or more of the aforementioned substances; atoms; or some combination thereof. They showed little interest in epistemology or ethics. The ranks of the nature philosophers included Thales (626–548 BCE), Anaximander (610–546 BCE), Anaximenes (586–526 BCE), Anaxagoras (500–428 BCE), and Democritus (460–370 BCE).

Pythagoras (570–495 BCE) was not a nature philosopher *per se*, but he, too, focused on the nature of reality. Espousing a complex quasi-religious framework, Pythagoras and his followers claimed that the concrete things we encounter in the sensible world are associated in some sense with numbers or various ratios of numbers. This view anticipated Plato's theory of Forms in some respects.

The "proto-metaphysicians"—our third category of presocratic philosophers—focused on the nature of change and hence causation. They shared a common question: "How do we account for the persistent identity of anything in the sensible world when everything seems—on the surface, at least—to be in flux?" At one extreme, Heraclitus (sixth century–fifth century BCE) contended that there is no such thing as permanence. Everything is constantly changing. He famously observed

---

well. It is certainly arguable that these streams of thought lie more closely at the heart of philosophy as envisioned by Plato, Aristotle, and Thomas Aquinas than the narrow pursuits favored by those in the academy who promote analytic philosophy to the near exclusion of all other thinking.

30. This identifier is not employed in most textbooks. Nevertheless, it accurately describes the primary focus and the impact these proto-philosophers had upon the subsequent development of philosophy. It also serves to distinguish them from the other presocratics.

that "you can never step into the same river twice." Opposing this view, Parmenides (sixth century–fifth century BCE) argued that everything is "one" and that nothing really changes at all. In Parmenides's view, all change is illusory. Taking a different tack, Empedocles (494–434 BCE) taught that the cosmos is eternal and that the changes we perceive in the sensible world result from the cyclical interplay of "Love" and "Strife." Plato and Aristotle would both take up the proto-metaphysicians's concerns about the nature of change and causation.

Our fourth category—the sophists—were not interested in metaphysical, epistemological, or ethical truth *per se*. Protagoras (490–420 BCE), Crates (365–285 BCE), and their followers were more concerned with winning arguments in the public square. Since they disdained the search for truth, as such, they are excluded by many from among the ranks of true philosophers. Nevertheless, the sophists contributed to the development of rhetoric and, hence, to a certain method—albeit a "morally neutral technique"[31]—employed in academic philosophy.

Like the sophists, the skeptics of the ancient world were concerned with arguments. They questioned, however, our capacity to know much of anything about the sensible world. The skeptics believed truth to be elusive or even illusory. Their ranks included Zeno (334–262 BCE) and Pyrrho (360–270 BCE), the most uncompromising of the ancient skeptics. Aristotle credited Zeno with having invented dialectic argument as an alternative to the eristic argumentative methods employed by the sophists. Skepticism would later find a home among the rationalists of the seventeenth and eighteenth centuries.[32]

109. THE "GOLDEN AGE" OF GREEK PHILOSOPHY

The "golden age" of Greek philosophy featured Socrates, his student Plato, and his student Aristotle, of course. Indeed, the discipline of philosophy is thought to have truly emerged with these three giants. That said, the cynics, epicureans, stoics, and neoplatonists thrived as well. Many of their contributions would be reprised again and again over the course of philosophy's long history.

---

31. MacIntyre, *A Short History of Ethics*, 27.

32. Skepticism should not be confused with methodological doubt. As noted by A. C. Cotter, "the tyro, i.e., beginner or novice, in philosophy is not to doubt reality, but to proceed as if he doubted philosophy." See Cotter, *An Introduction to Catholic Philosophy*, 252.

INTRODUCTION TO THE ARISTOTELEAN-THOMIST TRADITION

We only know of Socrates through Plato's dialogues, and it is difficult, in fact, to separate Plato's views from Socrates's teachings in these works. It is clear, nonetheless, that Socrates had a profound impact on his disciples. As far as we know, he did not show any interest in metaphysics. His primary focus was the good life and all that makes life worthwhile. Socrates is also the namesake for the "Socratic dialogue," a style of questioning and argumentation in which an instructor leads his interlocutors step-by-step towards an ever clearer understanding of this or that term or concept of interest.

Plato's contributions to philosophy were manifold. He was the first to have developed a comprehensive philosophical scheme. As noted by A. C. Grayling, "Plato's philosophy is a system . . . Its different components were meant to fit together to provide answers to the fundamental questions that he, more clearly and more comprehensively than his predecessors, saw had to be answered so that all the answers together make sense. Those questions are, 'What is the right kind of life and best kind of society?' 'What is knowledge and how do we get it?' 'What is the fundamental nature of reality?' These questions have a fundamental order: to answer the first you need an answer to the second, and to answer the second you need to answer the third."[33] Our primary focus in this text is the realist tradition associated with Aristotle and Thomas Aquinas. We would be remiss, however, if we failed to note Aristotle's debt to Plato. To this end, Plato's metaphysical teaching are addressed in some detail in section 212 and his epistemology in section 305.

As we shall see, Aristotle abandoned Plato's conception of reality and his epistemology, too.[34] In their place, he articulated the robust version of realist thought we associate with the Aristotelian-Thomist Tradition. Aristotle's views are addressed in considerable detail in sections 104, 203, 206, 303, 309, 404, and 407. Suffice it for now to note that Plato and Aristotle are generally viewed as the most important philosophers of all time.[35]

---

33. Grayling, *The History of Philosophy*, 67.

34. Again, Plato's work is sometimes described as a kind of idealism. This conflates the terms "realism" and "materialism," however. In this mistaken view, Plato's Forms or Ideas cannot be located in the material or sensible world; therefore, he must be an idealist. Metaphysical realism holds, however, that that which is asserted is "real," e.g., Plato's Forms *or* Aristotle's panoply of substances, accidents, mind-dependent beings, the mean, etc.. These entities exist independently of our knowing anything about them or even our existence. This is why Plato's metaphysics is more appropriately described as platonic or strong realism.

35. Some add Thomas Aquinas to this list and others Immanuel Kant.

The cynics of the ancient world hoped to live as "naturally" as possible and so disparaged all forms of social convention, doing so in ways that sometimes scandalized their contemporaries. They asserted the enduring value of a simple life, material self-sufficiency, and peace of mind. Their exemplars included Antisthenes (446–366 BCE) and Diogenes (414–313 BCE). Echoes of cynic belief can be discerned in the nineteenth century's romantic movement and in the bohemian lifestyle embraced by some artists and writers in the early twentieth century.

Like the cynics, the epicureans of the ancient world abjured any interest in metaphysics or epistemology. Like Socrates, Epicurus (341–270 BCE) and his followers focused on the nature of the good life, which they defined exclusively in material terms. Further, the epicureans viewed all change in the sensible world as fully determined. The proper goal of life—they professed—is the experience of pleasure and the avoidance of pain, twin goals best achieved—in their view—by a life of *ataraxia*, i.e., clear-minded equanimity or peace of mind. In some respects, the epicureans of the ancient world anticipated the hedonistic utilitarianism of the late eighteenth and nineteenth centuries.

The stoics of the ancient world proved more influential over time than the cynics or the epicureans. Zeno is considered the founder of stoicism, but three Romans, Seneca the Younger (4–65), Epictetus (50–135), and the Emperor Marcus Aurelius (121–180) were exemplars as well. Indeed, stoicism emerged as a popular alternative to Christianity and other religions and philosophies in the Roman Empire. It is primarily an ethical philosophy. Like epicureanism, however, stoicism is constructed on a material understanding of the world. The stoics believed that all that we know and experience in life is determined by the *logos*, i.e., fate or god narrowly conceived of as coterminous with nature. In their view, we are free only to the extent that we can choose either to resist or to acquiesce to the inevitable. Stoics embraced duty to one's state of life, family, and society as ideals and a stance of *apatheia*, i.e., courageous indifference, in the face of life's vicissitudes.

In the third century of the common era, Plotinus adopted Plato's metaphysics and epistemology as a starting point, but then developed his own unique and quite comprehensive philosophy. Plotinus emphasized two principles in particular. First, the mind is more fundamental than matter. Indeed, mind precedes matter. In making this pivot, Plotinus abandoned Plato's strong realism in favor of idealism. Indeed, Plotinus anticipated the idealism of George Berkeley (1685–1753) and Arthur

Schopenhauer (1788–1860). Second, Plotinus taught that the cosmos and everything in it are part of a single reality: the "One, the First, or the Good." According to neoplatonists, all human beings participate in the divine and the goal of life is to revert to unity with the One. Plotinus's student Porphyry (234–305) edited his master's teachings, and under Iamblichus (245–325) and Proclus (412–485), neoplatonism would evolve into a quasi-religious or mystical belief system. Neoplatonism would exert a significant influence on Christian thought in the West, primarily through Augustine, who was deeply impacted—it seems—by his personal encounter with neoplatonist thought.

110. MEDIEVAL PHILOSOPHY

Reading some accounts, one could easily conclude that little if any scholarly thinking occurred between the fall of Rome in 476 and the dawn of the Enlightenment in the seventeenth century. This ignores the fact that formal thinking about the nature of reality, knowledge, the good life, and moral and ethical behavior assumed a distinctly theological and spiritual focus between the second and eighth centuries of the common era. Two groups of ecclesiastics can be credited with this development. The first, the early church fathers, wrote and preached between the second and seventh centuries. Various lists of these churchmen have been advanced over the years, with one citing some 167 names. In the East, John Chrysostom (347–407) is widely acknowledged as the greatest of the early church fathers. Together with Basil (330–378) and Gregory Nazianzus (329–390), Chrysostom is recognized as one of the "Three Hierarchs." Together with Ambrose (374–397), Jerome (342–420), and Gregory the Great (540–604), Augustine is considered one of the four most prominent of the Latin Fathers.

A number of the early church fathers embraced aspects of Plato's metaphysics and concepts drawn from neoplatonism as well. The changeable and the unchangeable, on the one hand, and the temporal and the eternal, on the other, thus emerged as important considerations in the work of the early church fathers. The central task of Christians—they argued—is to "purify" themselves by ascending, in turn, from a fear of God to piety, to charity, to fortitude, to mercy, to purification of the heart, and finally to wisdom. Indeed, the early church fathers viewed the spiritual life as a progression in holiness.

Monasticism also absorbed much of the intellectual energy that might otherwise have been devoted to philosophy during this era. The monastic traditions of the Egyptian Desert were conveyed to the West by John Cassian (360–475) and would be adopted, in time, by Benedict of Nursia (480–587), whose Order would emerge as the most revered expression of Christian piety in the West up to the time of the Reformation and Counter-Reformation of the sixteenth century. In fact, Benedictine spirituality retained much of its influence across Catholic Europe until the disruption unleashed by the French Revolution in 1789.

Augustine is acknowledged by some as the first of the medieval philosophers even though he wrote and preached before the fall of Rome. This is so because his writings provided a bridge from the ancient world to the Christianized version of platonic and neoplatonic thought that provided an intellectual foundation for theology in the West over the course of some six or seven centuries. As noted in section 104, Aristotle's works were largely unknown in the West during this era.

Boethius (470–524) also served as a conduit of sorts between the philosophic patrimony of the ancient world and the Middle Ages. In his *Consolations of Philosophy*, Boethius addressed a number of enduring questions, including the problem of free will and the extent to which the changes we see in the sensible world may or may not be determined. He also examined the nature of universals, thereby anticipating one of the most contentious issues of the high and late Middle Ages. Eschewing the determinism of the epicureans and stoics, Boethius followed Augustine in his understanding of free will, but anticipated nominalism, i.e., the view that universals do not exist independently of their manifestations in individual things. Boethius also served as a primary source in the teaching of logic over the course of several centuries.

Anselm (1033–1109), a Benedictine, and Peter Abelard (1079–1142) also prepared the stage for the development of scholasticism. Anselm defined philosophical terms and famously advanced an ontological proof for God's existence. And Abelard's influential *Sic et Non*, i.e., *Yes and No*, articulated rules for the reconciliation of competing interpretations of Scripture. He thus anticipated the development of the scholastic method. Like Boethius, Abelard promoted a type of nominalism, a perspective pertaining to the nature of universals that would later be employed in opposition to Thomas Aquinas's metaphysics.

Three developments contributed to the subsequent emergence of scholastic thought. First, those who engaged in intellectual pursuits moved over time from monastic settings to the great universities that would be established across Europe from the eleventh through the fifteenth centuries.[36] Second, a unique style of philosophical investigation emerged in these settings: *quodlibetical* disputation, a public process in which an instructor responded to questions put to him. As noted above, the deductive reasoning associated with the *quaestio disputatae* would be accepted as a privileged pedagogy by the scholastics. Third, Plato's version of realism would be increasingly pitted against Aristotle's metaphysical, epistemological, and ethical realism, with Franciscan scholars, including Bonaventure, Duns Scotus (1266–1308), and William of Ockham, advocating on behalf of a Christianized version of platonic and neoplatonic thought and Dominicans, most notably, Thomas Aquinas, promoting a Christianized version of Aristotelianism. They wrestled—for the most part—with metaphysical questions, including the relationship shared by faith and reason; proofs for God's existence; the distinction between existence and essence; the vexing question of evil, i.e., theodicy; free will; and the nature of universals. In the end, these disputes would narrow into an extended debate between the metaphysics of the Aristotelian-Thomist Tradition and William of Ockham's version of nominalism. See section 205.

Roger Bacon (1214–1292) was something of an outlier in medieval philosophy. Indeed, he was well ahead of his time. Bacon focused on the underlying causes of errors in judgment, thereby anticipating the epistemological interests of the rationalists and empiricists of the Enlightenment. In some respects, his focus on language and its uses presaged twentieth century philosophy's "linguistic turn."[37] In his ethics, Bacon showed a marked sympathy for stoicism, most notably, the moral philosophy of Seneca the Younger.

---

36. According to John Aumann, two factors "contributed greatly to the rise of scholasticism: the concordances of Patristic texts on theological questions; and the bitter dispute concerning the respective roles of faith and reason, revelation and speculation, theology and philosophy." See Aumann, *Christian Spirituality in the Catholic Tradition*, 123. A third factor can be added as well: the rediscovery of Aristotle's philosophical works, which had been lost to the West for centuries.

37. Philosophy's "linguistic turn" represented "a radical re-conception of the nature of philosophy and its methods, according to which philosophy is neither an empirical science nor a supra-empirical enquiry into the essential features of reality; instead, it is an *a priori* conceptual discipline which aims to elucidate the complex interrelationships among philosophically relevant concepts, as embodied in established linguistic usage, and by doing so dispel conceptual confusions and solve philosophical problems." Glock and Kalhat, "Linguistic turn."

111. RENAISSANCE PHILOSOPHY

The Renaissance of the fifteenth and sixteenth centuries is more closely associated with humanism than any particular philosophy *per se*. That said, humanism is a somewhat amorphous term. It is best understood, perhaps, as a cultural development that prioritized human beings over God, the cosmos, metaphysics, and ideology as a focal point for human activity. Scholars note that humanism opened conceptual space that would lead, in time, to the development of science, the emergence of deist beliefs, and the legitimation of feelings and emotions in literature and in the arts.[38] The exemplars of this cultural moment included Dante Alighieri (1265–1321), Petrarch (1304–1374), Erasmus (1466–1536), Niccolò Machiavelli, and Thomas More (1478–1535).

The most important development in philosophy *per se* during this time period pertained to politics. A long-standing belief that the way in which society is organized and governed is preordained and unalterable was abandoned by some, including, most notably, Machiavelli and Thomas More. *Contra* the wisdom of Plato, Aristotle, Augustine, Marcus Aurelius, and others who had opined on politics over the centuries, Machiavelli's *The Prince* abandoned any appeal to God or tradition. In Machiavelli's view, the only virtue that should concern the ruler is the effective and ruthless exercise of power, and the only legitimate goal of governance is the achievement and maintenance of power. More's *Utopia* took a different tack. That said, this unusual text has been interpreted in conflicting ways. Indeed, *Utopia* has been described both as satire and as a straightforward prescription for a socialist state oriented to the personal flourishing of its citizens.

It is difficult to imagine the publication of either of these texts prior to the Renaissance. Although they are very different in tenor and in the kinds of society they envisioned, both demonstrated the extent to which the European imagination had been unleashed during the time of the Renaissance.

112. ENLIGHTENMENT PHILOSOPHY

To a considerable extent, our "social imaginary"—to use Charles Taylor's term—remains fully ensconced in the Enlightenment. In our day-to-day

---

38. Ruse, "Humanism," 375–277.

activities, we tend to view the world in material terms. Most of us trust in science. And many of us—in the West, at least—agree with Winston Churchill that "democracy is the worst form of government, except," of course, "for all of the others."

Few thinkers showed any interest in metaphysics during the Enlightenment. In fact, the most notable philosophers of the Enlightenment devoted themselves to epistemology, i.e., the science or philosophy of knowledge and truth. Others focused on politics, thereby demonstrating some interest in justice. Only one, i.e., Immanuel Kant, wrote extensively about moral behavior.

The philosophers of the Enlightenment can be organized into four camps or schools: rationalism, empiricism, transcendental idealism, and contract theory. Each will be introduced in turn.

The epistemologies of the rationalists, whose ranks included René Descartes (1596–1660), Baruch Spinoza (1632–1677), and Gottfried Leibniz (1646–1716), are described in some detail in section 305. Suffice it for now to note their overarching skepticism regarding our ability to know much of anything about the sensible world. Given their distrust of sense data and empirical methods, too, the rationalists searched for certain *a priori* truths that can provide a foundation of sorts for knowledge about ourselves and the world.

In contrast, the empiricists, including Francis Bacon, Thomas Hobbes (1586–1679), John Locke, and George Berkeley, believed sense data to be quite reliable. (David Hume was an exception in this regard.) Further, they celebrated science's potential to disclose truths about the sensible world, which they viewed exclusively—for the most part—in material terms. Again, the respective epistemologies of the empiricists are addressed in some detail in section 305.

Immanuel Kant (1724–1804) tried to reconcile the epistemologies of the rationalists and the empiricists of the Enlightenment. Kant's transcendental idealism discounts our ability to know things we encounter in the real world as they truly are, i.e., their noumena. He argued, instead, that certain innate structures in our minds organize our perceptions into the phenomena that constitute our knowledge—such as it is—of the sensible world.

Unlike most other Enlightenment philosophers, Immanuel Kant showed an interest in moral behavior and proffered a select set of principles in this regard. Kant's "categorical imperatives" are addressed in some detail in section 413.

With respect to political philosophy, Thomas Hobbes, John Locke, and Jean-Jacque Rousseau (1712–1778) all proposed social contracts as alternatives to polities long legitimized on the basis of a supposed divine right of kings. Their views in this regard are addressed in section 415.

113. NINETEENTH CENTURY PHILOSOPHY

The nineteenth century was a heady time in philosophy. This was in keeping with the tenor of the times. Indeed, change was in the air. To many, the prospect of ongoing progress seemed assured. After all, the hard sciences were in their ascendency. Charles Darwin (1809–1882) had advanced a new way of understanding creation. The modern nation-state was assuming a recognizable form, most notably in Germany and Italy. The several continental revolutions of 1848 had shaken the hereditary monarchies of Europe to their cores. The industrial revolution was gathering steam. New ways of imagining the church were emerging as well. Biblical scholarship in Germany was stripping away centuries of staid Biblical exegesis. And Friedrich Schleiermacher (1768–1834), a notable cleric and scholar in the Reformed Tradition, was busy formulating an alternative vision for Christianity, a "liberal" conception that reconciled—in his view—the wisdom of the Enlightenment and the *kerygma* of the early church.

Five distinct philosophies achieved prominence in the nineteenth century: a highly speculative brand of idealism, utilitarianism, Marxist materialism, positivism, and an early expression of existentialism. With a notable exception, these several philosophies embodied the optimism that was evident in so many quarters in nineteenth century Europe.

The idealism of the nineteenth century found root in two locations: Germany and England. Although their respective styles differed considerably, both versions reprised the sweeping and highly imaginative reach of Plato's metaphysics. In several works, including *The Phenomenology of Spirit* (1807), G. W. F. Hegel (1770–1831) posited the existence of an absolute mind or *Geist* which had grown in self-awareness over time as society had evolved from one form or structure into another. According to Hegel, our individual minds are a part of or participate in some way in this world-mind or world-spirit. For his part, Arthur Schopenhauer asserted the existence of a universal will that underlies the whole of nature. According to Schopenhauer, we experience this will in our "desires,

INTRODUCTION TO THE ARISTOTELEAN-THOMIST TRADITION

cravings, yearnings and inevitable dissatisfaction . . . "[39] Unlike Hegel's *Geist*, this universal will is unaware of itself. In the face of unavoidable suffering, Schopenhauer prescribed aesthetic experiences—especially music—as a salve and a compassionate attitude toward others since the predicament in which we find ourselves is universal in nature.[40]

Analogues to Hegel's idealism flourished in England from the mid-nineteenth century to the early decades of the twentieth century. Its chief proponents were T. H. Green (1836–1882), F. H. Bradley (1846–1924), and J. M. E. McTaggart (1866–1925). Green hypothesized the existence of an "eternal consciousness," which "is immanent (indwelling) in humanity and fully exists only when people themselves properly understand that it is within them, and accordingly help to actualize it in themselves."[41] Bradley echoed Hegel in positing the existence of a monistically-conceived "Absolute." In contrast, however, McTaggart described the Absolute in pluralistic terms. In McTaggart's view, "reality is fundamentally a community of minds which in their interrelationships constitute the Absolute, a single divine consciousness with which an inconceivably vast number of streams of finite experience interact and interweave."[42]

The hubris exuded by nineteenth century idealism needed the oxygen of the nineteenth century's belief in the inevitability of progress. It would not survive the trench warfare of the First World War, a worldwide depression, the subsequent rise of fascism and Stalinism, the holocaust, and the threat of annihilation implicit in the Cold War's doctrine of mutually-assured destruction. Indeed, idealism has few adherents in contemporary philosophy. Étienne Gilson's epitaph is apt: "As for those idealist philosophies which are most rigorously consistent, they are marvelous edifices, magnificent intellectual constructions whose artifice one cannot admire enough, but whose essential fault is their not being attached to reality."[43]

Utilitarianism is a consequentialist philosophy. At its core, it concerns social justice, i.e., the way in which life's benefits and burdens are distributed among citizens. Utilitarianism is a hedonistic belief system that defines human beings as sentient animals who seek pleasure all the

---

39. Grayling, *The History of Philosophy*.

40. Many, including Schopenhauer himself, have noted a similarity between his metaphysics and the metaphysics implied in some Hindu and Buddhist beliefs.

41. Grayling, *The History of Philosophy*, 322.

42. Graying, *The History of Philosophy*, 326.

43. Gilson, *Methodological Realism*, 58.

while hoping to minimize the experience of pain. According to utilitarians, the various pleasures and pains individuals in a community might be expected to experience with the implementation of any given policy proposal can be mathematically calculated using "utiles" as a measure. Once this is done, the option that promises the greatest net pleasure and the least amount of pain, i.e., its overall utility, should be adopted. Utilitarianism's originators included Jeremy Bentham (1747–1832) and John Stuart Mill (1806–1873).

Utilitarian thought continues to undergird all kinds of decisions made in all kinds of social settings. This includes business firms and government. It is commonly expressed in the guise of cost-benefit analyses and in the interest group politics now endemic in public life. Because utilitarian thought continues to rival the virtue ethics of the Aristotelian-Thomist Tradition, it is addressed in some detail in section 415.

Karl Marx had little use for the soaring speculation that defined G. W. F. Hegel's idealism. He was a thoroughgoing materialist. Marx borrowed Hegel's dialectic, i.e., the interplay of thesis, antithesis, and synthesis, however, and adapted it to economics and to social analysis more generally. His seminal work, *Das Kapital* (1867), followed his joint publication of the *Communist Manifesto* (1848) with Friedrich Engels (1820–1895). Although Marxist thought had little impact on the politics of nineteenth century Europe, it found its political footing in the Russian Revolution of 1917. The results were unremittingly tragic and long-lasting. Marxist ideology holds little credibility in contemporary philosophy.[44]

Positivism is closely associated with its founder Auguste Comte (1798–1857). Comte embraced the empiricism of the Enlightenment, but went a step further. He boldly critiqued the metaphysical claims that undergird the Aristotelian-Thomist Tradition, the "wooliness" of Kantian and Hegelian idealism, and any and all forms of religious belief as well. In the view of committed positivists, all such talk is utter nonsense and should be discarded forthwith from public discourse.[45] The positivism of

---

44. The one exception, perhaps, is the critical theory of the Frankfort School, which continues to inform the work of Jürgen Habermas. As originally conceived, critical theory drew on a pre-Leninist understanding of Marxist thought and the psychoanalytic theories of Sigmund Freud (1856–1939) as well. Habermas has since steered critical theory in a pragmatic direction.

45. Comte's overreach was evident in his effort to found a secular religion "complete with a catechism, a calendar of saints, priests, rituals, prayers, sacraments, and places of worship. He borrowed all the lineaments of his Religion of Humanity from the Catholicism of his native France, except for God and Christ . . . " In pursuing this objective,

the nineteenth century would give way in the next century to the logical positivism associated with the Vienna Circle. Whereas Comte's primary concerns included political and social beliefs and practices, the logical positivists of the twentieth century focused more intently on language and epistemology more generally.

Existentialism would not take hold in European thought until the twentieth century. Its roots are traceable, however, to two philosophers from the nineteenth century: Søren Kierkegaard (1813–1855) and Friedrich Nietzsche. Kierkegaard wrote in direct opposition to both the soaring idealism espoused by Hegel and the culturally accommodating version of liberal Christianity promoted by Schleiermacher and others. Friedrich Nietzsche's approach to philosophy—and to life more generally—differed dramatically from Kierkegaard's. He asserted a universal "will to power."[46] Whereas Kierkegaard prescribed a seemingly irrational "leap of faith" into the hands of a transcendent God, Nietzsche counseled self-confident living into one's true identity as an *Übermensch* or Overman. It is Nietzsche's path—rather than Kierkegaard's—that reflects the supreme confidence so characteristic of nineteenth century philosophy.

In a very real sense, philosophy reclaimed its Socratic roots in existential thought. Its key question is this: "What is the meaning of this life?" Key concepts in existential thought include the angst or dread we experience in the face of inevitable decline and death, alienation, our consciousness of having been "thrown" into an uncertain future, our unavoidable responsibility for creating meaning in our lives, and—for religious existentialists—the "leap of faith" that is required of true believers.

114. TWENTIETH CENTURY PHILOSOPHY

In the twentieth century, philosophers abandoned the unbounded optimism and grand ambitions of the preceding century. Analytic philosophy—the dominant philosophy of the English-speaking academy in the

---

Comte was following the well-worn path of the Pythagoreans of ancient Greece and the neoplatonists of the first century of the common era as well. Not surprisingly, "the endeavor collapsed in ridicule." See Grayling, *The History of Philosophy*, 303.

46. As shocking as Nietzsche's view in this regard was at the time, it was not unknown in the history of philosophy. As noted by A. C. Grayling, "Plato has Gorgias's pupil Callicles argue thus: conventional morality was invented by the weak to protect themselves against the strong, inhibiting the latter from doing what by nature they have a right to do, which is to use their inferiors for their convenience." See Grayling, *The History of Philosophy*, 54.

twentieth century—focuses almost exclusively on the subdiscipline of epistemology.[47] It is highly technical in nature and circumscribed in its reach. The various "continental philosophies" that competed with analytic philosophy throughout the twentieth century tend to be inward looking and—some would argue—pessimistic in their worldview. And the political philosophies that took root in the twentieth century are defensive in nature, designed—for the most part—to protect individuals and communities from each other, in other words, to keep the wolf of anarchy at bay. Little more is promised by libertarians and contract theorists than a bare modicum of social justice; and pragmatism is dismissed by some as a kind of "muddling through." For their part, postmodernists have abandoned any pretense at systems building. They do little but critique and challenge. Again, the twentieth century will be remembered for its many traumas. The several philosophies that emerged during this time period certainly testify to these scars.

That said, the dominant trends in twentieth century philosophy are best organized by their objects of interest: language; the linguistic turn; the human person; the turn to the self; the "text," i.e., hermeneutics; and politics and culture. Each of these foci will be briefly examined in turn.

Three distinct groupings or schools of philosophy adopted language—and, hence, epistemology—as their chief concern. The first—logical positivism—shared the unbounded confidence in science that had informed the work of the Comtean positivists of the prior century. Eschewing politics and society writ large, however, the logical positivists of the Vienna Circle investigated language and its uses. They found common cause in the informal gatherings of the Vienna Circle hosted by Rudolf Carnap (1891–1970) and Moritz Schlick (1882–1936) between 1924 through 1936. Carnap notably used set theory to expand the kinds of discourse that can be grounded scientifically. Over time, W. V. Quine (1908–2000) and Karl Popper (1900–1994) would make important contributions as well. Quine advocated for a kind of linguistic behaviorism, i.e., an account that attributes all utterances to sensory stimulations of

---

47. Meta-ethics, i.e., the logical meaning ethical claims, is of interest to analytical philosophers. They have little to say about the implications of particular ethical claims *per se*, however, which they tend to view as expressions of psychological states, emotive dispositions, or personal intuitions. This is not to say that analytic philosophers do not hold ethical positions as individuals, however. Bertrand Russell, for instance, participated in public protests against war and nuclear proliferation. These actions had little to do with his philosophy, however.

one kind or another; and Popper proffered the principle of falsifiability as a way to test the truth value of scientific theories.

Analytic philosophers also focused on language. Logic rather than science provided the lens though which they conducted their studies, however. Indeed, analytic philosophy represented "a radical re-conception of the nature of philosophy and its methods, according to which philosophy is neither an empirical science nor a supra-empirical enquiry into the essential features of reality; instead, it is an *a priori* conceptual discipline which aims to elucidate the complex interrelationships among philosophically relevant concepts, as embodied in established linguistic usage, and by doing so dispel conceptual confusions and solve philosophical problems."[48] Analytic philosophy is best understood, perhaps, as a method or set of methods in which complex propositions are broken down into discrete elements for investigation, hence the term "analytic."[49] That said, analysis in this context can be understood in various ways. As noted by A. C. Grayling, "It can mean breaking something down into its constituents; that is 'decomposition.' It can mean showing that something can be explained in terms of something else which is more basic than it; that is 'reduction.' It can involve looking for the 'essence' or defining properties of something. It can involve putting a concept into an illuminating relationship of 'necessity.' It can involve interpreting or translating a concept into other, clearer concepts. It can involve tracing the history of the development of a concept."[50] This range of strategies is very broad, indeed, so much so that some question the coherence of analytic philosophy even at the level of method.

Gottlob Frege (1848–1925) set the agenda for analytic philosophy by developing a complex notation system based on logic, i.e., his *begriffsschrift*, as a technique for analyzing propositions. Following Frege's lead, Bertrand Russell (1872–1970) developed a somewhat simpler notation system in partnership with Alfred North Whitehead (1861–1947). Ludwig Wittgenstein (1889–1951)—referred to in this iteration as the "early Wittgenstein"—went even further. In his *Tractatus Logico-Philosophicus*

---

48. Glock and Kalhat, "Linguistic turn."

49. Analytic philosophers hoped to fulfill Gottfried Leibniz's dream of a "*characteristica universalis*, a perfectly clear and ordered language, in which mathematics, science, and metaphysics can be expressed without ambiguity, and in which problems can be solved by 'calculation,' thus overcoming disagreement." See Grayling, *The History of Philosophy*, 347.

50. Grayling, *The History of Philosophy*, 344.

(1921), he argued that we can only know "facts," not "things in the world." (To this point in his analysis, Wittgenstein echoed Kant.) He argued further, however, that propositions about facts constitute "states of affairs," which should conform to a rigorous logic if they are to convey any meaning whatsoever. This is sometimes referred to as the verification principle of meaning.[51] According to Wittgenstein, this means that metaphysical propositions—indeed, all kind of philosophical, religious, and aesthetic discourse—stand outside the "bounds of sense."[52] In his own words, "what can be said at all can be said clearly, i.e., logically, and what we cannot talk about, we must consign to silence."[53]

Not surprisingly, the reduction of language to logical and mathematical notation engendered a backlash, a third wave in the linguistic turn of the twentieth century. G. E. Moore (1873-1958) pointed to the enduring value of "common sense."[54] (Although Moore aimed his critique at his idealist colleagues, it hit home among scholars in the analytic wing of language philosophy as well.) Much to the consternation of his colleagues and students, Ludwig Wittgenstein—the "later Wittgenstein"—then repudiated his earlier contributions to analytic philosophy in a posthumous publication, *Philosophical Investigations* (1953). He confessed to having abandoned his belief that language should be subjected to the rigors of logic in order to be accepted as meaningful. Wittgenstein argued, instead, that language is a "form of life," which is crafted in the context of particular life settings. Indeed, different "language games" are practiced in different communities. Given this, a universal logic makes no sense in the case of language. In this same vein, Gilbert Ryle (1900-1976) disparaged correspondence theory, an understating of knowledge that associates particular utterances with particular things in the sensible world. He focused, instead, on the myriad "connections" that make language meaningful.

---

51. Peterson and Pugh, "Introduction to Analytic Thomism," xviii.

52. Hacker, "Ludwig Josef Johan Wittgenstein," 913. More than one observer has noted that Wittgenstein succeeded in sawing off the philosophical branch on which he had been sitting.

53. Quoted in Grayling, *The History of Philosophy*, 373-374.

54. The pragmatist William James famously derided scholasticism as "common sense's college-trained younger sister . . . " According to James, scholasticism "was nothing but common sense rendered pedantic." As noted by F. C. Copleston, "This was not intended exactly as a compliment; nor would James's verdict be accepted by everyone. But there is some truth in the remark. For Aquinas, to confine one's observations to him, did not think that the philosopher enjoys private access to a sphere of realty from which ordinary people are excluded." See Copleston, *Aquinas*, 43-44.

Indeed, Ryle thought of philosophy as a kind of "conceptual geography" or "cartography."55 And John Austin (1911–1960) would describe "speech acts" as performances of a sort that should be analyzed as such.

As the term implies, the "turn to the self" characteristic of the various "continental philosophies" of the twentieth century is oriented, less to language *per se*, than to the lived experience of human beings. In this view, the key questions of interest include: How should we understand ourselves? How can we experience meaning in our lives? And what stance should we assume in the face of the challenges life inevitably poses?

Together, Edmund Husserl (1859–1938) and Maurice Merleau-Ponty (1907–1961), the two leading lights of philosophical phenomenalism, would have a significant impact on continental philosophy, but—for the most part—through the work of others. Indeed, Husserl's version of phenomenalism would be absorbed to a considerable extent into the science of cognitive psychology. Husserl focused intently on the subjective experience of consciousness. If philosophy can be defined as "thinking about thinking," then phenomenalism can be understood as "thinking about thinking about thinking." To this end, he developed a unique set of tools, e.g., the *epoche*, bracketing, eidetic reduction, and more, for isolating and then reflecting on consciousness. In Husserl's view, consciousness has both a personal dimension and a subjective dimension and a communal dimension as well. With respect to the latter, Husserl coined the term "lifeworld" or *lebenswelt*, a concept that would be further developed by others in the continental wing of twentieth century philosophy. In a similar way, traces of Merleu-Ponty's focus on the body as an "ambiguous mode of existence that infects knowledge"56 can be detected in Pope John Paul II's theology of the body.

The secular existentialism of Martin Heidegger (1889–1976)—one of Edmund Husserl's students—and Jean-Paul Sartre (1905–1980) inherited the somewhat dour worldview associated with Søren Kierkegaard's seminal contributions, but discarded his religious orientation.57 The impact of

---

55. Grayling, *The History of Philosophy*, 406–407.

56. Bernasconi, "Maurice Merleau-Ponty," 554.

57. *Faith Connection: Contra* Heidegger and Sartre, a number of twentieth century existentialists grounded their views on faith. Paul Tillich (1886–1965), a Lutheran, focused on the individual's need to "create" a personal sense of meaning: "Man's being includes his relation to meanings." See Tillich, *The Courage to Be*, 50. Further, "spiritual self-affirmation occurs in every moment in which man lives creatively in the various spheres of meaning. 'Creative,' in this context, has the sense, not of original creativity as performed by the genius, but of living spontaneously in action and reaction . . . "

twentieth century existentialism on Thomism is addressed in some detail in section 504. It is sufficient for now to note that the foci of nineteenth century existentialism were carried over in its twentieth century variants.

The "turn to the text," i.e., the artifact or any other object or subject of interest, in fact, including truth claims, is also thought of as a continental philosophy. Hermeneutics is the "science of interpretation." The term "science" is misleading in this context, however. In the hands of Hans-Georg Gadamer (1900–2002) and Paul Ricoeur (1913–2005), interpretation was reframed as a mutually-experienced and—at times—life changing encounter. Gadamer believed that each generation is challenged to interpret a text, an event, or a life to meet its own needs.[58] In this sense, there is no such thing as an original and inviolable meaning; upon inspection, every text, event, or life makes a truth claim. The object of study is approached as something quite independent of its creator and the time in which it was produced or occurred.[59] Understanding is achieved through a distinctive back-and-forth process called the "hermeneutic circle," in which the interpreter wrestles with anomalies and discontinuities in the artifact. The interpreter engages the object of study in the back-and-forth of the hermeneutic circle.[60] A successful encounter then leads to a "fusion of horizons" in which understanding takes place.[61] Again, this understanding may or may not reflect the author's intended meaning. Ricoeur's account of interpretation is similar to Gadamer's in several respects, but emphasizes to a greater extent the potential for a life-changing impact on the interpreter.

Two prominent political philosophies were revived in the twentieth century: libertarianism, a reprise of classic liberalism, and contract

---

See Tillich, *The Courage to Be*, 46. Martin Buber drew on his roots in Hasidic Judaism in affirming authentic relationships with people and with God as precursors to the existential experience of meaning: "The basic word I-You can only be spoken with one's whole being. The basic word I-It can never be spoken with one's whole being... You has no borders." See Buber, *I and Thou*, 54–55. Michael De Unamuno, a Catholic, linked his understanding of meaning to the stance one takes against an unwanted future over which he or she has little or no control. In doing so, he invoked the tragic-comic hero of Miguel de Cervantes's novel *Don Quixote*: "This personal and affective starting point for all philosophy and all religion is the tragic sense of life." See De Unamuno, *Tragic Sense of Life*, 37. Further, "this tragic sense is the spring of heroic achievements." See De Unamuno, *Tragic Sense of Life*, 125.

58. Gadamer, *Truth and Method*, 296.
59. Gadamer, *Truth and Method*, 287.
60. Gadamer, *Truth and Method*, 266.
61. Gadamer, *Truth and Method*, 306.

INTRODUCTION TO THE ARISTOTELEAN-THOMIST TRADITION

theory. Both are addressed in some detail in section 415. Suffice it for now to note that F. A. Hayek (1899–1998), Milton Friedman (1912–2006), Ayn Rand (1905–2002), and Robert Nozick (1938–2002) all contributed significantly to the development of contemporary libertarianism. John Rawls (1921–2002) played a similar role in the case of contract theory.

In contrast, pragmatism only emerged as a political theory in the twentieth century. Like utilitarianism, pragmatism is a consequentialist political philosophy. Its first generation of theorists included John Dewey (1859–1952), William James (1842–1910), and C. S. Peirce (1839–1914). Jürgen Habermas (b. 1929) and Richard Rorty (1931–2007) have proven more influential of late, however. Pragmatism is also addressed in considerable detail in section 415.

In the latter half of the twentieth century, postmodernism emerged as a counter-narrative to the philosophies of the nineteenth and twentieth centuries. Like existentialism, postmodern thought owes much to Edmund Husserl. The postmodern critique is about power and how it is exercised in ways that are both obvious and covert. Michael Foucault (1926–1984) argued that institutional, political, and personal power now determine what "counts as knowledge, madness, crime or acceptable sexual expression." This insight, according to Foucault, awakens us to "the perennial need to resist, to be suspicious and alert."[62] To pursue this objective, Jacques Derrida (1930–2004) recommended methodological "deconstruction" in order to reveal the contexts, histories, and perspectives that now masquerade as truth. For his part, Jean-François Lyotard (1924–1998) dismissed the "grand narratives" of modernism, including progress, science, and rationality, as deceptions that need to be subverted and replaced by a new sets of life-giving and life-sustaining narratives of a personal and more local nature.[63]

The foregoing analyses should not imply that the Aristotelian-Thomist Tradition has been forgotten or set aside of late. It is alive and well, especially in the philosophical subdiscipline of ethics. As detailed in section 506, the personalism of Karol Wojtyla, in particular, would complement the resurgence of virtue ethics in the late twentieth century, a renaissance that would be prompted by Gertrude Elizabeth Margaret Anscombe (1919–2001) and led by Philippa Foot (b. 1920) and Alasdair MacIntyre (b. 1929).

62. Grayling, *The History of Philosophy*, 510.
63. Grayling, *The History of Philosophy*, 511.

2

Metaphysics

201. METAPHYSICS

Metaphysics is the branch of philosophy that explores the nature of reality. As we shall see, this concern was of the utmost importance to the ancient Greeks and to the scholastic philosophers of the high and late Middle Ages as well. With a few notable exceptions, philosophers since the time of the Enlightenment have tended to focus more on epistemology (sixteenth to the eighteenth centuries), language (nineteenth and twentieth centuries), personhood and the experience of meaning (twentieth century), and culture (twentieth and twenty-first centuries) than metaphysics *per se*.

For the most part, realists who have followed Aristotle cordon off or "bracket" the sensible or material world in their pursuit of metaphysical knowledge. Paul J. Glenn thus defines metaphysics as "the science of non-material real being."[1] Metaphysical realists in the Aristotelian-Thomist Tradition typically relegate cosmology—a discipline sometimes identified as a sub-branch of metaphysics—to the natural sciences.[2] Realists in the Aristotelian-Thomist Tradition thus tend to focus more narrowly

---

1. Glenn, *An Introduction to Philosophy*, 258.

2. Different taxonomies of metaphysics abound, in fact. Paul J. Glenn, for instance, locates theodicy and criteriology, together with ontology, under the rubric of metaphysics. See Glenn, *An Introduction to Philosophy*, 259. Others include logic, the philosophy of language, phenomenology, the philosophy of religion, the philosophy of science, and rational psychology as well.

on the study of non-material and non-temporal[3] real being and mind-dependent or logical being as well, i.e., ontology or general metaphysics.[4]

As has been noted, we are all children of the Enlightenment, and so the realist conception of metaphysics can be challenging. We rarely think in terms of metaphysical categories, e.g., being, substance, essence, form, etc.. Indeed, the Enlightenment's foundational commitment to a material and non-spiritual worldview generally precludes the possibility of any kind of "being" as such, i.e., being that is non-material and non-temporal in nature.

202. KEY CONCERNS OF METAPHYSICS

To a considerable extent, the metaphysical realism of the Aristotelian-Thomist Tradition inherited its key concerns from the presocratics:

- How do we explain the variety and diversity of the existent "things" we encounter in the sensible world?
- And how do we account for the persistent identity or integrity of anything in the sensible world when everything seems—on the surface, at least—to be in flux?

As we shall see, Aristotle approached both of these questions from the same vantage point: a disciplined investigation of substances. Thomas Aquinas would adopt Aristotle's approach to these questions, but would focus more intently on existence. Most importantly, he would do so in a way that accommodated and complemented Christian theology.

203. METAPHYSICAL REALISM

Metaphysical realism in the Aristotelian-Thomist Tradition holds that "things" manifest in the world independently of our experience of them or our knowledge of them. According to metaphysical realists, the

3. The terms "non-material" and "non-temporal" are used here in lieu of the more frequently used term "eternal," since the latter can suggest a continuous existence in time and space. Foundational concepts employed in the realist metaphysics of the Aristotelian-Thomist Tradition tend to be supra-physical or supra-natural in nature. They "transcend" all material and sensible categories of knowledge, including both space and time.

4. Ontology can also be understood more narrowly as a kind of philosophical taxonomy or listing of relevant metaphysical categories.

sensible world is not illusory or dependent on our conception of it. On the contrary, reality—as we experience it—has a structure and a nature that exists quite independently of us. Further, these "things" in the world include "universals," e.g., a color, a virtue, a species, etc., and notional or mind-dependent beings as well. See sections 210 and 215.

Realists in the Aristotelian-Thomist Tradition argue that this view holds two advantages over idealism and other versions of anti-realist thought, most notably nominalism and conceptualism: first, it accords well with our everyday understanding of the world; and second, it accounts for universals and other forms of abstract thought that enable us to make sense of our world. Indeed, Aristotle anticipated a key argument against nominalism in celebrating metaphysical realism's sense-making capacity: "If there is nothing apart from individual things, and the individuals are infinite in number, how then, is it possible to get knowledge of the infinite individuals? For all things that we come to know, we come to know in so far as they have some unity and identity, and in so far as some attribute belongs to them universally."[5] (As we shall see, the understanding of universals is a key fault line in metaphysics. As explained by Michael J. Loux, "the phenomenon of similarity or attribute agreement gives rise to the debate between realists and nominalists. Realists claim that where objects are similar or agree in attribute, there is some one thing that they share or have in common; nominalists deny this. Realists call these shared entities universals; they say that universals are entities."[6])

Thomas Aquinas embraced Aristotle's metaphysics. In doing so, he sought to synthesize Aristotle's philosophical realism and Christian beliefs, and he achieved considerable success in doing so. Critical differences in their views are evident, nonetheless. Whereas substance served as the primary lens through which Aristotle approached his work,[7] Thomas Aquinas organized his reflections around the concept of existence and hence being. Whereas Aristotle was primarily concerned about the "whatness" of things, Aquinas focused more on their "isness." Further, Aquinas posited a personal God who loves us.[8] In contrast, Ar-

---

5. Aristotle, *Metaphysics*, 47.
6. Loux, *Metaphysics*, 20.
7. Aristotle, *Metaphysics*, 145.
8. *Faith Connection*: In the Christian tradition, God is best understood as pure existence or pure actuality, a view seemingly confirmed in the story of the burning bush in the Book of Exodus: "Moses said to God, 'If I go to the Israelites and say to them, "The God of your ancestors has sent me to you," and they ask me, "What is his name?" what do I tell them?' God replied to Moses, 'I am who I am.' Then he added, 'This is what you

istotle described an "unmoved mover" existing outside of time and space, a portrayal that falls well short of the personal God revealed in the Judeo-Christian Tradition.[9] Still further, Aquinas emphasized the importance of teleology, i.e., the orientation of everything in all of creation to one or more particular purposes, to a greater extent than did Aristotle.

204. THE CATHOLIC CHURCH AND METAPHYSICAL REALISM

Although the Catholic Church does not endorse any particular philosophy as such, it has tended to privilege metaphysical realism over certain other perspectives, including idealism, nominalism, conceptualism, constructivism, monism, and pluralism.[10] First, metaphysical realism affirms our everyday understanding of the sensible world. Indeed, metaphysical realism acknowledges the sensible world to be both real *and* knowable. It thus underwrites a belief in God's providential and loving purposes, which inform both the creation story that begins the Book of Genesis and our Christian understanding of the Incarnation. Second, metaphysical realism can accommodate Christian moral thinking in a way that the alternatives noted above cannot. See section 405.

The metaphysical positions proffered by some other Catholic philosophers, e.g., Bonaventure, William of Ockham, and John Duns Scotus notwithstanding, the church has demonstrated a marked preference for Thomas Aquinas's metaphysical framework. See section 102.

205. ALTERNATIVE VIEWS

At the broadest level, the very possibility of metaphysical inquiry is rejected by some scientists and positivists, too. Scientism is a pejorative term that is applicable, nonetheless, to extreme materialists who reduce all philosophical questions to scientific questions, all of which have been

---

will tell the Israelites, "I AM has sent me to you"'" (Exodus 3:13–14).

9. Aristotle, *Metaphysics*, 189. Aristotle also described the "unmoved mover" in terms remarkably amenable to a Christian conception of God: "Life also belongs to God; for the actuality of thought is life, and God is that actuality; and God's self-dependent actuality is life most good and eternal. We say therefore that God is a living being, eternal, most good, so that life and duration continuous and eternal belong to God; for this is God." See Aristotle, *Metaphysics*, 256.

10. John Paul II, *Fides et Ratio*, no. 49–51.

or will be answered—they claim—at some future date. To the extent that philosophical questions are being gradually "eliminated" by science, those who adhere to this view are sometimes referred to as "eliminativists."[11]

Logical positivists dismiss the claims of metaphysical realists whose "transcendental" concepts lie—by definition—entirely outside of time and space. In their view, nothing asserted by metaphysical realists is verifiable and so—according to positivists, at least—it is all meaningless. (Although logical positivism has fallen by the academic wayside, its focus on the concrete meaning of terms and its materialist presuppositions persist in analytic philosophy and in other philosophies of language.)

Unlike many scientists and positivists, some idealists affirm the ongoing relevance of metaphysical inquiry. That said, idealism comes in two varieties: one that postulates a reality that transcends the sensible world, i.e., metaphysical idealism, and another that asserts the priority of our minds—or God's—over matter, i.e., critical idealism.[12] Plato's metaphysics is an example of the first version[13] and so, too, the idealism advanced by G. F. W. Hegel, who argued that all changes in nature and in all of human history, too, can be attributed to an "absolute mind." Like Plato's Forms, this absolute mind is thought to be prior to and, hence, more "real" that anything in the sensible world. The idealism espoused by certain Enlightenment and nineteenth century philosophers is of a different sort. It prioritizes mind over matter. George Berkeley argued, for instance, that the physical world is nothing more than a collection of ideas in the mind of God. Immanuel Kant's transcendental idealism asserted that the innate structures of our mind order our inchoate perceptions of the world. In Kant's view, we project meaning on the phenomenal world. And Arthur Schopenhauer followed Kant in holding that "the physical world exists only for the subject of knowledge."[14] Again, idealism—broadly construed—comes in two forms.

The idealist perspectives noted above share a particular point of view, however: an underlying belief that the sensible world is *either* illusory *or* subordinate in some fundamental sense to a non-material or ideal realm of some sort or to the innate structures of our own minds. As

11 Lowe, "Opposition to Metaphysics," 559.

12. Étienne Gilson, *Methodological Realism*, 85.

13. According to Plato, the Forms we intuit are more "real" than anything we might encounter in the sensible world. Given this, his metaphysics are better described as a kind of metaphysical realism.

14. Sprigge, "Arthur Schopenhauer," 802.

Ernest Sosa puts it, "idealists view reality as ultimately spiritual *or* mental. For them the basic particulars are subjects of thought or experience, souls or sprits or monads, the world of matter in motion being nothing more than a stable appearance to our minds . . . For idealists, physical bodies are rather like images in a rich and stable dream."[15]

With respect to the more narrow but critical question of universals and other kinds of abstract or mind-dependent beings, nominalists assert that they add nothing to our understanding of reality. Nominalism is associated with William of Ockham, a Franciscan, who dismissed all nonmaterial concepts, e.g., being, substance, essence, nature, etc., as superfluous. According to nominalists, the term "tree" has no meaning beyond that which can be obtained by encountering any number of individual trees. Similarly, there is no such thing as "humanity" outside of our minds. We can only know individual human beings. In this sense, "humanity" does not exist in any real sense; at best, it is a mental construct or "set" that helps us cope on a day-in, day-out basis. William of Ockham thus employed his "principle of parsimony," i.e., Ockham's razor, in attempting to dismantle the structure of Aristotelian-Thomist metaphysics. Because nominalism can undermine our confidence in the everyday language we use in communicating with others, however, it can engender epistemological skepticism.[16]

Conceptualism is also opposed to metaphysical realism's understanding of universals and other abstract or mind-dependent beings. Indeed, conceptualism is often conflated with nominalism. They both deny the existence of universals and other kinds of abstract or mind-dependent beings whose independent existence is asserted by metaphysical realists. Still, some nominalists uphold the existence of a spiritual realm. In contrast, conceptualism is more commonly associated with the materialism that undergirded Enlightenment thought. Immanuel Kant, whose "transcendental idealism" acknowledges the external world to be

---

15. Sosa, "Problems of Metaphysics," 560.

16. This version of nominalism is sometimes called "austere nominalism." Other versions of nominalism resist the charge of incoherence that attends to nominalism more broadly, however. Drawing on the presuppositions of analytic philosophy, metalinguistic nominalists, for instance, reduce our everyday use of attributes, i.e., the supposed universals of metaphysical realists, to "ways we make claims about language." And trope theorists define all attributes as particulars. An example of trope theory is shared by Michael J. Loux: "When I focus on the color of the Taj Mahal, I am not thinking of pinkness in general, but of that unique pinkness, the pinkness that only the Taj Mahal has . . . " See Loux, *Metaphysics*, 58. It is difficult, in fact, to understand how either approach overcomes the inherent incoherence of this view that was first noted by Aristotle.

"real" but unknowable, as such, can thus be viewed as a conceptualist rather than a nominalist. According to Kant, knowledge of the sensible world and universals and other kinds of abstract or logical thought, too, are entirely dependent on certain categories of thinking, e.g., space and time, causality, etc., all of which are attributable to the innate structures of our minds.

With respect to its understanding of universals and other forms of abstract or logical thought, metaphysical realism can be contrasted with constructivism as well. Constructivism is a foundational perspective associated, most notably, with postmodern philosophers, many of whom attribute our understanding of the sensible world to certain social, cultural, and linguistic practices. In their view, knowledge cannot be discovered or encountered as such; on the contrary, knowledge is created or "constructed" by human beings in human settings. In their view, there is no such thing as an objective reality that exists independently of our social, cultural, and linguistic practices.

There is a third way in which the metaphysical realism of the Aristotelian-Thomist Tradition can be contrasted with other philosophical perspectives. It pertains to the nature of the reality we encounter in the sensible world. Indeed, metaphysical realism represents a kind of middle position between two rather extreme views: monism and pluralism.

Monism is the belief that reality is composed of just one thing. Following Parmenides, monists view change as illusory and deny the diversity of existent things. Because pantheism identifies God with nature, it can be thought of as a kind of monism and so, too, the idealism of Baruch Spinoza, who asserted that "God is nature and nature is God." In claiming that God stands within the natural order, Spinoza denied the belief that God summoned creation forth from nothing. To the extent that it dismisses the reality of a supernatural or spiritual order, the scientism now so prevalent in the academy can also be thought of as a kind of monism. Scientism views reality as material in nature and fully determined.

In contrast, extreme pluralism holds that there is no underlying unity, substance, or principle to the "things" we encounter in the sensible world. Metaphysical pluralists struggle to explain the regularity of events we experience in our day-to-day lives, however. Further, they generally deny the existence of a personal God who intervenes in creation or any kind of teleology or ultimate purpose to existence.

In contrast to monism and extreme pluralism, metaphysical realism affirms that the world is made up of various kinds of beings—including actual real beings, potential beings, and mind-dependent beings, too—and that these various manifestations or potential manifestations of being are knowable through one or more of our five senses and/or by way of our ability to reason.[17]

206. A GRAPHICAL DISPLAY OF METAPHYSICAL REALISM

We turn more specifically now to key concepts in the metaphysics of the Aristotelian-Thomist Tradition, several of which are displayed graphically below.[18]

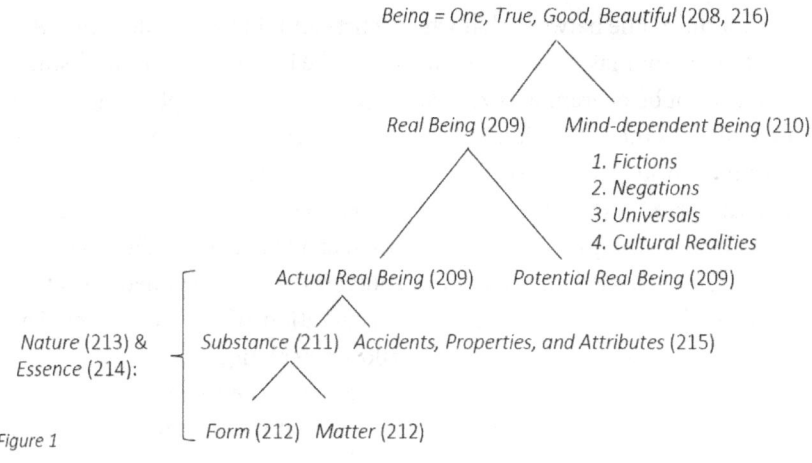

Figure 1

---

17. *Faith Connection*: This middle ground between monism and extreme pluralism is reflected in the story of creation in the very first chapter of the Book of Genesis. God created various kinds of things and declared them all to be good. In his apostolic exhortation *Evangelii Gaudium* (*The Joy of the Gospel*), Pope Francis embraced this view in quoting Thomas Aquinas's celebration of the sheer richness of God's creation: "St. Thomas Aquinas noted that multiplicity and variety 'were the intention of the first agent,' who wished that 'what each individual thing lacked in order to reflect the divine goodness would be made up for by other things,' since the Creator's goodness 'could not be fittingly reflected by just one creature.' Consequently, we need to grasp the variety of things in their multiple relationships." See Francis, *Evangelii Gaudium*, no. 44.

18. The graph that follows is a modest revision of a version developed by James M. Jacobs. See Jacobs, *Seat of Wisdom*, 123.

The relationships between and among these various concepts are more formal than real. All of the subordinate or "inferior"[19] terms displayed are aspects of being or being viewed from a particular perspective. They are not separate or distinct realities *per se*. As A. C. Cotter puts it, "differences in being are not extrinsic additions, but more distinct expressions of what is in the inferiors. They are modes of 'being.'"[20] That said, the formal distinctions displayed here can be helpful in a survey of Aristotelian-Thomist metaphysics. Each of these concepts will be examined in turn.

207. EXISTENCE

Metaphysical realists begin with the enigma of existence. In doing so, they draw a sharp line between that which exists and that which does not. According to Thomas Aquinas, in particular, the importance of this distinction cannot be overemphasized. Materialists simply accept the "given" of existence. In their view, it is sufficient to reflect on concrete things in the sensible world. Metaphysical realists in the Aristotelian-Thomist Tradition disagree. In their view, existence itself has to be explained. After all, why do some things—including us—exist at all? Further, philosophers in the Aristotelian-Thomist Tradition contend that a disciplined reflection on existence inevitably leads to a consideration of pure existence, i.e., God, the source and summit of all philosophical inquiry.

Embedded as we are in a worldview inherited from the Enlightenment, our first instinct may be to think that the distinction between that which exists and that which does not juxtaposes the material world against the non-material world, i.e., tangible things in space and time *vis-à-vis* anything else that might be imagined. Metaphysical realism holds, however, that nothing at all can be said about that which does not exist or could not potentially exist. And since we clearly talk about non-material "things," e.g., species and genera, numbers, ideas, propositions, events, states of affairs, etc., these "things" must exist, too, in some "real" sense, albeit in some non-material and non-temporal sense or in some analogous way, at least. (In lieu of the verb "exists," the term "subsists"

---

19. Cotter, *An Introduction to Catholic Philosophy*, 310.
20. Cotter, *An Introduction to Catholic Philosophy*, 315.

is often used to describe the way in which these kinds of non-material "subsistents" manifest in the world.[21])

The precise relationship shared by existence and essence, i.e., substance viewed from a particular perspective, is debated among metaphysical realists. Whereas Thomists argue that the difference between existence and essence is real and that existence, i.e., the "isness" of a thing, precedes essence, i.e., its "whatness," others, including Francisco Suarez (1548–1617), claim that the distinction between the two is merely formal or conceptual in nature.[22]

208. BEING

The concept of "being"[23] is of the utmost importance in metaphysical realism, and it plays a significant role in realist epistemology, too. The idea of "being" can be enormously challenging, however.

In fact, being has two formal meanings in the metaphysical realism of the Aristotelian-Thomist Tradition: *ens*, i.e., that which is, and *esse*, i.e., that by which a thing is. *Ens* pertains to existence and so characterizes everything that exists, including all real beings, both actual and potential, and all mind-dependent or logical beings, i.e., beings of reason, too, in effect, anything that exists or can be thought to exist and anything that subsists or can be thought to subsist. All things in existence in the sensible world or having the potential for existence in the sensible world can thus be referred to as "existents." In an analogous way, mind-dependent beings that we encounter in thought or in communications with others are said to "subsist"[24] and so can be referred to as "subsistents." To say that anything has being is simply to say that it exists or participates in existence or that it subsists or exhibits subsistence. Drawing on both Aristotle[25] and Thomas Aquinas, Paul J. Glenn affirms that "everything is a being,

---

21. Aquinas also differentiated between "subsisting existence" and "material existence." See Thomas Aquinas, "On Being and Essence," 197.

22. Suarez, "Essence and Existence," 235.

23. Philosophers tend to use a variety of synonyms for the term "being," including "thing," "reality," "entity," and "object." Antonyms include "nothing," "non-entity," "unreality," and "nil." See Cotter, *An Introduction to Catholic Philosophy*, 318.

24. Mind-dependent or logical beings do not exist in the same way that tangible things, i.e., existents, manifest in the sensible world. Given this, the verb "subsist" and the noun "subsistence" are used in referring to the ontological status of mind-dependent beings. Technically, "subsistence" refers to the particular manner of a being's existence.

25. Aristotle, *Metaphysics*, 223.

every difference of things is a being, every special character is a being, every conceivable thing is a being."[26] This is the sense in which the term "being" is transcendental in nature,[27] in fact; it pertains to everything that exists or subsists. Still further, other concepts in realist metaphysics, e.g., substance, matter, form, nature, essence, etc., cannot truly be separated from the concept of being. They each speak to "being" viewed from a particular perspective; they are "aspects"[28] or "categories"[29] of being.

Esse is the causal principle that explains why anything exists at all. Since no being can conjure itself into existence, *esse*, the cause of existence, must come from outside of each and every entity that exists or subsists or could potentially exist or subsist. *Esse* thus addresses a concern that is entirely ignored in nominalism, conceptualism, constructivism, and various other philosophies that are grounded exclusively on a materialist conception of reality.[30]

Whereas Aristotle attributed both *ens* and *esse* to the form of any given substance, Thomas Aquinas attributed independent ontological

---

26. Glenn, *An Introduction to Philosophy*, 261.

27. Cotter, *An Introduction to Catholic Philosophy*, 311.

28. Aquinas, *The Summa Theologica and The Summa Contra Gentiles*, 236–237.

29. Loux, *Metaphysics*, X. See also Cotter, *An Introduction to Catholic Philosophy*, 299.

30. *Faith Connection*: We tend to think of "being" as a noun. In the Aristotelian-Thomist Tradition, however, being is better understood as a verb. This is particularly so in Thomas Aquinas's reflections on being. In Aquinas's view, our being—and the being of all other creatures, as well—is not our own *per se*: "Everything that is is from God . . . Therefore, all beings other than God are not their own being, but are beings by participation." See Aquinas, *The Summa Theologica and The Summa Contra Gentiles*, 234. Elsewhere, Aquinas was more circumspect in this regard. See Aquinas, "The Principles of Nature," 190. Today, the Catechism of the Catholic Church seems to follow Bonaventure more closely than Aquinas in endorsing a remarkably fulsome understanding of the relationship shared by God as Being and all other beings: "The world, and man, attests that they contain within themselves neither their first principle nor their final end, but rather that they participate in Being itself, which alone is without origin or end. Thus, in different ways, man can come to know that there exists a reality which is the first cause and final end of all things, a reality that everyone calls God." See *Catechism*, no. 34. In contrast, James M. Jacobs echoes Aquinas's hesitation in this regard in describing our participation in God's Being as once-removed, as it were: "This participation in being is in God directly but in *esse commune*, the common being that is the foundation for the existence of things other than God." See James M. Jacobs, *Seat of Wisdom*, 109. Pursuing the logic of this view, it may be inappropriate to think of God himself as Being, since God is better understood as pure actuality or pure existence. Others in the Aristotelian-Thomist Tradition attempt to resolve this conundrum by treating Being in God—or more appropriately, perhaps, God as Being—as merely analogous to all other manifestations of being, a view formally adopted by Pope Pius X in 1914 in thesis four of his twenty-four theses on authentic Catholic philosophy. See Pius X, "Twenty-four Thomistic Theses," 294.

status to being itself and, in doing so, positioned both existence and subsistence in this more foundational and transcendental reality.[31] That said, Aquinas agreed with Aristotle in privileging being exhibited or instantiated in substances of various kinds. According to Aquinas, "being is absolutely and primarily said of substances, and only secondarily and in a certain sense said of accidents . . ."[32]

209. ACTUAL VS. POTENTIAL BEING

The concept of being can be further disaggregated—albeit only formally so—into two distinct ontological categories. The first encompasses real beings and the second beings of reason or mind-dependent or logical beings. Real beings—both actual and potential—are addressed here. (Again echoing A. C. Cotter, "being is that which can exists, whether it actually exists or not."[33]) Mind-dependent beings are examined in section 210.

Actual real being includes things that are wholly "extended," "instantiated," or realized in space and time. According to the Aristotelian-Thomist Tradition, a rock, a fully grown tree, and a fully developed human being are all ontologically endowed with actual real being. They "extend" or manifest in space and time.

In contrast, potential real being or "possibles" includes beings that could come into being, but have yet to do so, and beings that are in the process of "becoming" as well. It is important to note that every potential being must be capable of existence.[34] For example, a square circle cannot be considered a being as such, nor can a mermaid. Neither are capable of existence; both are imaginary and "necessarily un-exemplifiable."[35] As noted by A. C. Cotter, "possibles are neither nothing nor mere 'logical beings' for they have the capacity to exist, which neither absolute nothing nor the logical being has."[36]

Objective potency is the "capacity of a non-existent" but possible being to exist.[37] According to Aristotle, "potency is prior to the actual

---

31. Jacobs, *Seat of Wisdom*, 103.
32. Aquinas, "On Being and Substance," 193.
33. Cotter, *An Introduction to Catholic Philosophy*, 318.
34. Glenn, *An Introduction to Philosophy*, 263.
35. Loux, *Metaphysics*, 45.
36. Cotter, *An Introduction to Catholic Philosophy*, 299–319.
37. Cotter, *An Introduction to Catholic Philosophy*, 328.

cause, and it is not necessary for everything that is potential to be actual ... Even that which is not yet is capable of being; for that which is not comes to be, but nothing that is incapable of being comes to be."[38] Thomas Aquinas agreed: "That which can be and is not is said to exist in potency, while that which already is is said to exist in act."[39] Think, for instance, of a seed, a sapling, an embryo, and a teenager, none of which or whom have yet to realize their full potential or—in the Christian view—to have fulfilled their ultimate purpose or *telos*. For some metaphysical realists, the ontological status of potential real being extends even to plants that have yet to be pollinated and human beings who have yet to be conceived.

As noted by James M. Jacobs, "existence perfects or actualizes the potential of an essence."[40] See section 214. Metaphysical realists describe this movement from potential real being to actual real being in terms of two "acts" through which potential real being manifests in the sensible world and then develops over time.

- In the first act, i.e., *actu primus*, an actual real being manifests with a particular nature or way of being in the world and an essence that differentiates it both from actual real beings in other species or genera and from other actual real beings in its own species and genera. The essence of a tree and the essence of a human being are thus embodied—quite literally—in particular trees and particular human beings. Again, this movement from potentiality to actuality is referred to as "becoming"[41] or *in fieri*, i.e., in the making. Prior to becoming, a being is said to have "objective potential."[42]

---

38. Aristotle, *Metaphysics*, 56–57.
39. Copleston, *Aquinas*, 97.
40. Jacobs, *Seat of Wisdom*, 118.

41. *Faith Connection*: The Catholic Church locates human dignity, which it believes to be inviolable, in this first movement from potential real being to actual real being. "*Human life is sacred* because from its beginning it involves the creative action of God and it remains forever in a special relationship with the Creator, which is its sole end. God alone is the Lord of life from its beginning until its end . . . " See *Catechism*, no. 2258. In this view, human dignity is not dependent on the physical or mental development, perceived worthiness, social "convenience," merits, or moral faults of a particular man or woman, all of which manifest in the context of *actu secundus*: "It is not intellect, consciousness, and freedom that define the person, rather it is the person who is the basis of the acts of intellect, consciousness, and freedom. These acts can even be absent, for even without them, man does not cease to be a person." See Pontifical Council for Justice and Peace, *Compendium*, no. 131.

42. Glenn, *An Introduction to Philosophy*, 265.

- In *actu secundus*, developmental change occurs. For instance, a newborn baby comes into existence with all of the basic equipment that defines him or her as a human being, i.e., the essence of a human being, including, for instance, an as-yet undeveloped ability to reason, to will this or that, and even to walk. See section 214. A newborn comes into the world with a particular nature as well. He or she is oriented to "be in the world" in a particular way. See section 213. It is only in *actu secundus* that the various abilities and dispositions we associate with a fully functioning adult develop over time. It is only in *actu secundus* that an acorn develops into a fully individuated and mature oak tree.[43] Viewed from the perspective of potential, *actu secundus* can take one of two forms: "active potentiality is a capacity for *doing* . . . And passive potentiality is a capacity for *receiving*"[44] or being acted upon.

The concept of being in the Aristotelian-Thomist Tradition is complex, however. Grounded in the materialism of the Enlightenment as we are, we tend to conflate the concept of being with another metaphysical concept: substance. We tend to reduce all manifestations of being to that

---

43. *Faith Connection*: This understanding of *actu secundus* holds an important implication for our understanding of identity and the extent to which it manifests uniquely in this or that present moment or persists—in some sense—over time. *Contra* other perspectives pertaining to space and time, perdurantism holds that actual real beings manifest in four dimensions. The first three, i.e., height, width, and depth, are referred to as "extensions" in the sensible world and the fourth as "time," a fact that was well understood by Thomas Aquinas. See Aquinas, *The Summa Theologica and The Summa Contra Gentiles*, 257. According to perdurantism, a substance persists over time even as the accidents, properties, and attributes associated with it emerge, develop, or dissipate. A somewhat surprising implication follows from this insight: at any given moment in time, actual real beings manifest incompletely or only partially. Imagine a flip book in which movement over time is demonstrated by drawing a young girl walking in a slightly different position on each page. When the pages are "flipped" one after the other, it appears as though the girl is walking across the surface of a single page. Each page is analogous to a particular moment in time. In effect, the "identity" of the young girl, i.e., her nature, her essence, and her way of being in the world, cannot be confined to any single page of the flip book. The young girl's identity—as an integrated whole—persists over time. As counter-intuitive as this might seem, this perspective is well-expressed in Psalm 139: "LORD, you have probed me, you know me: you know when I sit and stand; you understand my thoughts from afar. You sift through my travels and my rest; with all my ways you are familiar. Even before a word is on my tongue, LORD, you know it all. Behind and before you encircle me . . . You formed my inmost being; you knit me in my mother's womb." The implication is that God knows each of us in the entirety of our lives—past, present, and future—and not just in the seemingly disconnected moments in which we live out our existence.

44. Glenn, *An Introduction to Philosophy*, 266.

which is physically tangible and fully present in the sensible world. Recall, however, that the first meaning of being is *ens*, i.e., that which is. The concept of being pertains to the existence of a thing, not the thing as we sense it or experience it in the sensible world. Given this, metaphysical realists hold that being can persist even beyond death and disincorporation, even if it is only so in some notional sense or in memory.

To further complicate the matter, metaphysical realists hold that actual real beings participate in existence to differing degrees. Some actual real beings come into existence in a very limited fashion. Inanimate objects do not have the ability to sense the world around them or to move or to know anything about the world they inhabit. Living beings have a greater potency for action. They can develop and change over time. This potency is still quite limited in plants, however. In contrast, animals are endowed with senses that enable them to interact with the world. As human beings, we stand at the apex of this "ladder of being"[45] because of our ability to reason and our free will, both of which Thomas Aquinas identified as powers of the human soul, the subsistent form of every human being. According to Aquinas, "the intellectual soul approaches to the divine likeness more than inferior creatures, in being able to acquire perfect goodness, although by many and various means . . . "[46] Relying on our ability to reason and our free will, we can choose—to some extent—the way in which we interact with our environment. In this sense, we participate in existence to a fuller degree than do inanimate objects, plants, and other animals. James M. Jacobs has employed a useful metaphor in this regard: "Consider an electrical line supplying energy to three light bulbs: forty watts, sixty watts, and one-hundred watts. The same electricity is given to all three bulbs, but the forty-watt bulb has much less potential to illuminate because its potency to receive electricity is more limited. The act of electricity is the same; yet the results differ because of the different potential of the bulbs."[47]

---

45. Jacobs, *Seat of Wisdom*, 126. See also Cotter, *An Introduction to Catholic Philosophy*, 382.

46. Aquinas, *The Summa Theologica and The Summa Contra Gentiles*, 316.

47. Jacobs, *Seat of Wisdom*, 105.

210. MIND-DEPENDENT BEING

The second category of being is even more challenging to describe. Indeed, Aristotle himself referred to mind-dependent beings as "paradoxical" and "baffling."[48] These abstract entities include such things as fictions; negations, i.e., "mere absence conceived of as something";[49] universals, accidents, or properties, e.g., color, shape, texture, location, etc.; certain cultural realities, e.g., poverty, justice, etc.; propositions or truth claims; events; and states of affairs.

Whereas actual real beings are believed to exist independently of our thinking about them or our interactions with them, the existence or—more appropriately—subsistence of mind-dependent beings depends on us, it seems, either to be conceived of at all or to be apprehended in some sense, depending on one's understanding of their ontological status.

In our everyday lives, we tend not to think of mind-dependent beings, logical beings, or beings of reason as "real." We struggle to think of anything as existing or subsisting outside of space and time. After all, we employ these beings of reason—more often than not—in time-delimited thoughts or in interpersonal communications. We use numbers and mathematical expressions in transacting business. We create fictional worlds in telling bedtime stories. We argue against this or that assertion or claim. We reference universals and other abstract groupings—species, genus, and class, for instance—in trying to make sense of the world. And we often find ourselves "co-constructing" cultural narratives in social and political conversations. Most mind-dependent or logical beings seem to exist or subsist—if they do so at all—only fleetingly. As A. C. Cotter puts it, mind-dependent beings "exist as long as someone thinks of them and not a second longer."[50] They arise in the moment from the ethereal realm of potentiality, are actualized or employed in some way, and then fade again into non-existence. Or so it seems.

Metaphysical realists assert, nonetheless, that mind-dependent beings are "real," if only so by analogy. Their reasoning can seem somewhat fuzzy, however, or even to veer in the direction of a materialist version of conceptualism or towards a platonic conception of Forms or Ideas. Still, mind-dependent beings, logical beings, or beings of reason convey meaning and, hence, can be the subject of interpersonal dialogue.

---

48. Aristotle, *Metaphysics*, 43.
49. Cotter, *An Introduction to Catholic Philosophy*, 306.
50. Cotter, *An Introduction to Catholic Philosophy*, 306.

Mind-dependent beings can be known "extra-mentally,"[51] as it were. Oxford historian Yuval Noah Harari echoed this view in his examination of certain narratives that have long persisted in our culture: "The imagined order[52] is not a subjective order existing in my own imagination—it is rather an inter-subjective order, existing in the shared imagination of thousands and millions of people."[53] *Contra* nominalists, metaphysical realists ascribe ontological status to the meaning-conveying capacity of mind-dependent beings. More to the point, they recognize this inter-subjective capacity as an analogue to the "knowability" of existents we encounter or could potentially encounter in the physical world.

That said, Aristotle did not believe that universals, e.g., red, the virtue of courage, a particular genus or species, etc., enjoy an ontological status independent of our minds. He had—after all—rejected Plato's conception of Forms. In Aristotle's view, we can only know what terms like "humanity" mean by knowing any number of individual human beings. (This is why Aristotle is sometimes described—*contra* Plato—as a moderate or immanent realist or even a conceptualist.)

In contrast, Thomas Aquinas was somewhat ambivalent with regard to the status of mind-dependent beings. On the one hand, he agreed with Aristotle that we abstract mind-dependent beings from our knowledge of one or more actual beings in the sensible world; for instance, "human nature has in the intellect existence abstracted from all individuals . . . The intellect invents the notion of species . . . The intellect is what makes universality in things . . . "[54] On the other, he affirmed that universals do, in fact, enjoy a certain ontological status independent of our minds, if only so in the mind of God. In this view, mind-dependent beings are not so much conceived of in the mind as accessed or apprehended by thinking human beings. This latter understanding is sometimes described as "strong realism."

Despite their different views on this matter, Aristotle and Aquinas agreed that we can know the meaning conveyed by such terms as "tree" separate and apart from our knowledge of particular trees. In this instance, our knowledge of "tree" is abstracted from our knowledge of one

---

51. Copleston, *Aquinas*, 94.

52. Realist metaphysicians would prefer the term "conceptualized order" rather than "imagined order" in order to differentiate beings that could potentially exist from imagined fancies that have no potential to exist in the real world.

53. Harar, *Sapiens*, 117.

54. Aquinas, *On Being and Essence*, 15.

or more trees in the sensible world. According to A. C. Cotter, logical beings do, indeed, "have a foundation in reality. While they themselves are mental constructions, reality may offer us a solid reason for conceiving of them as such, e.g., the similarity and dissimilarity between the various groups of beings."[55] In this abstracted sense, the term "tree" constitutes a universal being or "universal" for short. See section 215.

Although this kind of knowledge is acquired by way of abstraction, the universal referents to which these terms apply can be considered real being. Because we can know what "tree," the number "four," and the color "red" mean conceptually, they constitute real being according to those who adhere to the Aristotelian-Thomist Tradition. If these referents did not pertain to real beings of some sort—if the idea of "tree" or "tree-ness" did not subsist or could not possibly subsist, for instance—we could not know anything or say anything about the realities to which these abstracted terms apply.

Still, considerable controversy pertaining to the precise ontological status of these types of mind-dependent beings or beings of reason persists in the world of academic philosophy. This is especially so in the case of universals and propositions.

211. SUBSTANCE

We return now to the concept of actual real being. In the Aristotelian-Thomist Tradition, actual real being is thought to consist of two elements: substance and accidents, also called properties or attributes.[56] Substance is examined here. This will be followed by a further word about the two components of substance, i.e., matter and form. See section 212. And this will be followed, in turn, by an investigation of two terms that are often conflated with "substance": "nature" and "essence." See sections 213 and

---

55. Cotter, *An Introduction to Catholic Philosophy*, 307.

56. Empiricists entirely reject the idea of "substance." As explained by Michael J. Loux, "Empiricists have typically found the idea of an underlying substratum objectionable and have been bundle theorists . . . A concrete particular is nothing more than a 'bundle,' a 'cluster,' a 'collection,' or a 'congeries' of the empirically manifest attributes that common sense associates with it . . . The account bundle theorists provide invariably involves the appeal to a special relation tying all the attributes in a bundle together. They have given the relation a variety of names. Some have called it 'compresence'; others speak of 'collocation'; still others use terms like 'combination,' 'consubstantiation,' and 'coactuality.'" See Loux, *Metaphysics*, 92.

214 respectively. Only then will the realist understanding of accidents, attributes, and properties be examined in section 215.

It is important to note, first, that any given substance is not the same as the "thing," i.e., the existent, we encounter in the sensible world. In realist metaphysics, the term "substance" refers to a metaphysical reality. In fact, the word "substance" is drawn from two Latin terms: "*sub*" meaning "under" and "*stare*" meaning "stand." A substance is that which "stands under" the sensible thing we encounter in the world. Indeed, it is not at all uncommon to think that "substance" refers to an entirely mysterious entity or "bare or denuded substratum" that underlies each and every unique object or thing that manifests in space and time.

Recall, however, that metaphysical realists tend to be concerned—first and foremost—with the question of "being"; and recall, too, that other key terms employed in the lexicon of metaphysical realism can be thought of as "aspects" of being or being examined from a particular perspective. Given this, the metaphysical concept of substance pertains more to the existence of a thing and its essential nature as an existent than the "thing" itself as it is perceived in the sensible world.[57] According to F. C. Copleston, "the distinction between substance and accident is a distinction, not between an unknowable substratum and knowable modifications, but between that which exists, if it does exist, as subject and that which exists only as a modification of a subject. In Aquinas's own terminology, the word 'substance' signifies an essence to which it pertains to exist by itself."[58]

A key question is thus prompted: How does any substance, i.e., the "isness" of any given existent we happen to perceive in the sensible world, relate to the corresponding "thing" itself? According to the Aristotelian-Thomist Tradition, substances are comprised of matter and form, i.e., that which gives shape and direction to matter, the fundamental building block of everything we encounter in the sensible world.[59] In order to maintain our focus on being, however, it is more helpful, perhaps, to

---

57. The relationship shared by the concepts "substance" and "being" can be examined etymologically. As noted by Michael J. Loux, "Aristotle and those following him have called concrete particulars substances. The English world 'substance' is etymologically close to the world 'substratum,' and that fact can lead to confusion. The Greek word for which 'substance' is our English translation is '*ousia*,' and it does a better job of expressing the force of calling something a substance. '*Ousia*' is a noun derived from the Greek verb for 'to be.'" See Loux, *Metaphysics*, 123–124.

58. F. C. Copleston, *Aquinas*, 85.

59. Aristotle, *Metaphysics*, 147.

say that the "isness" of a thing is "expressed" in matter and form. More to the point, metaphysical realists contend that we cannot perceive any given substance directly; we can only intuit or infer a substance, i.e., the "isness" of a thing, by way of the mix of accidents, attributes, and properties associated with it. (In fact, metaphysical realists tend to understand matter and form as types or causes of change rather than as things in the world or as components of things in the world *per se*.)

Again, the term "substance" denotes something other than the material presence in the physical world we perceive with one or more of our five senses. Sensible "things," i.e., actual real beings, which are composed of both substances, i.e., "isness," and accidents, properties, and attributes are perceptible solely by virtue of their attendant accidents, attributes, and properties. Isolated from any given set of accidents, attributes, or properties, substances are not perceptible. Given this, some realists describe "substance"—somewhat obscurely, to be sure—as that which is "in a thing" that is not or cannot be said, asserted, or "predicated" about it. In this sense, any given substance can be distinguished from the various accidents, attributes, and properties that we perceive with our senses or could possibly perceive. According to metaphysical realists in the Aristotelian-Thomist Tradition, substances are, nevertheless, believed to exist—in some sense—separate and apart from the accidents, properties, and attributes by which they can only be known by inference.

Further, substances perdure in time. Substances come into existence and go out of existence, and while in existence, they are entirely stable, according to most metaphysical realists. In contrast, accidents are subject to change and so, too, therefore, the concrete things we encounter in the sensible world.

Still further, substances are described in the Aristotelian-Thomist Tradition as subjects of inherence.[60] Accidents are "carried by" or inhere in substances.[61]

---

60. Cotter, *An Introduction to Catholic Philosophy*, 363.

61. *Faith Connection*: This understanding underlies the concept of "transubstantiation," the profound change by which bread and wine brought to the altar in the offertory procession become the body and blood of the Risen Christ. As noted in the Catechism of the Catholic Church, "the Council of Trent summarizes the Catholic faith by declaring: 'Because Christ our Redeemer said that it was truly his body that he was offering under the species of bread, it has always been the conviction of the church of God, and his holy Council now declares again, that by the consecration of the bread and wine there takes place a change of the whole substance of the bread into the substance of the body of Christ our Lord and of the whole substance of the wine into the substance of his blood. This change the holy Catholic Church has fittingly and properly called

Consider, for instance, a potted plant. When we encounter a potted plant, we perceive a certain color, a particular shape, a unique texture, and an attractive scent, i.e., a unique combination of accidents, properties, and attributes. That said, we don't perceive the substance of the potted plant *per se*, according to metaphysical realists. Still, we can "know" the substance of the potted plant, first, because it shares an attribute with all other kinds of being: it exists. It has being that is expressed in matter and form. Beyond that, however, we can only intuit or infer the "concreated" matter and form that constitute the substance of the potted plant and the potted plant itself by virtue of its sensible accidents, properties, and attributes, all of which are carried by it or inhere in its associated substance.

Finally, substances enjoy both a formal nature and a formal essence, to the extent that they participate in one or more non-material, non-temporal, and non-individuated, but nonetheless, real genus or species and a fully-individuated nature and essence as well.[62] The species "homo sapiens" can be considered an essence—it exists and so has being—in a formal sense, i.e., *substantia secunda*, and so, too, a particular human being in a fully-individuated sense, i.e., *substantia prima*.

In the metaphysical realism of the Aristotelian-Thomist Tradition, an individuated substance is referred to as a "suppositum" or "hypostasis"[63] if it is or could potentially be self-sustaining. A particular tree can thus be considered a suppositum or hypostasis, but not so a leaf or a branch. Similarly, an individual human being can be considered a suppositum or hypostasis, but not so an arm or a kidney.[64] In the words of A. C. Cotter, "*substance* is something existing by itself or in itself (*ens per se, ens in se*) . . . "[65]

212. FORM AND MATTER

Again, substance is comprised of two elements: form and matter. The concept of "form" is challenging and can best be understood, perhaps, in terms of Aristotle's re-conception of Plato's Forms. Plato's allegory of the cave, as described in his classic work *Republic*, theorizes that the world

---

transubstantiation." See *Catechism*, no. 1376.

62. To further complicate the matter, perhaps, Aristotle's fourth definition of "substance" identifies it as a synonym of "essence," a term that is further defined in section 214.

63. Cotter, *An Introduction to Catholic Philosophy*, 381.

64. Aquinas, *The Summa Theologica and The Summa Contra Gentiles*, 287.

65. Cotter, *An Introduction to Catholic Philosophy*, 362.

we inhabit is illusory. The things we see and experience in the world are poor replicas of their corresponding Forms, all of which exist entirely outside of space and time. For instance, for every tree we see, there is a Form for Tree, according to Plato; the individual trees we see "participate" in a hypothesized Form, i.e., Tree, which is far more real than any individual tree.

Aristotle abandoned Plato's fanciful depiction of "Forms," but added considerable ambiguity to the concept in doing so. In the Aristotelian-Thomist Tradition, a form[66] can be described as a kind of blueprint, model, formula, or organizing principle. Form determines the "shape" of an existent. According to Aristotle, form can thus be understood as a "such" as opposed to a "this."[67] And in Thomas Aquinas's view, "matter is contracted by form to a determinate species."[68] Further, "matter is for the sake of form."[69] Things in the world "instantiate, exhibit, or exemplify" form.[70] Form thus defines the nature of a sensible thing or existent, i.e., its purpose, its fundamental way of "being in the world" of space and time, its orientation to its own existence and to other existing substances, its mode of operation, and its essence, i.e., that which distinguishes its species and genera from other species and genera and that which constitutes it as a unique and fully individuated existent, too.[71]

Like Aristotle, Thomas Aquinas did not believe that forms preexist—either ontologically or in the sensible world—substances: "Form is not there until the thing has been made to be."[72]

66. By convention the first letter in the word "Form" is capitalized when referring to Plato's concept of Forms. It is not capitalized in conceptions of forms advanced by Aristotle and by other metaphysical realists.

67. Aristotle, *Metaphysics*, 143.

68. Aquinas, *The Summa Theologica and The Summa Contra Gentiles*, 236.

69. Aquinas, *The Summa Theologica and The Summa Contra Gentiles*, 260.

70. Loux, *Metaphysics*, 22.

71. *Faith Connection*: As challenging as this idea might be, it is quite consistent with our theology. According to Thomas Aquinas, "this determination of forms must be reduced to the divine wisdom as its first principle, for divine wisdom devised the order of the universe residing in the distinction of things. And therefore we must say that in the divine wisdom are the models of all things, which we have called ideas, i.e., exemplary forms existing in the divine mind." See Aquinas, *The Summa Theologica and The Summa Contra Gentiles*, 238. As James M. Jacobs puts it, "the unity of being in God's causal activity is reflected in the Christian transformation of Plato's Forms into divine Ideas. God knows himself as the infinite act of existence. But he therefore also knows in his Ideas all the finite ways things can participate in existence." See Jacobs, *Seat of Wisdom*, 110.

72. Aquinas, "The Principles of Nature," 183.

Although Thomas Aquinas assigned a higher ontological status to forms found in nature, he attributed a kind of "form" to artifacts designed and manufactured by humans as well: "All artificial forms are accidental forms. For art works only on what has already been put into existence by nature."[73]

The concept of "matter" in realist metaphysics can also be confusing. Thomas Aquinas distinguished between *materia primus*, i.e., undesignated matter,[74] and *materia secunda*, i.e., designated or signate matter, the visible "stuff" that we encounter in the sensible world. According to Aquinas, "prime matter cannot be known or defined by itself..."[75] Matter yet to be "in-formed" and so rendered capable of expressing existence in this or that substance is better understood as "a purely indeterminate constitutive principle which is capable of existing successively in union with an indefinite multiplicity of forms... [For example], when the oak tree perishes, its substantial form disappears, relapsing into the potentiality of matter, but the first matter of the tree does not disappear. It does not, and indeed cannot, exist by itself; for an existent material substance is something definite and determinate. When an oak tree perishes, the matter immediately exists under another form or forms. When a human being dies and his or her body disintegrates, the body's matter is at once informed by other forms. But there is continuity, and it is first matter that ensures this continuity. According to Aquinas, every material thing of substance is composed of a substantial form and first matter. Neither principle is itself a thing or substance..."[76] Aristotle referred to this indeterminate first matter as "pure potential"[77] and as a kind of "heap."[78]

Again, form and matter are "concreated," i.e., constituted simultaneously,[79] in all actual real beings.[80] This understanding has a name, in fact: hylomorphic theory.[81] When form and matter come to-

---

73. Aquinas, "The Principles of Nature," 181.
74. Jacobs, *Seat of Wisdom*, 113.
75. Aquinas, "The Principles of Nature," 182.
76. F. C. Copleston, *Aquinas*, 90.
77. Aristotle, *Metaphysics*, 190.
78. Aristotle, *Metaphysics*, 162.
79. Jacobs, *Seat of Wisdom*, 103.
80. Thomas Aquinas used the term "hypostasis" in the case of human beings, creatures comprised of bodies and souls as their corresponding forms. See Aquinas, *The Summa Theologica and The Summa Contra Gentiles*, 287.
81. Aristotle and Thomas Aquinas were men of their times. Neither had access to the insights of contemporary science. At first glance, at least, metaphysical realism's

gether in this way, a non-material, non-temporal, and non-individuated essence is "expressed" in a fully individuated substance in time and space, and this fully individual substance can be known and experienced in the sensible world by way of the various accidents, properties, and attributes that inhere in it.

Like all actual real beings, a human being or person can be described as an "actualized" essence that constitutes its own ordered but now individuated[82] being in the world. This newly created essence is comprised of a particular substance, i.e., concreated form and matter, which can be apprised by way of the accidents, properties, and attributes that inhere in him or her.[83]

---

distinction between form and matter may seem to bear a resemblance to our understanding of DNA, chemical reactions, and electrical interactions, on the one hand, analogues, perhaps, of form, and chemicals and minerals, on the other, analogues, perhaps, of matter. How might the findings of contemporary science have been incorporated into Aristotle's work or Thomas Aquinas's hylomorphic theory? F. C. Copleston considered this intriguing question at some length: "Those followers of Aquinas who maintain the truth of (hylomorphic) theory, even in its application to the inorganic world, insist on its metaphysical character and on its independence of the changing hypotheses of science... There are, however, other followers of Aquinas who consider that the theory was the result of a speculative attempt to cope with that problem, which is solved, in so far as it can ever be finally solved, by scientific research. I do not feel inclined to hazard any opinion as to what Aquinas himself would say on this matter if he were alive. Questions of this sort cannot be answered in a definitive manner. It is sufficient to say that Aquinas regarded the theory as being independent of contemporary 'scientific' ideas." See Copleston, *Aquinas*, 93. That said, Aquinas, in particular, demonstrated a remarkably modern understanding of human biology in his description of substantial change. This is clear if we substitute the word "nutrients" for the word "bread" in the quote that follows: "Bread is the matter of blood, but blood is not generated unless the bread is corrupted. Whence bread does not remain in blood, and so bread cannot be said to be an element of blood. Elements must remain in some way, (however), since they are not entirely corrupted." See Aquinas, "The Principles of Nature," 185.

82. The word "independent" in this instance does not deny our manifest reliance on God to sustain our existence from one moment to the next. It is intended, instead, to rebut the mistaken concept of a universal soul in which all human beings participate while alive and to which individual souls return after death. See Aquinas, *On Being and Essence*, 24. Aquinas followed the tradition of the early church fathers and Aristotle, too, in denying this view. See Aristotle, *Metaphysics*, 248.

83. *Faith Connection*: This distinction between matter and form has profoundly influenced our Christian understanding of the soul. Like Aristotle, Thomas Aquinas equated the human soul with the form of any given human being. According to Aquinas, our bodies do not carry or contain our souls as such, nor do our souls inhabit our bodies. We are a single, concreated essence or manifestation of being. Nevertheless, our subsistent souls—as forms—persist beyond our deaths and the dissolution of our bodies. See Aristotle, *Metaphysics*, 153. See also Aquinas, *The Summa Theologica and The Summa Contra Gentiles*, 280.

213. NATURE

Before moving on to a description of metaphysical realism's understanding of accidents, i.e., the second component of actual real being, two terms often conflated with the concept of substance, i.e., nature and essence, will be examined. Indeed, the term "nature" is often used interchangeably with the word "substance" and the word "essence."[84] Some degree of confusion inevitably results.

In the Aristotelian-Thomist Tradition, nature determines the teleology of any given actual real being. This includes its fundamental way of "being in the world" of space and time, i.e., "those activities that are characteristic of a fully mature instance of that species,"[85] its orientation to its own existence and to other existents and subsistents, its mode of operation, and its purpose. Aristotle described this way of "being in the world" as movement: "Nature in this sense is the source of movement of natural objects being present in them somehow, either potentially or in complete reality."[86] Further, the nature of any given actual real being is determined or caused by its form when it is concreated with matter as substance and is, hence, knowable by way of the accidents, properties, and attributes that inhere in it. See section 215.

214. ESSENCE

Like the term "nature," the term "essence," i.e., quiddity or "whatness," is often conflated with the term "substance." Essence is best understood, however, as a concept or linguistic tool we use to distinguish—in two distinct ways—between and among the characteristics that uniquely define any two existents. In other words, "essence is substance considered as definable"[87] or, as Aristotle put it, "essence belong(s) to substance."[88] The first of these two ways pertains to distinctions drawn between the different species or genera to which any two existents belong, if, in fact, they belong to different species or genera, e.g., tree, for instance, *vis-à-vis* human being, etc., and the second pertains to differences between any

---

84. Cotter, *An Introduction to Catholic Philosophy*, 377.
85. Jacobs, *Seat of Wisdom*, 110.
86. Aristotle, *Metaphysics*, 90.
87. Copleston, *Aquinas*, 100.
88. Aristotle, *Metaphysics*, 135. See also Cotter, *An Introduction to Catholic Philosophy*, 301.

two or more actual real beings that or who happen to share a species or genera, e.g., any particular tree *vis-à-vis* any other tree, any one human being *vis-à-vis* any other human being, etc..

The concept of essence is important because it allows metaphysical realists to explain why we encounter such a variety of "things" in the sensible world, even though everything we could conceivably encounter, i.e., all actual and potential beings, all mind-dependent beings, and all accidents, properties, and attributes, too, share in being. According to James M. Jacobs, "to get different beings, there must be another principle to account for the difference. That principle is essence, which causes the differences between nature and individuals. Thus, existence and essence are the two principles whose composition is necessary to account for the unity of being and the diversity of beings."[89]

With respect to the first distinction, i.e., differences between and among two or more natures, an essence encompasses that which every member in any given species or genera, e.g., tree, human being, etc., shares by virtue of its membership in that species or genera. As noted by Thomas Aquinas, "essence signifies something common to all natures through which the various beings are placed in the various genera and species, as humanity is the essence of man, and so on."[90] This first distinction does not encompass all such commonalities, but only those that are definitive or central to the essence of a species or genera. A human being can thus be differentiated from all other animals by virtue of its ability to reason.

With respect to the second distinction, essence accounts for the ontological uniqueness of fully individuated beings in the world, i.e., their "thisness" or *haecceitas*. For instance, a particular human being or person can be said to "participate in" or "instantiate" the essence of human nature, which exists—in some sense—separate and apart from his or her own unique essence.

The concept of "essence" can also be conflated with the Aristotelian-Thomist Tradition's understanding of form. Again, essence can be examined from two perspectives: it pertains, first, to that which differentiates any particular species or genera from any other species or genera, and, second, to that which differentiates one member of a species or genera from another member of the same species or genera. In contrast, the

---

89. Jacobs, *Seat of Wisdom*, 104.
90. Aquinas, *On Being and Essence*, 6.

term "form"—as it pertains to essence—is better understood as one of four possible causes of change or development in the essence of any given actual real being that we might encounter over time in the sensible world. See section 217.

As is suggested above, the term "essence" can be understood as a differentiating tool. Some metaphysical realists contend, however, that essences subsist—in some real sense—independently of or prior to any member of a species or genera coming into existence. In this view, the essence of "tree" exists separate and apart—in some non-material, non-temporal, and undifferentiated sense—from any given tree. Similarly, the essence of a "human being" subsists independently of any particular human being who has or could come into existence. For some, this "strong" conception of essence veers far too close to Plato's idealized conception of Forms, however. After all, Aristotle had rejected this hyper-idealized understanding of reality. According to some who uphold the wisdom of metaphysical realism, we can, nonetheless, abstract a non-material, non-temporal, and non-individuated "essence" from any unique and fully individuated essences we may encounter in the sensible world.

215. ACCIDENTS, PROPERTIES, AND ATTRIBUTES

At a metaphysical level, any given actual real being consists of two elements: a substance, on the one hand, and a particular mix of accidents, properties, and attributes, on the other. Metaphysical realism's understanding of accidents, properties, and attributes is examined here.[91]

According to Aristotle, the various ways in which we come to know the sensible world can be organized into ten distinct categories. Paul J. Glenn refers to these ten categories as "the philosopher's map, his guide, and his plan of work."[92] These ten categories pertain exclusively to actual real being, i.e., to any being that is single, real, and finite in the sensible world[93]; they do not pertain to potential real beings, spiritual beings, or mind-dependent or logical beings.

---

91. To this point, we have described accidents as sensible attributes, such as red, soft, or sweet. Thomas Aquinas, however, attributed certain "accidents" specifically to the form that is concreated with matter in all substances. In human beings, this includes understanding and our ability to sense things in the world. See Aquinas, *On Being and Essence*, 28–29.

92. Glenn, *An Introduction to Philosophy*, 277.

93. Glenn, *An Introduction to Philosophy*, 278.

These ten categories do not all enjoy the same ontological status, however. The first, "substance," has already been addressed. Aristotle considered the remaining nine categories to be accidents, attributes, or properties, all of which inhere in substances. Whereas substances can only be known by way of inference, accidents can be perceived via one or more of our five senses. Although both substances and accidents are types of "being," accidents are considered to be of a lesser or inferior type.[94]

To be perceived, any given accident, property, or attribute must be associated with a substance. Although accidents are real, they are entirely dependent. Accidents cannot exist on their own. The accident "red," for instance, can only be perceived if it is associated with a substance in the sensible world. Accidents exist only as "marks, determinants, modifications, or characteristics of some other thing."[95] Further, some accidents can be considered incidental and others "essential" or "absolute" because "*whatever* has them must have them essentially."[96] For instance, we can differentiate between a tree's location, i.e., an incidental accident or attribute, and its roots, i.e., an essential or absolute accident or attribute.

Moreover, when an accident or property is associated with or ascribed to a substance, it can function as a predicate. Whereas accidents, properties, and attributes pertain to particular substances in the sensible world, "predicate terms express or connote universals."[97] According to Aristotle, a predicate is anything that can be said about a substance.[98] In the sentences "the car is red," "the house is large," and "Jerry is in New Jersey," "red," "large," and "in New Jersey" are predicates. Each of them refers to a corresponding subject, i.e., the associated metaphysical substances that underly the "car," the "house," and "Jerry." As a class, predicates are called predicamentals. As noted by F. C. Copleston, "A substance is that of which we say primarily that it exists and which is not predicated of something else in the way in which we predicate pallor of John or redness of a rose, while an accident is that which exists only as a modification of a substance or thing and which is predicated of a substance."[99]

To illustrate the difference between a substance and an accident, consider the following sentence: "the man is tall." The accident, attribute,

---

94. Cotter, *An Introduction to Catholic Philosophy*, 363.
95. Glenn, *An Introduction to Philosophy*, 277.
96. Sosa, "Essence," 250–251.
97. Loux, *Metaphysics*, 29.
98. Aristotle, *Metaphysics*, 119.
99. Copleston, *Aquinas*, 85.

or property "tall" is a predicate that pertains to a particular substance: "man." The converse would make no sense, i.e., "the tall is man," since the term "man," in this instance, refers to a substance about which something can be predicated or asserted. Generally speaking, a substance cannot be predicated about another substance, unless it denotes a species-genus relationship. For example, it would make no sense to say that "the warehouse is a man." "Warehouse" and "man" are entirely unrelated to each other as substances. It would be appropriate, however, to say that "man is a primate," since "man" can be defined as a primate who reasons and exercises free will. In this instance, the implied relationship lies between a particular species, i.e., human being, and a particular genus, i.e., primate.[100]

The predicamentals, i.e., categories two through nine in Aristotle's taxonomy, were subsequently affirmed by Thomas Aquinas.[101] They can be thought of as all-inclusive divisions or types of accidents, attributes, or properties that can be associated with particular substances.

- "Quantity" refers to any measurable attribute.
- "Quality" pertains to dispositions, habits, or ways of being in the world, abilities and capacities, passive characteristics such as color or scent, and qualitative descriptions of shape or size, e.g., big, round, tiny, etc..
- "Relations" concern positional dispositions *vis-à-vis* any two or more substances, e.g., under, between, alongside, ahead, etc..
- "Action" includes all kinds of self-directed or self-engendered movements.
- "Passion" pertains to actions imposed on a substance.
- "Place" refers to physical location.
- "Time" orients a substance in terms of "before," "now," and "after."
- "Posture" addresses the arrangement or disposition of a subject's various parts.
- "Habit" includes clothing, external accoutrements, and adornments.

---

100. The distinction made here between substances, on the one hand, and accidents or properties, on the other, follows the second of four definitions of substance stipulated by Aristotle in Book V of his *Metaphysics*. See Aristotle, *Metaphysics*, 97.

101. Other taxonomies abound.

216. TRANSCENDENTAL PROPERTIES

Like being itself,[102] certain properties are distinguishable from all other accidents and properties in the metaphysical realism of the Aristotelian-Thomist Tradition because they are part and parcel of everything that exists. As such, they do not inhere in any particular individual being or class of beings, essences, substances, or accidents. These attributes are described as transcendental properties. They apply to everything that exists and, hence, to all types of being. In the metaphysical realism of the Aristotelian-Thomist Tradition, three transcendental properties are ascribed to all manifestations of being: unity, truth, and goodness. A fourth transcendental is sometimes added: beauty. And a fifth is asserted by some as well: perfection.

First, every being—by definition—must be united. Aristotle thus includes being and unity among the highest of conceivable genera.[103] If a being was metaphysically divided, it would be two beings rather than one. We refer to this unity as concrete when it pertains to an existent in the sensible world. Abstract unity refers to that which unifies groupings or classes of individual existents, e.g., species, genus, etc., and to mind-dependent beings as well. Predicamental unity denotes the unique combination of accidents, properties, and attributes that inhere in a particular substance in the sensible world.

The apprehension of unity is important because it allows us to make distinctions between and among beings in the sensible world, potential real beings, and beings of reason, too. Recall that nominalism denies that these distinctions are real; according to nominalists, they do not exist outside of our minds. *Contra* nominalists, metaphysical realists affirm the ontological status of these distinctions.

Second, all being is true. In this context, truth can be defined as the "apprehensibility" or "knowability" of being.[104] Whereas epistemological

---

102. Glenn, *An Introduction to Philosophy*, 261.

103. Aristotle, *Metaphysics*, 220.

104. *Faith Connection*: The transcendental understanding of truth explains why the Catholic Church has so vigorously resisted the appeal of relativism in contemporary life. The church affirms objective truth, even if it may be obscure or opaque in any given situation or in any particular moment. "It is always from the truth that the dignity of conscience derives. In the case of the correct conscience, it is a question of the *objective truth* received by man; in the case of the erroneous conscience, it is a question of what man, mistakenly, *subjectively* considers to be true." See John Paul II, *Veritatis Splendor*, no. 49, no. 71.

truth pertains to logic, ontological truth pertains to anything that might be perceived to exist in the sensible world or in the world of reason and the extent to which it conforms to the mind, i.e., its "intelligibility,"[105] or to its form.[106] Alexander Brodie uses the metaphor of a house in making this point: "The relation in which the house stands to the mind of the passer-by is accidental, for the house does not depend upon the passerby ... It is primarily the idea in the mind of the architect that is true, and the house built according to his plan is said to be true only derivatively. If the house constructed by the builder does not correspond to the architect's plan, then the builder has made a mistake—the house is not true to the architect's plan. It is not that the plan does not fit the house, but that house does not fit the plan."[107]

Third, all being is good to the extent that it reflects the richness of being and is thus desirable. The term "good" used in this sense does not refer to moral approbation or to physical health, but to a being's transcendental goodness,[108] i.e., that which can "perfect" it and that which can help it pursue its telos or purpose in existing.[109]

Beauty and perfection, i.e., the "rounded completeness of a created nature,"[110] are sometimes described as aspects of goodness, sometimes as widespread—but by no means universal—attributes, and sometimes as transcendental properties in their own right and, as such, predicable of any and all manifestations of being.[111]

---

105. Cotter, *An Introduction to Catholic Philosophy*, 344.

106. *Faith Connection*: The Christian belief that God not only created us but sustains us in existence, too, aligns well with this view. As affirmed by A. C. Cotter, "God did not create blindly, but fashioned the world and all its parts in accordance with a definite plan or idea; also those creatures which are merely possible, are possible only because they are in conformity with God's intellect." See Cotter, *An Introduction to Catholic Philosophy*, 345. The truth or intelligibility of being in the Aristotelian-Thomist Tradition thus mirrors the Christian understanding of God's providence.

107. Brodie, "Thomas Aquinas," 45.

108. *Faith Connection*: The *Catechism of the Catholic Church* cites Thomas Aquinas in locating all forms of human affection in this transcendental property: "'To love is to will the good of another.' All other affections have their source in this first movement of the human heart toward the good." See *Catechism*, no. 1767.

109. Cotter, *An Introduction to Catholic Philosophy*, 348.

110. Glenn, *An Introduction to Philosophy*, 275.

111. *Faith Connection*: Augustine reflected this understanding, in fact, in a moving prayer in his autobiography, *The Confessions*: "O my God, for me you are loveliness itself; yet for all these things, too, I sing a hymn and offer a sacrifice of praise to you who sanctify me, because the beautiful designs that are born in our minds and find expression through clever hands derive from that Beauty which transcends all minds."

According to the Aristotelian-Thomist Tradition, every being can thus be described as one, true, and good. The transcendental property of truth will be further examined in the next chapter.

Critics of metaphysical realism generally deny the existence of transcendental properties. Some dismiss them as a kind of "backdoor" into an understanding of God as one, true, and good.[112]

217. CAUSATION AND CHANGE

Recall that the problem of change was uppermost on the minds of the nature philosophers who had preceded Socrates, Plato, and Aristotle. "How," they wondered, "can identity and continuity be maintained in a world that is constantly in flux?" Causation was thus a key concern for the presocratics. It was a key concern, too, for rationalists during the Enlightenment and beyond, many of whom questioned our ability to firmly associate any given effect with any particular cause. In contrast to the skeptics of the seventeenth and eighteenth centuries, philosophers in the Aristotelian-Thomist Tradition have consistently affirmed the essential "knowability" of the sensible world and, hence, the intelligibility of change.

Whereas Plato attributed the changes we experience and witness in the sensible world to his ethereal conception of Forms, Aristotle grounded his understanding of change in the concrete world of things. Indeed, Aristotle's understanding of change follows from his understanding of actual real being.

We must first distinguish between the twin concepts of "substantial change" and "accidental change." As noted by F. C. Copleston, "if the tree is burned down and reduced to ashes, we don't speak of the ashes

---

See Augustine, *The Confessions*, 232. See also *Catechism*, no. 2500.

112. *Faith Connection*: In fact, openness to God and to the transcendental properties associated with God can be understood as a defining characteristic of human nature. "*Openness to transcendence belongs to the human person: man is open to the infinite and to all created beings. He is open above all to the infinite—God—because with his intellect and will he raises himself above all the created order and above himself, he becomes independent from creatures, is free in relation to created things, and tends toward total truth and the absolute good. He is open also to others, to the men and women of the world, because only insofar as he understands himself in reference to a 'thou' can he say 'I.' He comes out of himself from the self-centered preservation of this own life, to enter into a relationship of dialogue and communion with others. The human person is open to the fullness of being, to the unlimited horizon of being.*" See Pontifical Council for Justice and Peace, Compendium, no. 130.

as an oak tree. When bread has been digested, we no longer speak of it as bread."[113] Substantial change has occurred in both instances. Indeed, one substance can arise—in a metaphysical sense, at least—from another substance, but only as something entirely new.

The subject of substantial change is a matter of some controversy among metaphysical realists, however. The more common view is that substances do not change while they are in existence. In keeping with this view, A. C. Cotter notes that "change supposes a *common subject*, that is, something which passes from one state to another, yet remains the same . . ."[114] Metaphysical realists offer a number of proofs for this understanding, in fact. The most compelling, perhaps, is grounded in our conception of ourselves as stable identities. As described by Cotter, "I am conscious not only of my present internal experiences: thoughts, feelings, desires, etc., but also of *my Ego* of which there are modifications and in which they inhere. Moreover, my memory assures me that *my same Ego* has had other or similar modifications in the past. Therefore, the existence of some common substances is not mere inference, but is *perceived immediately* in and with the facts of consciousness."[115] My sense of myself as "I" and "me" persists over time in a remarkably stable way. This way of talking about ourselves and what we do in the world also reflects an implicit understanding of ourselves—our substance or identity—as separate and apart in some real way from the physical parts that make up our bodies. An example provided by Cotter is sufficient to demonstrate this point: "It is not so much my feet that walk, but *I* walk."[116]

Some metaphysical realists, however, assert the existence of certain "incomplete substances"—all of which are still more or less stable—that can engender or experience a certain degree of change over time.[117] That said, realists tend to reserve the terms "change" and "alteration" to additions, subtractions, and modifications in accidents, properties, and attributes associated with particular substances. The capacity of a stable substance to support this kind of "accidental change" is referred to as its "subjective potency."[118]

---

113. Copleston, *Aquinas*, 89.
114. Cotter, *An Introduction to Catholic Philosophy*, 323.
115. Cotter, *An Introduction to Catholic Philosophy*, 367.
116. Cotter, *An Introduction to Catholic Philosophy*, 381.
117. Cotter, *An Introduction to Catholic Philosophy*, 376.
118. Cotter, *An Introduction to Catholic Philosophy*, 329.

We must also distinguish between the processes by which actual real beings come into and go out of existence, on the one hand, and the processes by which the accidents, properties, and attributes associated with substances transition from one mode of being to another, on the other. Because the term "change" is used somewhat loosely at times, realists prefer "creation" and "generation" when referring to the process by which a potential real being comes into existence and the terms "annihilation" and "corruption" when referring to the process by which an actual real being goes out of existence. According to Thomas Aquinas, "generation is a kind of change from nonexistence to existence, and corruption conversely from existence to non-existence. Generation does not take place from just any kind of non-being, but from the non-being which is being in potency."[119] If the word "change" is used at all in these contexts, it tends to be referred to as "substantial change."[120]

It is also important to distinguish between and among four causes of change. Metaphysical realism in the Aristotelian-Thomist Tradition posits four causes: formal causes of change, material causes, efficient causes, and final causes.[121] The first two were examined in section 212. Again, form gives shape and direction to matter and so accounts for the nature and essence of substances. Form and matter are understood to be intrinsic causes of change.

An efficient cause, an extrinsic cause of change, is that "which by its activity gives existence to something or brings about a change."[122] Some efficient causes are proximate or immediate in their effects; others produce their effects indirectly or in combination with other extrinsic causes.

A final cause is that "for the sake of which the efficient cause acts."[123] As affirmed by Thomas Aquinas, "the end is the cause of causes, because it is the cause of the causality in all the causes."[124] Final causes, too, are understood to be extrinsic causes of change. They pertain to teleology, i.e., purposes, objectives, or aims.[125] As A. C. Cotter puts it, "it is that

---

119. Aquinas, "The Principles of Nature," 180.
120. Cotter, *An Introduction to Catholic Philosophy*, 376.
121. Aristotle, *Metaphysics*, 85.
122. Cotter, *An Introduction to Catholic Philosophy*, 393.
123. Cotter, *An Introduction to Catholic Philosophy*, 393.
124. Aquinas, "The Principles of Nature," 186.
125. *Faith Connection*: It is easy to understand why Aristotle's understanding of final causes, in particular, would appeal to a committed Christian such as Thomas

which is desired (intended) by the efficient cause or as that for the sake of which the efficient cause acts."[126] In our experience of time, final causes precede most efficient causes; purpose generally precedes any action that is not entirely random. Whereas Aristotle located a being's movement toward the full realization of its potential in its inherent properties or its nature,[127] Aquinas grounded his understanding of movement, i.e., change, and causation in God as the first or prime mover and as the one who sustains all of creation in what we perceive to be time.

Aristotle employed a particular example in explaining how these four causes can operate on a single substance: "The same thing may have all the kinds of causes, e.g., the moving cause of a house is the art of the builder, the final cause is the function it fulfils, the matter is earth and stones, and the form is the definition."[128] Another example involving a statue of George Washington is provided by A. C. Cotter: "The sculptor himself is the efficient cause through his chiseling; the motive from which he works (money, fame, esthetic pleasure, etc.) is the final cause. The marble out of which the statue is made is the matter or material cause; and the figure of the hero, which the sculptor produces in the marble, is the formal cause."[129]

Aquinas. According to Aristotle, "the final cause is an end, and that sort of end which is not for the sake of something else, but for whose sake everything else is . . . " See Aristotle, *Metaphysics*, 35.

126. Cotter, *An Introduction to Catholic Philosophy*, 406.
127. Aristotle, *Metaphysics*, 235.
128. Aristotle, *Metaphysics*, 40.
129. Cotter, *An Introduction to Catholic Philosophy*, 393.

3

Epistemology

301. EPISTEMOLOGY

Epistemology is the science or philosophy of knowledge and truth, "the branch of philosophy that concerns the nature and scope of human knowledge."[1] Epistemology is also referred to as "critical philosophy" or "major logic," the latter in order to distinguish it from the philosophical sub-discipline of logic.[2]

Our investigation of epistemology from the perspective of the Aristotelian-Thomist Tradition is complicated by the fact that it does not "own the field" as such. Whereas the various philosophies of the Enlightenment—and most contemporary philosophies, too—have abandoned metaphysics altogether, epistemology emerged as *the* central concern of the rationalists and empiricists of the Enlightenment. Contemporary philosophies, e.g., analytic philosophy, phenomenalism, existentialism, pragmatism, postmodernism, etc., have articulated their own epistemologies, too, or critiqued—in some cases severely—what they perceive to be the dominant epistemology of the day. This is particularly so in the case of postmodernism.

---

1. Littlejohn and Carter, *Epistemology*, 1.
2. Glenn, *An Introduction to Philosophy*, 216.

302. KEY CONCERNS OF EPISTEMOLOGICAL REALISM

At the most basic level, the questions taken up by epistemological realists are the same as those taken up by philosophers who have promoted alternative epistemologies:

- What can be known?
- What constitutes belief?
- What constitutes knowledge?
- What kinds of knowledge are there?
- Can beliefs be justified?
- What constitutes the justification of belief?
- What kinds of evidence can be mounted in asserting a truth claim?
- What methods can be employed to this end?
- How should questions pertaining to belief and knowledge be framed?

These questions are addressed below, largely from the perspective of epistemological realism. The perspectives of key Enlightenment philosophies, i.e., rationalism, empiricism, and Immanuel Kant's transcendental idealism, will be summarized as well.

303. EPISTEMOLOGICAL REALISM

The two pillars of philosophical realism—Aristotle and Thomas Aquinas—were generally of one mind with respect to their epistemologies. Aristotle viewed epistemology as a foundational concern and, hence, on a par with metaphysics. This abiding interest prompted—not just his detailed reflections on knowledge and its justification, chief concerns of any epistemology—but his foundational work in logic as well.[3] In contrast, Thomas Aquinas's epistemological reflections were mounted—for the most part—in service to his more central focus on metaphysics and ethics. Aquinas adopted Aristotle's epistemology uncritically.[4] That said,

---

3. Copleston, *Aquinas*, 49.

4. It seems likely that Aquinas would have been somewhat surprised by the Enlightenment's privileging of epistemology over metaphysics. It is prudent, therefore, to proceed somewhat cautiously in speculating about how he might have responded to the epistemological skepticism of the rationalists in particular. Whereas the ancient skeptics had been content to pit one belief against another, thereby revealing them through

Aristotle relied more on definition, classification, and logic in developing his epistemology than did Aquinas, who tended to emphasize the role of reason and reflection. These differences in approach do not constitute an essential difference in their epistemologies, however.

That said, today's epistemological realists espouse different views with respect to the way in which we come to know anything about the sensible world. Étienne Gilson (1884–1978) noted three such alternatives. The first, immediate or naïve realism, discounts the need to posit any process between an entity in the sensible world and our knowledge of that entity. Sensible entities are simply "apprehended" as such.[5] Mediated realism—the second alternative—argues that this is not sufficient. A "bridge" is required and so the principle of causality must be applied in order for us to have knowledge of an entity. In other words, "their manifest contingency obliges us to look for a cause."[6] Gilson himself endorsed a third view, immediatism, which he attributed to Léon Noël. In this view, the distance between the thing in itself and the one who apprehends it breaks down in an intensive encounter. The entity is "grasped," as it were, in a "lived and experienced unity of an intellect with an apprehended reality."[7] The relationship between realist immediacy and Thomas Aquinas's epistemology is explained by Gilson: "(Noël) appeals to Thomistic principles of the most authentic kind . . . The object of the understanding is not the material thing in its concrete individuality but its nonmaterial quiddity which, as such, can form a real unity with an intellect . . . We must, he tells us, give up the illusory idea of an outside and an inside."[8] (This view is reminiscent of the hermeneutics associated with Hans-Georg Gadamer and Paul Ricoeur described in section 114.) That said, "we are by no means saying that the intellect infallibly so grasps it, but that only when it does grasp it as it is will there be knowledge. Still less do we mean that knowledge exhausts the content of its object in a single act. What knowledge grasps in the object is something real,

---

disputation to be equally valent, the skepticism of the Enlightenment was something entirely new. The extreme rationalists of the Enlightenment declared most beliefs concerning the sensible world to be inherently unreliable. See Littlejohn and Carter, *Epistemology*, 19, 391. We are on firmer ground, perhaps, in imagining how Aquinas might have responded to the empiricists, most of whom were committed to materialism.

5. Gilson, *Methodological Realism*, 49.
6. Gilson, *Methodological Realism*, 30.
7. Gilson, *Methodological Realism*, 94.
8. Gilson, *Methodological Realism*, 56.

but reality is inexhaustible, and even if the intellect had discerned all its details, it would still be confronted by the mystery of its very existence."[9]

304. THE CATHOLIC CHURCH AND EPISTEMOLOGY

Again, the Catholic Church does not endorse any particular philosophy as such. This includes the epistemological realism of the Aristotelian-Thomist Tradition.

That said, the church has forthrightly resisted the appeal of skepticism, an epistemological stance that undergirds a great deal of Enlightenment thought. Although the tone of the church's censure has moderated somewhat, the vigor of its opposition to skepticism has not. Consider two telling documents: Pope Pius X's encyclical letter *Pascendi Dominici Gregis* (*On the Doctrine of the Modernists*) (1907) and Pope John Paul II's encyclical letter *Fides et Ratio* (*On the Relationship Between Faith and Reason*) (1998). In *Pascendi Dominici Gregis,* Pius X groups rationalists and empiricists among the "modernists" he condemns in no uncertain terms: "Modernists place the foundation of religious philosophy in that doctrine which is usually called *Agnosticism*. According to this teaching, human reason is confined entirely within the field of *phenomena*, that is to say, to things that are perceptible to the senses, and in the manner in which they are perceptible; it has no right and no power to transgress these limits."[10] This assessment is echoed in John Paul II's *Fides et Ratio*: "As a result of the exaggerated rationalism of certain thinkers, positions grew more radical and there emerged eventually a philosophy which was separate from and absolutely independent of the contents of faith. Another of the many consequences of this separation was an ever-deeper mistrust with regard to reason itself. In a spirit both skeptical and agnostic, some began to voice a general mistrust, which led some to focus more on faith and others to deny its rationality altogether."[11]

With respect to the more narrow concern of knowledge acquisition, thinkers associated with the Catholic Church have endorsed a variety of views.[12] Thomas Aquinas followed Aristotle in attributing all knowl-

---

9. Gilson, *Methodological Realism*, 102.
10. Pius X, *Pascendi Dominici Gregis*, no. 6.
11. John Paul II, *Fides et Ratio*, no. 9.

12. In chapter 1, a deep suspicion of all forms of philosophical speculation among some was noted. This included, for instance, certain expressions of early monasticism and the *devotio moderna* movement, too.

edge—first and foremost—to sense data. Although Aristotle privileged the role reason plays in reflective thinking, he insisted that all knowledge arises—not from some ethereal realm—but from the senses. We are, in effect, blank slates, i.e., *tabula rasa*, prior to our encounters with the sensible world. Thomas Aquinas endorsed this view.[13] In *Fides et Ratio*, John Paul II echoed it as well. In a distinction the pontiff drew between faith and philosophical knowledge, he notes: "Faith is of an order other than philosophical knowledge, which depends upon *sense perception and experience* and which advances by the light of the intellect alone."[14] (Emphasis added.)

In contrast, Bonaventure discounted the role reason plays in the "apprehension, enjoyment, and judgment" of certain higher truths, thereby attributing the acquisition of knowledge to direct divine illumination.[15] Bonaventure followed Augustine in asserting this view.[16] The Bishop of Hippo's understanding of original sin—and hence our fallen nature as human beings—and grace can, in fact, undermine confidence in our ability to reason or, at least, to reason well. As has been noted, this was certainly evident in the moral thinking of the Reformation. Thomas Aquinas, for one, was more sanguine with respect to the relationship shared by faith and reason: "Faith presupposes natural knowledge, even as grace presupposes nature, and perfection supposes something that can be perfected.[17]

Given Bonaventure's reference to certain "higher truths" and Augustine's prominence as both a philosopher and a churchman, we can easily miss a telling difference between the epistemological stances advanced by Aristotle and Aquinas, on the one hand, and Augustine and Bonaventure, on the other. Indeed, both camps seem—on the surface, at least—to espouse a "two-track" understanding of knowledge: divine

13. Jacobs, *Seat of Wisdom*, 162.

14. John Paul II, *Fides et Ratio*, no. 45.

15. *Faith Connection*: Given this, it is not surprising that contemplation played a more significant role than reason in Bonaventure's spirituality: "God can be contemplated not only outside us through His traces and inside us through His image, but also through a light that shines upon our mind—the light of eternal truth; for 'our mind itself is created by Truth in person without intermediary.' Therefore, those who are experienced in the first way have entered the vestibule of the Dwelling; those experienced in the second way have entered the Holy Place; but those who practice the third way enter with the High Priest into the Holy of Holies." See Bonaventure, "The Mind's Journey to God," 2005, 169.

16. Augustine, *The Confessions*, 240. See also MacIntyre, *A Short History of Ethics*, 48.

17. Aquinas, "The Existence of God," 161–162.

illumination or revelation, on the one hand, and sense knowledge and reason, on the other. Thomas Aquinas, however, was an epistemological optimist. Like Aristotle, he believed that the senses—guided by reason—can engender true knowledge. The two tracks he postulated were entirely distinct, but complementary and mutually enhancing. Augustine and Bonaventure may have endorsed a two-track epistemology of sorts, but they left no doubt as to the superiority of one, e.g., divine illumination or revelation, over the other, i.e., sense perception informed by reason. In his autobiography, *The Confessions*, Augustine goes on at some length, in fact, concerning the futility of his search for truth in the teachings of Mani (216–274), Plato, Aristotle, and Plotinus, and he disavows the appeal of hedonism and the "world's values" as well. Unlike Aristotle and Aquinas, Augustine was an epistemological pessimist.

305. ALTERNATIVE VIEWS

Aristotle developed his epistemology in opposition to Plato's concept of Forms or Ideas. Plato believed in the pre-existence of souls and so posited a process of *anamnesis* by which we can "recollect" knowledge—however partial and vague it may be—about the non-material and non-temporal Forms or Ideas on the basis of which the various existents of the sensible world are modeled. As described by Alasdair MacIntyre, Plato believed that "knowledge is already present in us and has only to be brought to birth by a philosophical midwife."[18]

In comparison to epistemological realists and platonic idealists, too, the philosophers of the Enlightenment narrowed their understanding of knowledge. Rationalists such as René Descartes, Baruch Spinoza, and Gottfried Leibniz generally ascribed true belief, i.e., knowledge, exclusively to tautological statements, i.e., propositions deemed true by virtue of their logical form, and certain analytic truths, i.e., propositions deemed true by virtue of the concepts employed in them. (The equation "A = A" is an example of a tautological truth, and the statement "a square has four sides" is an instance of an analytic truth.)[19] The rationalists of the

---

18. MacIntyre, *A Short History of Ethics*, 21.

19. Aristotle and Thomas Aquinas both acknowledged the validity of these kinds of self-evident truths. That said, Aquinas, for one, "did not think that we can deduce a whole system of philosophy from these abstract propositions." See Copleston, *Aquinas*, 34. Given this, he would likely not have been surprised at the severely circumscribed boundaries of rationalist thought.

Enlightenment were philosophical pessimists. They were skeptical of our ability to know much if anything for certain about the sensible world.[20]

In contrast, the empiricists of the Enlightenment, most notably Francis Bacon, Thomas Hobbes, John Locke, and George Berkeley, trusted sense data and believed, in fact, that all knowledge is "constructed on the basis of experience obtained through the traditional five senses."[21] They affirmed, too, the need to subject all truth claims to verification using the scientific method, induction, and empirical inference, i.e., conclusions drawn from direct observation and experience. Given the materialist underpinnings of their work, the empiricists were dismissive of truth claims formulated on the basis of other conceptual foundations, especially metaphysics and religion. In contrast to the rationalists of the seventeenth and eighteenth centuries, the empiricists tended to optimism concerning what we can know about the sensible world. All that is needed—in their view—is more data and more refined techniques.

Immanuel Kant hoped to reconcile the insights of the rationalists and the empiricists. He had been significantly influenced by David Hume (1711–1776), one of the great minds of the eighteenth century. Although Hume is best classified as an empiricist, he, nonetheless, shared the profound skepticism of the rationalists, albeit for very different reasons.

Kant hoped to overcome the skepticism that had so occupied his rationalist counterparts and David Hume, too; indeed, he referred to skepticism as the "euthanasia of pure reason."[22] At the same time, Kant harbored grave doubts about the way in which Bacon, Hobbes, Locke, and Berkeley had seemingly reduced all knowledge to sense data. In Kant's view, the empiricists had not adequately accounted for the role our minds play in sense-making. As described by Graham Bird, Kant's "Copernican revolution reversed the usual way of viewing cognition . . . Instead of thinking of our knowledge as conforming to a realm of objects, we [should] think of objects as conforming to our ways of knowing."[23]

Kant acknowledged the reality of the world outside of our minds, but perceived an unbridgeable gulf between our perceptions of things in

---

20. This observation pertains to a rather extreme form of rationalism. As noted by Alan Lacey, "rationalism does not have to take an extreme form. It can content itself with claiming simply that some of our knowledge, though not all of it, can come to us otherwise than through the senses." See Lacey, "Rationalism," 743. The distinctions made in this chapter are cast in sharp relief in order to facilitate comparisons and contrasts.

21. Lacey, "Empiricism," 226.

22. Kant, "Immanuel Kant," 436.

23. Kant, "Immanuel Kant," 436.

the sensible world, i.e., phenomena, and their corresponding noumena, i.e., the things in themselves, which exist independently of our perception of them. "Kant calls this thinkable-but-not-knowable reality behind experience the noumena. Knowledge of the material world is restricted to that which is experienced, the world of necessity and determined by the laws of science. Kant calls this *phenomena*: the world as it appears to us in our experience as ordered by the judgments of the mind."[24]

According to Kant, all is not lost. Because of certain ways in which our minds invariably structure or organize our experiences of the sensible world, i.e., transcendental categories,[25] some truths about the world outside of our minds can be known with some degree of certainty.[26] Indeed, "Kant argues that understanding is equipped with a set of *a priori* concepts or categories, including substance and causality, which are required for the knowledge of an object or an objective realm. From this, he concludes that all objects of possible experience must conform to these categories."[27] Kant can thus be described as a qualified optimist with respect to what we can know.

306. A CHART COMPARING ASPECTS OF EPISTEMOLOGICAL REALISM TO CERTAIN ALTERNATIVE EPISTEMOLOGIES

The chart below displays the epistemological positions defended by realists in the Aristotelian-Thomist Tradition alongside those of Plato and key Enlightenment thinkers.

---

24. Jacobs, *Seat of Wisdom*, 153.

25. Kant's use of the word "transcendental" differs profoundly from its meaning in the Aristotelian-Thomist Tradition. As noted in section 216, Aristotle and Aquinas distinguished certain "transcendental" properties, i.e., unity, truth, and goodness, from all other accidents and properties because they are part and parcel of everything that exists. They do not inhere in any particular individual being or class of beings, essences, substances, or accidents. As noted by Henry E. Allison, Kant argued that we "are equipped with a set of *a priori* concepts or [transcendental] categories, including substance and causality, which are required for the knowledge of an object or an objective realm. From this, he concludes that all objects of possible experience must conform to these categories." Kant's transcendental categories are thus attributable to the basic framework of our minds. See Allison, "Transcendental Analytic," 878.

26. "Certainty," in this sense, refers rather narrowly to the coherence and consistency of our knowledge.

27. Allison, "Transcendental Analytic," 878.

	Epistemological Realism (Aristotle and Aquinas)	Platonic Idealism (Plato)	Rationalism (Descartes, Spinoza, Leibniz, et al.)	Empiricism (Bacon, Hobbes, Locke, Berkeley, et al.)	Transcendental Idealism (Kant)
Privileged Form of Truth Claims (314):	Propositions				
Method(s) (313):	• Demonstration by Syllogism • Inductive Inference • Intuition	• Socratic Questioning • Dialectic Debate	• Deductive Reasoning • Intuition	• Scientific Method • Induction • Inference	• Empirical Investigation • Transcendental Reflection
Evidence (312):	• Sense Data • Memory • Testimony	• Contemplative Recollection • Innate Ideas	• Innate Ideas • Sense Impressions	Data Derived from Direct Observation or Experience	• Insights into How Our Minds Shape Our Sense Perceptions • Data Pertaining to Phenomena
Theories of Justification (310, 311):	• Foundationalism • Coherentism • Intersubjective Agreement	Alignment of Our Perceptions and Unchanging Forms	Rational Certitude	• Scientific Certitude • Probability	Coherency and Consistency in Our Philosophical Thought
Impediments to the Justification of Knowledge (311, 312):	Infinite Regress	Illusion	Skepticism	• Insufficient Data • Inadequate Techniques	The Inaccessibility of Noumena
Types of Knowledge (310):	• A Priori • A Posteriori	A Priori	A Priori	A Posteriori	• A Priori • A Posteriori • Synthetic a Priori
The Nature of Knowledge (309):	Justified Belief				
That Which Can Be Known (308):	• Actual Real Being • Potential Being • Mind-dependent Being	Forms or Ideas	The Mind	The Sensible World	• Transcendental Categories of the Mind • Phenomena
Philosophical Assumptions that Underlie Various Epistemologies (304, 305):	• Metaphysical Realism • Epistemological Optimism	Idealism	Epistemological Pessimism	• Materialism • Epistemological Optimism	• A Noumena-Phenomena Divide • Qualified Epistemological Optimism

Figure 2

307. EPISTEMOLOGICAL REALISM AND THAT WHICH CAN BE KNOWN

Different epistemologies tend to focus on different mixes of subject matter. Since epistemological realism is grounded on metaphysical realism, it is not surprising that real being serves as the primary subject of investigation in the epistemological realism of the Aristotelian-Thomist Tradition. As explained by James M. Jacobs, "human knowledge is the result of the act of existence in substances acting on the potency of humans to learn, so that the essence of a real being is grasped in the mind as a being of reason pointing to a universal essence that defines that object."[28] Further, given that "everything that exists is being," everything is "fair game" for

---

28. Jacobs, *Seat of Wisdom*, 129.

epistemological realists. This includes any and all manifestations or potential manifestations of actual real being and mind-dependent beings, too.

This could suggest, however, that all meaningful knowledge is theoretical in nature. This was certainly not Aristotle's understanding. The ancient Greeks parsed knowledge into three distinct categories: *episteme* encompasses all types of theoretical knowledge, including knowledge of being; *phronesis* pertains to practical knowledge gleaned from the world of experience and expressed, in turn, in sound judgments; and *techne* concerns the kind of practical know-how required in "doing" and in "making" things in the world. Again, epistemological realism encompasses all kinds of knowledge.

308. OTHER PERSPECTIVES PERTAINING TO THAT WHICH CAN BE KNOWN

This all-encompassing focus differs considerably from Plato's more narrow interest: knowledge concerning the ethereal Forms or Ideas that serve as models for the changing, impermanent, and imperfect existents we encounter in the sensible world.

The philosophers of the Enlightenment differed significantly among themselves with respect to the subjects of investigation they recognized as knowable or potentially knowable. They agreed, however, that the scope of that which can be known is considerably smaller than either Aristotle and Thomas Aquinas, on the one hand, or Plato, Plotinus, and the other idealists of the ancient world, on the other, had imagined. For René Descartes and his fellow rationalists, things in the sensible world cannot be known with any degree of certainty, hence Descartes's *cogito, ergo sum*, i.e., "I think, therefore I am."[29] Their epistemological interests were thus restricted to that which can be apprehended by reason quite apart from anything that might be encountered or experienced in the sensible world. The empiricists of the seventeenth and eighteenth centuries pursued the opposite tack; they were convinced that nothing meaningful can be said about anything purported to exist or subsist outside of the sensible world. Finally, Immanuel Kant's transcendental idealism restricted the scope of what can be known to the transcendent categories of our minds, our

---

29. Descartes's *cogito, ergo sum* was anticipated, in fact, by Aristotle: "If we perceive, we perceive that we perceive, and if we think, that we think; and if to perceive that we perceive or think is to perceive that we exist..." See Aristotle, *Nicomachean Ethics,* 153.

perceptions of things we encounter in the sensible world, i.e., phenomena, and certain *synthetic a priori* truths, a far cry from the portfolio of interests embraced by epistemological realists.

309. THE NATURE OF KNOWLEDGE

There is broad agreement concerning the nature of knowledge: knowledge is justified belief or truth. As affirmed by E. J. Lowe, "a candidate for truth is true if and only if it corresponds to the facts."[30] To be considered knowledge and, hence, truth, a belief must be justified in some satisfactory way. Although controversies in academic circles persist concerning the proper objects of knowledge, its form, and what constitutes justification, this formal definition of knowledge is quite straightforward and is sometimes referred to as the "correspondence theory of truth" or "logical truth."[31]

That said, two questions are prompted. First, what is belief? And second, what is required for a particular belief to be justified and so constitute knowledge? The nature of belief and the nature of knowledge are addressed in this section and in section 310. The critical question of justification is addressed in sections 311 and 312.

Belief can be understood as a mental or cognitive state.[32] It is important to note, however, that a belief may be consciously unknown to the believer or incompletely articulated or even unarticulated altogether. Further, beliefs are thought to imply the "deployment of concepts" or "action" of one sort or another.[33] This "deployment" could involve specific actions or—alternately—dispositions of one kind or another. Indeed, our beliefs hold implications for how we make our way in the world. Finally, some beliefs are thought to be involuntary in nature. I can pay someone to assert that Donald Duck is the president of the United States. It is unlikely that doing so, however, would lead him or her to "believe" that this is actually so.

---

30. Lowe, "Truth," 881. See also Glenn, *An Introduction to Philosophy*, 218.

31. Logical truth can thus be distinguished from ontological truth, which refers more specifically to metaphysical knowledge about being. See Glenn, *An Introduction to Philosophy*, 219. See also Cotter, *An Introduction to Catholic Philosophy*, 129.

32. Dretske, "Belief," 82.

33. Dretske, "Belief," 83.

310. TYPES OF KNOWLEDGE

If a belief is justified, it constitutes knowledge. Before considering how truth claims can be justified, however, we would do well to consider certain distinctions between and among three kinds of knowledge. This is important because the various positions espoused by epistemologists in this regard reveal certain fault lines that have contributed to the development of their very different epistemologies.

A priori knowledge does not arise from experiences in the sensible world. That said, there is little consensus as to what constitutes *a priori* knowledge.[34] As you might expect, few today subscribe to Plato's theory of recollection by which we supposedly recall—in an *a priori* fashion—our pre-birth knowledge of eternal Forms. Most would agree, however, that analytic assertions, e.g., a triangle has three sides, constitute *a priori* knowledge; and most would agree, too, that tautologies, e.g., A = A, can be understood as *a priori* knowledge. We simply know these kinds of propositions to be true.

Some further assert that raw sense perception, i.e., sense perceptions unmediated by reflection, can be understood as a kind of *a priori* knowledge and so, too, our sense of ourselves as beings in the world. This is especially so in the case of rationalists. Again, René Descartes's epistemology begins with his sense of himself as a thinking being: "*cogito, ergo sum*"; and Gotfried Leibniz argued that a number of other metaphysical concepts, including substance and causation, are innate in us as well.[35]

As we shall see, foundationalists in the camp of metaphysical realism and the rationalists of the seventeenth and eighteenth centuries, as well, uphold the validity of certain *a priori* truth claims. Extreme empiricists tend to reject the concept of *a priori* truth claims altogether.[36]

In contrast, *a posteriori* knowledge is entirely dependent on our senses and on our experience of the material world, not in a raw or unmediated sense, but as impressions carried to our minds by our senses and so rendered available for reflection. Epistemological realists put a premium on *posteriori* knowledge. They dismiss claims of *a priori* knowledge obtained independently of our sense experiences. Although certain non-material and non-temporal truths certainly exist, e.g., our

---

34. That said, the extent to which sense knowledge and experience actually underlie *a priori* truth claims is contested in the academic sub-discipline of epistemology.

35. Sleigh, Jr., "Gottfried Wilhelm Leibniz," 480.

36. Littlejohn and Carter, *Epistemology*, 79.

knowledge of being, for instance, in their view, these non-experiential or *a priori* truths only come to our attention by way of our experiences in the sensible world and only then acquire salience in our reflections on these sense experiences. Indeed, the exclusivity empiricists attribute to *a posteriori* truths distinguishes them from epistemological realists. Because their epistemologies are grounded on a materialist worldview, empiricists tend to deny the very possibility of any truth that is of a non-material and non-temporal nature. With respect to *a priori* truths, there is simply "no there there," according to empiricists.

In attempting to reconcile the epistemological positions of his rationalist and empiricist counterparts, Immanuel Kant posited a third kind of knowledge: *synthetic a priori* truths. Transcendental idealists attribute this kind of knowledge—not to particular *a priori* truths or to particular *a posteriori* experiences of one kind or another—but to the structures of our minds. Kant's understanding of *synthetic a priori* truths can be thought of as knowledge obtained through a kind of "bootstrapping" process, i.e., deductions drawn from certain *a priori* truths. This includes our understanding of causation, our sense of time, mathematical formulae, e.g., 2 + 2 = 4, and the fact that we know ourselves to be "extended" in three dimensions, i.e., height, width, and depth. According to Kant, these kinds of *synthetic a priori judgements* "are *a priori* because they are based in reason alone; but they are synthetic because they are capable of connecting two previously unconnected ideas with necessity so as to produce real knowledge."[37] Indeed, Kant attributed certain "transcendental categories" to our minds. (In contrast, a metaphysical realist in the Aristotelian-Thomist Tradition would assign these ways of thinking to our essence as rational beings. See section 214.)

311. EPISTEMOLOGICAL REALISM AND KNOWLEDGE JUSTIFICATION

The prospect of "infinite regression" poses the clearest epistemological threat to realists in the Aristotelian-Thomist Tradition. This challenge follows from the metaphysical concept of causation, more specifically, the third cause of change identified by Aristotle: efficient causation. Recall from section 217 that an efficient cause is one "which by its activity gives

---

37. Jacobs, *Seat of Wisdom*, 150.

existence to something or brings about a change."³⁸ Again, some efficient causes are proximate or immediate in their effects; others produce their effects indirectly or in combination with other extrinsic causes.

According to metaphysical realists, any change or event we might happen to witness in the sensible world must be attributable—in theory—to one or more efficient causes. The efficient cause of that event must itself have been caused, too, and so, too, the event that preceded it, and so on back to the "unmoved mover" hypothesized by Aristotle. We may have great confidence in the first cause; after all, we witnessed the event to which it is ascribed, but can we be so sure about the preceding cause or set of causes, or the cause or set of causes that preceded that event and so on back to the "unmoved mover"?

According to skeptics, the answer is "no." This view is sometimes called "infinitism."³⁹ After all, they claim, Aristotle had affirmed that "scientific knowledge"—as he broadly construed the term—requires a precise knowledge of causes.⁴⁰ Lacking an understanding of an event's efficient cause or set of causes, anything that might be said about it should be relegated to the domain of opinion; according to skeptics, our beliefs concerning events of this kind cannot be considered knowledge *per se*.⁴¹ Given the prospect of infinite regress, the rationalists of the seventeenth and eighteenth centuries concluded, in fact, that we lack a sure foundation for most of our beliefs and, hence, true knowledge. Because we cannot be certain about the efficient cause of sets or causes attributable to each and every link in impossibly long chains of causation that attend to each and every change we encounter in the sensible world, there is little that can be considered certain. On its face, at least, the skeptics seem to have a point.⁴²

---

38. Cotter, *An Introduction to Catholic Philosophy*, 393.

39. "Infinitism" is an epistemic stance that holds that "all justified beliefs are justified because of support from further justifiers. The chain of justifiers justifies beliefs only when it forms an infinite series of non-repeating justifiers." See Littlejohn and Carter, *Epistemology*, 20.

40. Aristotle, *Prior & Posterior Analytics*, 102.

41. Aristotle, *Prior & Posterior Analytics*, 143.

42. The idea of infinite regress as an insurmountable problem is not itself unproblematic. As noted by Paul J. Glenn, arguments in favor of this view tend to be circular in nature: "The defender of skepticism asks us to accept his doctrine that *it is certain that there is no certitude*. He offers evidence for a doctrine *which denies the value of all evidence*. He uses the mind to work out the argument *that there is no use of the mind*. By his own confession, the skeptic is confounded as well as confuted . . . In a word, the skeptic contradicts himself; one part of his doctrine cancels out the other, and the result

That said, the prospect of infinite regress does not seem to have troubled either Aristotle or Thomas Aquinas. In fact, Aristotle was well aware of this concern, which he attributed to the skeptics of his own day: "It is enough in some cases that the *fact* be well established, as in the case of the first principles; the fact is the primary thing or first principle. Now of first principles, we see some by induction, some by perception, some by a certain habituation, and others, too, in other ways."[43] He insisted that certain "basic truths" need no proof; they can be presumed to be true and then leveraged to engender new knowledge.[44] This view is called foundationalism. More recently, coherentism and a particular understanding of intersubjective agreement have also been advanced to counter the problem of infinite regress. Each will be addressed in turn.

Metaphysical realists tend to follow Aristotle in asserting that some truths are of an *a priori* nature. If this is true, it should be possible to short-circuit infinite regress if, in fact, a particular link in any given chain of reasoning can be determined to be *a priori* in nature. After all, *a priori* truths require no further justification. Some foundationalists go further, however; they contend that the causal links in any given chain of events may be more robust than we sometimes imagine. In fact, multiple causes—all of an efficient nature—attend to most changes. Indeed, many changes in the sensible world may be "over-determined." In other words, if one or more efficient causes was removed from any particular event in the long chain of events leading up to it, it is likely—or maybe even certain—that that event would have occurred anyway just as it did. According to some foundationalists, we can thus be confident in our understanding of at least some events in the sensible world and, hence, in any knowledge we might glean from witnessing these events.[45]

---

is zero." See Glenn, *An Introduction to Philosophy*, 225. See also Littlejohn and Carter, *Epistemology*, 360.

43. Aristotle, *Nicomachean Ethics*, 19. See also Aristotle, *Prior & Posterior Analytics*, 104.

44. Aristotle, *Prior & Posterior Analytics*, 114.

45. Foundationalism is not without its own problems. Particular links in chains of reasoning that rely on *a posteriori* truths, i.e., knowledge gleaned from the sensible world, still need to be justified, and academic epistemologists disagree about what might or might not be required to justify these kinds of beliefs. These debates tend to focus on the concept of "warrants" and are often framed as "arguments of defeasibility." See Littlejohn and Carter, *Epistemology*, 40.

Coherentism suggests that we need not rely solely on a chain of causation to justify our beliefs.[46] We can take epistemological solace, instead, in the way our understanding of the sensible world "hangs together" as a coherent whole. As E. J. Lowe explains, "accepting that truth cannot consist in a relation between truth-bearers and items which are not themselves truth-bearers (such as 'facts'), (coherence theorists) propose instead that it consists in a relation which truth-bearers have to one another, such as a relation of mutual support amongst the beliefs of an individual or a community."[47] In this view, our world and the events we witness in time "cohere" in a knowable reality. This can give us considerable confidence in the knowledge we glean from our day-to-day experiences and in the philosophical reflections underwritten by this knowledge.[48]

According to some epistemological realists, a certain kind of intersubjective agreement can also underwrite knowledge. To be clear, this kind of intersubjective agreement cannot be a matter of opinion or public polling. This would suggest a constructivist and, hence, subjectivist understanding of knowledge; epistemological realists in the Aristotelian-Thomist Tradition hold that truth is objective in nature and external to and fully independent of our reflections upon it. Although widespread agreement—even among knowledgeable parties—cannot justify knowledge *per se*, it can, nonetheless, attest to a deeper wisdom that itself can justify some truth claims. Metaphysical realists note that this kind of deeper wisdom is often embedded in axioms that may be quite general in nature or unique to particular communities of interest.[49]

---

46. The view that coherentism is a remedy for the problem of infinite regress is contested by some metaphysical realists.

47. Lowe, "Truth," 881.

48. *Faith Connection*: The Catholic Church has endorsed a version of coherentism in its reflections on certain proofs of God's existence: "Created in God's image and called to know and love him, the person who seeks God discovers certain ways of coming to know him. These are also called proofs for the existence of God, not in the sense of proofs in the natural sciences, but rather in the sense of '*converging and convincing arguments,*' which allow us to attain certainty about the truth." (Emphasis added.) See *Catechism*, no. 31.

49. *Faith Connection*: The Catholic Church has embraced a particular understanding of this kind of intersubjective agreement: *sensus fidelium*, i.e., the sense of the faithful: "The whole body of the faithful who have received an anointing which comes from the holy one cannot be mistaken in belief. It shows this characteristic through the entire people's supernatural sense of the faith, when 'from the bishops to the last of the faithful,' it manifests a universal consensus in matter of faith and morals." See Second Vatican Council, "*Lumen Gentium*," no. 12. See also *Catechism*, no. 92.

312. ENLIGHTENMENT EPISTEMOLOGIES AND KNOWLEDGE JUSTIFICATION

Extreme rationalists tend to think of the problem of infinite regress as an insurmountable barrier to the justification of most beliefs based on sense data and, therefore, to the engendering of true belief or knowledge. René Descartes went even further. In a thought experiment, he imagined the existence of a demon who manipulates our sense perceptions, thereby undermining any and all knowledge we might have of the sensible world.[50]

Having surrendered to the challenge of infinite regress, Descartes, Spinoza, Leibniz, and their fellow rationalists encountered another formidable challenge, however: skepticism. Indeed, the twin perils of infinitism, on the one hand, and skepticism, on the other, can be described as the Scylla and Charybdis of epistemology, indeed, as the opposing horns of an imposing dilemma. Lacking a firm foundation for knowing anything about the sensible world, the justification of knowledge seemed to them to be beyond reach. According to C. J. Hookway, this kind of philosophical skepticism or "hyperbolic doubt"[51] can undermine "our cognitive achievements, challenging our ability to obtain reliable knowledge. Global skepticism casts doubt upon all our attempts to seek the truth; more restricted forms of skepticism may question our knowledge of ethical matters of the past, of other minds, of the underlying structures of matter and so on,"[52] in short, everything!

In response, the rationalists of the seventeenth and eighteenth centuries went back to the drawing board. They looked for first principles—*a priori* truths, in fact—that are only marginally, if at all, dependent on sense knowledge. Much like their foundationalist cousins in the camp of metaphysical realism, these "Cartesian foundationalists"[53] concluded that certain links in some chains of causation may constitute *a priori* truths, i.e., truths that require no further justification. The rationalists

---

50. The so-called Cartesian demon has had remarkable staying power. It led in time to the "mind in a vat" imagery that is often used by contemporary epistemologists to "bracket" sensory experiences in their philosophical reflections. If this sounds familiar, it may be because you are a fan of the Matrix movies, which were based entirely on the "mind in a vat" meme.

51. Jacobs, *Seat of Wisdom*, 139.

52. Hookway, "Skepticism," 794. See also Littlejohn and Carter, *Epistemology*, 359. See also Cotter, *An Introduction to Catholic Philosophy*, 134.

53. Littlejohn and Carter, *Epistemology*, 50, 74–75.

of the Enlightenment were reluctant to go any further, however, and so eschewed a more robust understanding of foundationalism, coherency theory, or intersubjective agreement. In limiting themselves in this way, they set their epistemological sights—not on truth *per se*—but on something far less ambitious: rational certitude.[54] They relied on innate ideas in pursuing this more circumscribed objective. Relying on certain *a priori* truths, the rationalists argued, some beliefs—as meager as they might be and any beliefs subsequently derived from them, too—might be justifiable and so constitute true knowledge. Again, this particular defense of epistemological justification is called "foundationalism." Descartes's *cogito, ergo sum*, i.e., "I think, therefore I am," has already been noted as an example of this kind of thinking.

To epistemological realists, this is thin soup, indeed. In an influential essay entitled "Defense of Common Sense" (1925), G. E. Moore employed a *reductio ad absurdum* to "prove" the existence of the external world, thereby mocking all such skeptical musings. C. J. Hookway describes Moore's argument as follows: "Holding up his hands before him, (Moore) affirmed his knowledge that he had two hands, and since hands were objects in the external world, he concluded that there was an external world."[55] Clayton Littlejohn and J. Adam Carter further attest to the import of this argument using "explanationist theory": "If the hands-hypothesis provides the best explanation of these features of our evidence, we are justified in accepting it and rejecting the rival mind-in-a-vat hypothesis. Our experience of objects in the external world is, by and large, orderly and coherent. Things don't seem to us to pop in or pop out of existence or change without reason. There is a kind of agreement across sense modalities in the sense that the objects we see typically visually appear to have the shapes that we feel them to have. When there are sensory illusions, we can provide principled explanations as to why these illusions should occur by appeal to our common-sense beliefs about the nature of external objects and our relations to them. The rival mind-in-a-vat hypothesis seems to offer nothing but ad hoc explanations of these features."[56] Referring obliquely to René Descartes's evil demon hypoth-

---

54. Formal certitude can be defined as "firm assent (or dissent) which is necessarily true and known to be true, i.e., one in which the mind is necessarily conformed to its object and knows its own conformity . . . " Cotter, *An Introduction to Catholic Philosophy*, 234.

55. Hookway, "Skepticism," 795.

56. Littlejohn and Carter, *Epistemology*, 378.

esis, Paul J. Glenn similarly appeals to common sense: "Perhaps we are the creatures of a Power that delights to see us deceived. The sane answer to one 'perhaps' is another 'perhaps.' We might dismiss this silly assertion by saying 'perhaps not.' But we need not be so abrupt. No normal man can look upon existence as a hopeless confusion, a milling about in toils of error and deception."[57]

If the rationalists of the Enlightenment were ridden by epistemological doubt, their empiricist counterparts suffered from the opposite condition: overconfidence or—some would say—hubris. In their view, the only barriers to the justification of knowledge, i.e., scientific certitude or statistical probability, is insufficient data and the further development of the scientific tools, i.e., observation and experimentation, and the analytic tools needed to exploit it.[58] (David Hume was a notable exception in this regard.) Nicolas Rescher attests to the philosophical bravado of the empiricists in asking: "Is human knowledge completable? The incompletability of scientific progress is compatible with the view that every question that can be asked at any particular state of the art is going to be answered—or dissolved—at some future state: it does *not* commit one to the idea that there are any unanswerable questions placed altogether beyond the limits of possible resolution."[59]

As noted above, Immanuel Kant attempted to bridge the gap between the dueling epistemologies of his rationalist and empiricist counterparts.[60] As described by Owen Flanigan, "Kant's Copernican turn, the

---

57. Glenn, *An Introduction to Philosophy*, 227.

58. The empiricists of the Enlightenment thus joined their rationalist counterparts in severely constricting philosophy's scope of interest, but in a very different way. Pope John Paul II employed the pejorative term "scientism" in lamenting this development: "(Scientism) relegates religious, theological, ethical, and aesthetic knowledge to the realm of mere fantasy ... It dismisses values as mere products of the emotions and rejects the notion of being in order to clear the way for pure and simple facticity ... Scientism consigns all that has to do with the question of the meaning of life to the realm of the irrational or imaginary ... This leads to the impoverishment of thought, which no longer addresses the ultimate problems which the human being, as the *animal rationale*, has pondered constantly from the beginning of time." See John Paul II, *Fides et Ratio*, no. 88.

59. Rescher, "The Limits of Knowledge," 448.

60. Kant was concerned with sense-making, i.e., the processes by which we draw coherent understanding and meaning from our encounters with people and things in the sensible world, and in mapping the boundaries of human knowledge. Like his rationalist and empiricist counterparts, Kant eschewed any interest in metaphysics in pursuing these objectives. As we shall see, he, nevertheless, developed a moral system that—in the minds of some—rivals the moral system associated with the Aristotelian-Thomist Tradition.

proposal that the mind lays down certain *a priori* conditions for experience, was meant to answer the deep skepticism about causation, self, and transcendental matters, such as the existence of God, generated by Hume's epistemology."[61] As noted by James M. Jacobs, "the mind does not fit reality, reality fits the mind,"[62] at least in Kant's view. In making this claim, however, Kant conceded the existence of an unbridgeable gulf between our minds and the sensible world, that is, between "phenomena," i.e., things as they appear, and "noumena," i.e., things as they are in and of themselves, independent of our perceptions of them.[63] Despite this unyielding divide, Kant argued that some knowledge can be justified by the coherence and consistency revealed when we impose the "transcendental structures" of our minds on this or that phenomena we encounter in the sensible world, not things as they are, i.e., their noumena, to be sure, but things as they appear to us.

313. EPISTEMOLOGICAL REALISM AND EVIDENCE

Evidence can be defined as a "body of belief that supports some less well-established hypothesis."[64] As Paul J. Glenn notes, "evidence, to be of value, must be *objective*, or, more accurately, *trans-subjective*. It must not be the mere feeling or the mere viewpoint or the mere taste of the person who seeks it or is influenced by it; it must not be *subjective*. Objective *evidence* is the ultimate criterion of truth, the ultimate basis of certitude."[65] As you might expect, the several philosophers introduced in this chapter harbored very different views concerning the "bodies of belief" they believed to be germane to the acquisition of knowledge. Indeed, their perspectives in this regard followed from the different assumptions that guided their work and the very different views they harbored pertaining to the justification of true belief, i.e., knowledge.

Three sources of evidence are generally privileged by metaphysical realists: sense data and experience, memory, and testimony.[66] For meta-

---

61. Flanigan, "History of the Philosophy of Mind," 570.

62. Jacobs, *Seat of Wisdom*, 149.

63. Kant thus anticipated what would later be called the "mind-body problem," a concern that has been of abiding interest to generations of philosophers and scientists, too.

64. Downie, "Evidence," 254.

65. Glenn, *An Introduction to Philosophy*, 240.

66. Realists in the Aristotelian-Thomist Tradition dismiss Plato's conception of preexistent knowledge as fanciful and so, too, the rationalists's belief in innate ideas;

physical realists, however, it all begins with sense data and experience.[67] After all, our memories include physical sensations we have experienced; and testimony—in one way or another—goes back to the experiences of others. As Fred Dretske observes, however, the concept of sense data is broader than we sometimes imagine and includes such things as "twinges, tickles, pains, itches, thirst, hunger, feelings of sexual arousal, and so on."[68] As noted by James M. Jacobs, the Aristotelian-Thomist Tradition recognizes two additional "senses" as well, i.e., common sense and imagination, which together "organize information" about the sensible world into "a coherent image that can be thought about . . . "[69] That said, sense data can be distinguished from "propositional attitudes such as thought, belief, judgment, and knowledge" and from "discursive events such as reasoning, thinking, knowing and remembering," too.[70]

The salience of sense data and experience does not mean, however, that the role of reasoning is unimportant to epistemological realists. It certainly is. After all, Aristotle defines human beings as reasoning animals; our essence is grounded in our ability to reason. As affirmed by Aristotle, sense data and experiences in the sensible world constitute little more than "perceptions" until they are grasped in the mind.[71] Thomas Aquinas endorsed this view. As noted by F. C. Copleston, Aquinas believed that "truth is primarily in the mind . . . It is defined as conformity between the mind and the thing. Hence to know this conformity is to know truth."[72] Indeed, Aquinas identified the intellect as a defining "power of the soul."[73] Further, the kind of reasoning that makes use of sense data is accomplished in a series of steps that, in effect, link epistemological realism to metaphysical realism: "The first step, in which we form a concept as a sign of a thing's essence, is called *apprehension* of the form. This grasps the universal concept that allows us to understand a nature in terms of

---

and they attribute Immanuel Kant's concept of "transcendental categories" to human essence, a metaphysical aspect of actual real being, rather than to the mind as such.

67. Although they acknowledged the *a priori* nature of some truths, neither Aristotle nor Thomas Aquinas believed that knowledge can be attributable in any way to innate ideas that are entirely disconnected from sense experience.

68. Dretske, "Sensation," 821.

69. Jacobs, *Seat of Wisdom*, 159. See also Aquinas, *The Summa Theologica and The Summa Contra Gentiles*, 333.

70. Aquinas, *The Summa Theologica and The Summa Contra Gentiles*, 881.

71. Aristotle, *Prior & Posterior Analytics*, 141.

72. Copleston, *Aquinas*, 184.

73. Aquinas, *The Summa Theologica and The Summa Contra Gentiles*, 337.

its necessary properties... In *judgment*, we attribute real existence to the essence in a thing outside the mind. That is, we tie the essence as a conceptual being of reason to a real substance with *esse*, the act of existence ... The third act of the intellect is where we string a series of judgments together, and by doing so learn something new by logical inference that is not immediately evident in experience. This is *reasoning*." Indeed, true belief or knowledge requires the active engagement of the mind. For epistemological realists in the Aristotelian-Thomist Tradition, "sense data and reason are both directed to knowing being, but they grasp different aspects of being: sensation is ordered to the individuality of substances, while the intellect grasps the universal nature of substances."[74]

To epistemological realists, memory also provides a source of evidence.[75] There is a tendency, however, to think of memory as a simple storehouse of sense impressions that have been laid down in our minds—in some mysterious fashion—and so rendered available for later use.[76] Memory is certainly more complex than that. To be sure, some memories are tactile or olfactory in nature and so tied to past sense experiences, but we remember emotions, as well, and so, too, tasks that need to be done and the way in which we value something or someone. There is an additional problem: memories are often incomplete or error-prone. This is of no small consequence, particularly for epistemological foundationalists who hold that the validity of each and every link in any given chain of reasoning must be justified—or justifiable in theory, at least—if a belief that relies on these underlying beliefs is to be deemed justified.

Despite this concern, our sense of ourselves—our identities, if you will—would be severely impaired if we had no memories, a fact affirmed

---

74. Jacobs, *Seat of Wisdom*, 155. See also Glenn, *An Introduction to Philosophy*, 240. See also Cotter, *An Introduction to Catholic Philosophy*, 273.

75. *Faith Connection*: The adage "*lex orandi, lex credendi*" points to the power of memory in the church. As noted in *Catechism of the Catholic Church*, "the church's faith precedes the faith of the believer. When the church celebrates the sacraments, she confesses the faith received from the apostles—whence the ancient saying: *lex orandi, lex credendi* ... The law of prayer is the law of faith: the church believes as she prays." See *Catechism*, no. 1124. Shared prayer stores memories and makes them accessible to succeeding generations. See *Catechism*, no. 1124.

76. This understanding of memory was well-described by Augustine: "Now I arrive in the fields and vast mansions of memory, where are treasured innumerable images brought in there from objects of every conceivable kind perceived by the senses. There too are hidden away the modified images we produce when by our thinking we magnify or diminish or in any way alter the information our senses have reported. There too is everything else that has been consigned and stowed away, and not yet engulfed and buried in oblivion." Augustine, *The Confessions*, 204.

in recent studies of the kinds of brain injuries that rob victims of their short-term memories. Memories constitute evidence.[77]

Extreme rationalists are as suspicious of memory as they are of sense data. Their arguments in this regard encompass a host of epistemological, biological, and practical concerns that extend even to René Descartes's evil demon: "The kind of imagery and feelings of pastness that some take to be involved in episodic memory could have all sorts of causes, e.g., deceiving gods, drugs, knocks on the head . . ."[78]

Finally, epistemological realists affirm the value of testimony. Like memory, testimony is not unproblematic when viewed from an epistemological perspective, however. Indeed, Baruch Spinoza's *Tractatus Theologico-Politicus* (1670) had a significant impact in this regard. As described by T. L. S. Sprigge, it was "part biblical study, part political treatise. Its overriding goal is to recommend full freedom of thought and religious practice, subject to behavioral conformity with the laws of the land. As virtually the first examination of the Scriptures (primarily the Pentateuch) as historical documents, reflecting the intellectual limitations of their time, and of problematic authorship, it opened the so-called higher criticism."[79] In effect, Spinoza paved the way for the critical reassessment of a broad range of "authoritative" texts and—by extension—all kinds of testimony.[80]

---

77. In a notable passage, Aristotle described how sense perception and memory are both essential to knowledge: "Though sense-perception is innate in all animals, in some the sense-impression comes to persist, in others it does not. So animals in which this persistence does not come to be have either no knowledge at all outside the act of perceiving, or no knowledge of objects of which no impression persists; animals in which it does come into being have perception and can continue to retain the sense-impression in the soul: and when such persistence is frequently repeated a further distinction at once arises between those which out of the persistence of such sense-impressions develop a power of systematizing them and those which do not. So out of sense-perception comes to be what we call memory, and out of frequently repeated memories of the same thing develops experience; for a number of memories constitute a single experience. From experience again, i.e., from the universal now stabilized in its entirety within the soul, the one beside the many which is a single identity within them all, originate the skill of the craftsman and the knowledge of the man of science, skill in the sphere of coming to be and science in the sphere of being. We conclude that these states of knowledge are neither innate in a determinate form, nor developed from other higher states of knowledge, but from sense-perception." See Aristotle, *Prior & Posterior Analytics*, 170.

78. Littlejohn and Carter, *Epistemology*, 93.

79. T. L. S. Sprigge, "Baruch Spinoza," 845.

80. *Faith Connection*: According to Urban C. von Wahlde, John's entire Gospel is organized around several "witness" claims. The first three are revealed in John's account of Jesus's public ministry: "The first is the witness of John the Baptist . . . The second

We know, however, that most of our everyday knowledge comes from the testimony of others. It includes our family histories, the academic canons on the basis of which we were educated, and the reports that spill out endlessly on our newsfeeds, too. As Paul J. Glenn notes, "much if not most of our knowledge is based upon the objective evidence of *authority*, of *testimony*. All historical knowledge is so evidenced, and indeed much scientific knowledge even in the realm of the laboratory. For each experimental scientist cannot spend his life repeating the experiments made by his predecessors."[81] Testimony is essential to the way we think and to the way we make our way in the world.[82]

314. OTHER PERSPECTIVES AND EVIDENCE

The competing epistemologies examined in this chapter tend to view evidence quite differently. Consistent with his belief in the preexistence of souls, Plato concluded that true belief, i.e., knowledge, is attributable to certain innate ideas in our minds that pertain to eternal Forms or Ideas. In Plato's view, a process of contemplative recollection can bring this otherwise suppressed knowledge to the fore.[83]

Recall that the rationalists of the Enlightenment were dedicated "to exposing the limitations of reason and to explaining how we make

---

witness to Jesus is his works . . . And the third witness is his word." And two more "witnesses" are later associated more specifically with the church. In chapter 15, "Jesus speaks of the witnesses to him in the time *after his departure* . . . He uses the term 'witness,' showing conclusively that he had been referring to the other three witnesses previously . . . The first witness will be the Paraclete . . . And, second, the disciples, who themselves responded positively to Jesus during his public ministry, will now be qualified to be witnesses in their own right." See von Wahlde, "John," 1430. The connection to "testimony" is further underwritten by the NRSV's translation of the conclusion of chapter 15 of Matthew's Gospel: "When the Advocate comes, whom I will send to you from the Father, he will *testify* on my behalf. You also are to *testify* because you have been with me from the beginning" (John 15:26–27). (Emphasis added.)

81. Glenn, *An Introduction to Philosophy*, 248.

82. *Faith Connection*: The church's adherence to the Apostolic Tradition demonstrates its commitment to testimony and affirms, as well, the need to safeguard the integrity of testimony over time: "The church, 'the pillar and bulwark of the truth,' faithfully guards 'the faith which was once for all delivered to the saints.' She guards the memory of Christ's words; it is she who from generation-to-generation hands on the apostles' confession of faith. As a mother who teaches her children to speak and so understand and communicate, the church, our Mother, teaches us the language of faith in order to introduce us to the understanding and life of faith." See *Catechism*, no. 171.

83. Jacobs, *Seat of Wisdom*, 136.

judgements."[84] As noted above, René Descartes posited the existence of an evil demon—an epistemological trickster—as a way to sow doubt about our sense experiences. Few rationalists would go so far as Plato or the Buddha in denying the reality of sense experience; many would, nonetheless, join David Hume in reducing our experiences in the sensible world to mere "impressions." According to Hume, these sense impressions cannot be relied upon to generate rational certitude.

Given this, the rationalists of the seventeenth and eighteenth centuries tended to endorse the role of certain innate ideas that manifest in our intuitions[85] and inform our reasoning. According to Harold I. Brown, "rationalists typically hold that the mind has a set of innate ideas that provide the source of *a priori* knowledge on a wide variety of necessary truths."[86]

Like some epistemological realists, empiricists hold that all knowledge is derived from the senses and from our experiences in the sensible world, and they, too, believe that the human mind is best understood as a blank slate, i.e., a *tabula rasa*. The empiricists of the Enlightenment went further than Aristotle or Thomas Aquinas in this regard, however. In keeping with their materialist worldview, they denied the existence of "innate ideas," as such, instead attributing our intuitions, our remembering, and our imaginings to certain "powers of the mind,"[87] all of which are innate to our physical makeup. Again, the empiricists of the Enlightenment distrusted all assertions of *a priori* truths. Evidence is limited to that which can be demonstrated empirically.

In Immanuel Kant's view, evidence is twofold in nature. It draws, first, on sense data, but with a notable caveat: our apprehension of the sensible world is limited to the appearances or phenomena revealed to us; again, the noumena of things, i.e., things in and of themselves, are inaccessible to us. Second, true belief or knowledge requires some understanding of the way in which our minds inform or shape our perceptions and our understanding of the phenomena we encounter in the sensible world.

---

84. Broackes, "David Hume," 377.

85. "Intuition" is a challenging concept in epistemology. It is said by some to be analogous to seeing, albeit a capacity that relies less on the senses than on the mind. Others see it as a kind of remembering that draws indirectly on sense data. Still others think of intuition as a kind of informal reasoning process.

86. Brown, "Innate Ideas," 409.

87. Brown, "Innate Ideas," 409.

315. EPISTEMOLOGICAL REALISM AND METHOD(S)

Method pertains to the uses to which evidence is put in advancing a philosophical claim. As Paul J. Glenn describes it, "method is a way after truth, a reasonable and orderly procedure in the attaining of truth and certitude. It is a seemly mode of acquiring truth."[88] As might be expected, the several philosophers examined in this chapter differed rather dramatically with respect to their preferred methods as well as the evidence they marshaled in advancing their truth claims.

Metaphysical realists in the Aristotelian-Thomist Tradition tend to privilege three tools: deductive syllogisms, induction, and intuition. Deduction aims at the generation of new knowledge through the use of two or more bits of extant knowledge. In a perfect syllogism,[89] two fully justified or substantiated premises are used to "bootstrap" new knowledge, which is expressed, in turn, in a conclusion.[90] This new knowledge can be further leveraged when the conclusion in one syllogism is used as a premise in another syllogism. As described by Aristotle, "a syllogism is discourse in which certain things being stated, something other than what is stated follows of necessity from their being so. I mean by the last phrase that they produce the consequence, and by this, that no further term is required from without in order to make the consequence necessary."[91] (Examples of syllogisms pertaining to God's existence are provided in Appendix 2.)

The role of inference is particularly important in the case of inductive reasoning, in which certain conclusions are inferred as probable from a series of observations in the sensible world. Certainty is elusive in the case of inductive reasoning because it is virtually impossible to observe all instances of any given phenomenon or to think that all such observations in the future will produce the same result.[92] This is why physical

---

88. Glenn, *An Introduction to Philosophy*, 253.

89. "Perfect" in this instance should not be confused with the terms "unflawed" or "valid." An "imperfect" syllogism simply relies on three or more premises.

90. This is sometimes referred to as the "closure principle." As explained by Clayton Littlejohn and J. Adam Carter, "if one knows something, p, and competently deduces something else, q, from p, while retaining one's knowledge of p, then one knows that q." See Littlejohn and Carter, *Epistemology*, 4.

91. Aristotle, *Prior & Posterior Analytics*, 6.

92. Invoking René Descartes's evil demon and other such "mind in the vat" arguments, extreme rationalists dismiss the "principle of the uniformity of nature" as unreliable. In their view, causation—as we understand it—cannot be assumed as we move forward in time. See Littlejohn and Carter, *Epistemology*, 131.

scientists aspire to probabilities of 99 percent or better in their research and why social scientists aim for probabilities of 95 percent or better. As A. C. Cotter puts it, "probability admits degrees."[93] As noted by Clayton Littlejohn and J. Adam Carter, "inductive reasoning," unlike deductive reasoning, "leaves open the chance or the possibility that the argument's conclusion is false even if all the premises in an argument are true."[94]

Aristotle considered both deductive and inductive reasoning to be dialectic in nature, a concept connoting the opposition of two or more ideas, i.e., two or more premises *vis-à-vis* a conclusion in the case of a deductive syllogism *and* a hypothesis *vis-à-vis* multiple instances of an observed phenomenon in the case of inductive reasoning. Surprisingly, perhaps, Aristotle also thought of intuition—a non-dialectic form of reasoning—as a kind of method, even if only so in a preliminary sense: "Intuition apprehends the primary premises—a result which also follows from the fact that demonstration cannot be the originative source of demonstration, nor consequently, scientific knowledge . . . If, therefore, it is the only other kind of true thinking except scientific knowing, intuition will be the originative source of scientific knowledge. And the originative source of science grasps the original premise, while science as a whole is similarly related as originative source to the whole body of fact."[95]

316. OTHER PERSPECTIVES AND METHOD(S)

Plato's epistemological "method"—to the extent that the concept applies—can be described as a kind of contemplative recollection that promises to bring certain preexisting knowledge, which is normally suppressed, to the fore. As revealed in his Socratic dialogues, Plato believed that contemplative reflection is best preceded by Socratic questioning and dialectic debate.

Given their distrust of knowledge gleaned from the material world, the rationalists of the Enlightenment privileged deductive reasoning over inductive reasoning, which relies solely on sense data. David Hume's antipathy to induction similarly followed from his distrust of our everyday understanding of causation and, hence, his profound skepticism about our ability to know anything at all: "All inferences from experience

---

93. Cotter, *An Introduction to Catholic Philosophy*, 267.
94. Littlejohn and Carter, *Epistemology*, 140.
95. Aristotle, *Prior & Posterior Analytics*, 171.

suppose, as their foundation, that the future will resemble the past . . . If there be any suspicion that the course of nature may change, and that the past may be no rule for the future, all experience becomes useless, and can give rise to no inference or conclusion. It is impossible, therefore, that any argument from experience can prove this resemblance of the past to the future; since all these arguments are founded on the supposition of that resemblance."[96]

The empiricists of the seventeenth and eighteenth centuries took the opposite tack. For empiricists, both then and now, it is all about quantifiable data and inferences that can be sufficiently underwritten to ensure scientific certitude or, at least, a satisfactory level of probability. The methods relied upon by empiricists include the scientific method, which was first described by Francis Bacon, induction, and inference.

Immanuel Kant embraced the methodologies of his empiricists counterparts. Given his twin convictions that we have no true access to the noumena of the real world, however, and that empirical investigations—for this reason—can only speak to the phenomena we apprehend around us, Kant insisted that "transcendental reflection" is required as well. According to Kant, this requires a true willingness to critique what we know and how we have come to know it and great discipline and integrity in the pursuit of knowledge as well.

317. PROPOSITIONS

Although some contemporary philosophers argue that truth is a property or feature that pertains to a wide variety of linguistic structures and phenomena, e.g., sentences, the raw apprehension of "things" in the sensible world, emotional states, etc., the more traditional view holds that truth claims pertain to propositions, i.e., statements that contain both a subject and an assertion about the subject. E. J. Lowe thus distinguishes propositions from other more generic kinds of thoughts and utterances: "A *sentence* is a linguistic token or type, such as a string of written words . . . A *statement* is the assertoric use, i.e., an assertion that something is or is not the case, of a sentence by a speaker on a particular occasion. A *proposition* is what is asserted when a statement is made—its content."[97] A proposition asserts something about something, and it does so in a

---

96. Hume, "Induction," 405–406.
97. Lowe, "Truth," 881.

way that its truth value can be assessed.[98] As affirmed by Aristotle, propositions can take one of four forms: a universal affirmation, a universal negation, a particular affirmation, and a particular negation.[99] Most importantly, a proposition—as opposed to any other kind of thought or utterance—lends itself to philosophical investigation.

A question follows, however: What kinds of assertions can be advanced philosophically and thus qualify as propositions? To answer this question, we can begin with Aristotle's understanding of predicamentals. See section 215. Again, predicamentals can be thought of as all-inclusive divisions or types of accidents, attributes, or properties that can be associated with particular substances. Aristotle's predicamentals include the following nine "categories," all of which inhere in particular substances:

- "Quantity," i.e., any measurable attribute;
- "Quality," i.e., dispositions or habits or ways of being in the world, abilities and capacities, passive characteristics such as color or scent, and qualitative descriptions pertaining to shape or size;
- "Relations," i.e., positional dispositions *vis-à-vis* any two or more substances;
- "Action," i.e., all kinds of self-directed or self-engendered movements;
- "Passion," i.e., actions imposed upon a substance;
- "Place," i.e., physical location;
- "Time," i.e., the orientation of a substance in terms of "before," "now," "after," etc.;
- "Posture," i.e., the arrangement or disposition of a subject's various parts; and
- "Habit," i.e., clothing, external accoutrements, and adornments.

Do these nine predicamentals encompass all that can be meaningfully asserted? It does not seem so. Recall that the foundational concept of "being"—see sections 209 and 210—includes both "real beings" and "mind-dependent beings" of various kinds and that the category "real being" includes, in turn, both "actual real beings" and "potential real beings." Given this, it seems clear that other kinds of assertions can be meaningfully advanced as well. Meaningful propositions—assertions of

---

98. Littlejohn and Carter, *Epistemology*, 1.
99. Aristotle, *Prior & Posterior Analytics*.

something about something—seem to extend beyond assertions about accidents and the unique relationships they may or may not share with particular substances, the two components of "actual real being."

Unfortunately, both Aristotle and Aquinas are less than clear with respect to these other kinds of assertions. A taxonomy of "truth claims" proposed by Jürgen Habermas is more helpful. Habermas draws sharp distinctions between and among four distinct types of "truth claims," an analogue, in fact, for the word "proposition." According to Habermas, truth claims can be empirical, normative, expressive, or aesthetic in nature.[100] Further, Habermas argues that different evaluation criteria or modes of justification apply to each of these several kinds of truth claims. An empirical truth claim is either objectively true or untrue and should be justified as such. When asserted about substances, the nine predicamentals posited by Aristotle can be understood as empirical truth claims. A normative truth claim is an assertion about what *should* be done in a particular circumstance. A normative truth claim can be deemed appropriate or inappropriate or as prudent or imprudent. Appeals to rights and duties are often framed as normative truth claims. An expressive truth claim pertains to a belief about *me*—or more broadly *us*—and takes on "truth value"—according to Habermas—in terms of its authenticity. Truth claims that speak to the core of an individual's identity or to the identity of a particular community are often framed in this way. Using the language of the Aristotelian-Thomist Tradition, assertions about our essence and nature as human beings can be thought of as expressive truth claims. And an aesthetic truth claim concerns goodness or beauty or, alternately, a certain lack of goodness or lack of beauty. Indeed, Habermas's conception of truth claims extends beyond Aristotle's understanding of the nine predicamentals and their associations with particular substances. Again, the predicamentals pertain uniquely to this or that actual real being and so exclude propositions pertaining to this or that potential real being or to this or that mind-dependent being.

That said, Habermas's theory of communicative action relies on intersubjective agreement, i.e., "communicative action," to establish the "truth" of a proposition or truth claim. As a committed pragmatist,[101]

---

100. Habermas, *The Theory of Communicative Action*.

101. As a philosopher, Jürgen Habermas can be described as a pragmatist whose work has been influenced to a considerable extent by critical theory and the insights of philosophers associated with the Frankfort School. His work is cited here, however, in order to extend the breadth of the Aristotelian-Thomist Tradition's understanding of

Habermas does not believe in objective truths that exists independently of our perceptions and reasoning as such. He is anything but a metaphysical or epistemological realist, in fact. Nevertheless, Habermas's fourfold framework makes intuitive sense. We often advance propositions that are of a non-empirical nature. We would do well, therefore, to name these other kinds of assertions so that they can be examined philosophically.

Habermas's taxonomy serves another purpose, too. His framework aligns well with the major divisions of philosophy as we typically understand them, thus opening particular kinds of propositions to the theoretical and methodological resources of these several subdisciplines. Empirical truth claims concern "things in the world," a key interest of those who espouse extreme versions of empiricism and metaphysical realists, too. Normative truth claims clearly pertain to the philosophical subfield of ethics. Expressive truth claims—from the perspective of the Aristotelian-Thomist Tradition—can be thought of as empirical truth claims about human beings, i.e., our objective essence and nature. And aesthetic truth claims are clearly about goodness and beauty, key interests in aesthetics.

---

propositions framed as truth claims.

4

Ethics, Morality, and Justice

401. THE GOOD, THE MORAL, AND THE JUST

Ethics and morals are of enduring interest in philosophy and so, too, justice. These terms are often used interchangeably, however, and so some confusion can result.

For reasons that will soon become apparent, we will define "ethics" as conceptual schemes or frameworks in which the interrelationships—to the extent they exist—between one's conception of human nature, the good, the moral, and the just are articulated. The "good" will be defined as the end, objective, or *telos* of life; the "moral" as the manner in which one thinks about and treats oneself and others; and the just as the way in which a community ensures that the various benefits and burdens of life are shared.[1]

402. ETHICAL FRAMEWORKS

In the West, ethical systems have historically assumed an articulated form. Based on a particular human anthropology or ontology, a conception of the good is posited. From this conception of the good, an understanding

---

1. This type of justice is referred to as "distributive justice." Two other forms of justice lie beyond the scope of this text. Procedural, organizational, or particular justice pertains to the processing of individual claims. And retributive, compensatory, or restorative justice pertains to dispositions involving those who are believed to have wronged others and their purported victims, too.

of the moral can be advanced; and from the moral, a conception of justice can be proposed.

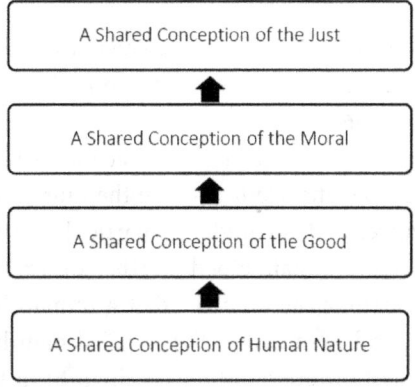

Figure 3

403. KEY CONCERNS OF ETHICAL REALISTS

The concerns addressed by ethical realists include the following:

- How should we understand what it means to be a human being?
- Given this, how should we live our lives?
- What do we mean when we refer to the "good" or to the "good life"?
- How should we think about and treat ourselves?
- How should we think about and treat others?
- What do we owe to others and what do they owe to us?
- How should we share life's benefits and burdens?

404. ETHICAL REALISM

Ethical realism affirms the existence of objective standards of right and wrong. Philosophical realists reject the ethical relativism and subjectivism endemic in much of contemporary philosophy. Further, certain standards of right and wrong can be known. According to Aristotle, the "mean" of various dispositions and behaviors can be used to identify certain virtues that can then be acquired by way of habit and so contribute to the pursuit of human fulfillment, i.e., *eudaimonia*. Thomas Aquinas embraced Aristotle's conception of the virtues, but drew on the Judeo-Christian Tradition, too, in invoking the natural law. See section 412.

Further, ethical realists affirm the efficacy of free will. In doing so, they reject the determinism asserted by some Enlightenment philosophers. See section 406.

Still further, ethical realists hold that moral behavior is possible. Human effort can be efficacious because the moral virtues of prudence, justice, temperance, and fortitude, in particular, can be cultivated by habit. Indeed, Aristotle maintained a rather optimistic view of human nature. We can assume, he argued, "that a human being is one of the things that are good by nature."[2] Further, "all men have some good in them and the way they are good makes them fit in with one another."[3] G. K. Chesterton (1841–1922), the renowned Catholic apologist and culture critic, certainly maintained this view. According to Fergus Kerr, "(Chesterton) does not conceal his own conviction that the Reformation—'the sixteenth-century schism'—was 'really a belated revolt of the thirteenth-century pessimists, a backwash of the old Augustinian Puritanism against the Aristotelian liberality.' He insists on seeing Thomas as 'the only optimist theologian'; and indeed on seeing Catholic Christianity as 'the only optimist theology.'"[4]

Aristotle did not have to wrestle with the concept of sin, of course, as Thomas Aquinas did. As we shall see, however, the Angelic Doctor advanced the twin concepts of the natural law, i.e., the law "written on our hearts," and grace in order to bolster Aristotle's presumption of moral efficacy. As we shall see, this stands in sharp contrast to certain Enlightenment philosophers who proposed various schemes intended to ensure the stability of society.

Finally, the Aristotelian-Thomist Tradition locates the motive for moral and just behavior in human nature. For this reason, the moral and the just are properly located in particular individuals rather than in particular acts or ethical systems, e.g., "categorical imperatives," social contracts, etc., designed to restrain our natural impulses, which—according to some non-Catholic theologians, in particular—are invariably corrupt,

---

2. Aristotle, *The Eudemian Ethics*, 118.
3. Aristotle, *The Eudemian Ethics*, 121.
4. Kerr, *After Aquinas*, 75.

sinful, or rapacious. Reflecting this view, Deirdra McCloskey (b. 1942) orients moral virtue to "being" rather than to "doing": "A virtue is a habit of the heart, a stable disposition, a settled state of character, a durable, educated characteristic of someone to exercise her will to be good."[5] Thomas Aquinas similarly described virtue as an inclination or power rather than as an act, a decision, or a behavior as such. As explained by Servais Pinckaers, "virtue is not a habitual way of acting . . . It is a personal capacity for action, the fruit of a series of fine actions, a power for progress and perfection. In the tradition of Aristotle, it is deemed a *habitus*."[6]

That said, according to ethical realists in the Aristotelian-Thomist Tradition, moral behavior should be oriented to the common good. See section 414.

405. THE CATHOLIC CHURCH AND ETHICAL REALISM

The impact of Thomas Aquinas's virtue ethics on the Catholic Church was short-lived, in fact. The formation of priests had emerged as a key concern following the Council of Trent, which had gathered in 25 sessions between the years 1545 and 1563. Thereafter, seminary training would be increasingly oriented to the development of effective confessors. By the time the dust of the Reformation and the Counter-Reformation had settled, Catholic moral theology had shifted away from the virtues to an explicit focus on sin. The situation is aptly described by Pinckaers: "From the beginning of the seventeenth century, [Thomas Aquinas's] treatise on *happiness* was passed over in silence. The earliest [confessors's] manuals actually excluded it from fundamental moral teaching. It was thought to be too speculative, but the fundamental reason was that at this time the question of obligation and law was substituted for that of happiness as the central theme of moral teaching."[7] Like Protestants, but for a very different reason, Catholic moral theologians of the modern era tended to view the Decalogue—rather than the virtues espoused by Aristotle and Aquinas—as the essential guide to faithful living. The moral virtues were set aside as something optional, as something exceptional, i.e.,

---

5. McCloskey, *The Bourgeois Virtues*, 17.
6. Pinckaers, *The Sources of Christian Ethics*, 364.
7. Pinckaers, *The Sources of Christian Ethics*, 364.

supererogatory, or as something reserved, in effect, for contemplatives and professed members of religious communities.

With respect to justice, we would do well to remember, too, that Aristotle and Thomas Aquinas were men of their times. Aristotle endorsed the extreme social stratification of the Greek city-state, which was comprised of a laboring class that constituted the majority of the populace, a "guardian" class that safeguarded the city-state and ensured its ongoing functioning, and a ruling class for which contemplation and the pursuit of the virtues was both possible—due to their perceived intellect, disposable wealth, and free time—and recommended. Although change was in the offing, society in the high Middle Ages, i.e., the eleventh to the thirteenth centuries, was organized in a highly structured fashion as well. The feudalism of Thomas Aquinas's day was thought of as a pyramid, with the church on top and the aristocracy, landowners, a slowly emerging merchant class, freemen, and serfs arrayed in order below. This commitment to a static social order would be considerably bolstered by several unanticipated shocks, i.e., the Reformation of the sixteenth century, the French Revolution, and the continental revolutions of 1848.

Despite this unpromising trajectory, the ethical realism espoused by Aristotle and Thomas Aquinas would be restored to pride of place in the church in the late nineteenth century and in the first half of the twentieth century. This recovery of the Aristotelian-Thomist Tradition was amplified by two movements in particular: the development of the church's social teaching tradition and philosophical personalism, both of which follow Aristotle and Aquinas in affirming the primacy of the individual in social and philosophical analysis and both of which affirm our nature as social beings who live in community. See sections 506 and 508.

406. ALTERNATIVE VIEWS

Although different ethical systems espouse different perspectives on human nature, the good, the moral, and the just, three broad perspectives—all of which are recurring in the long history of Western philosophy—stand in opposition to ethical realism more generally: relativism and subjectivism, determinism, and fideism. Each of these alternatives will be addressed in turn.

Relativists and subjectivists both hold that there are no immutable standards pertaining to human behavior as such. Today's relativists argue that our ethical allegiances are culture-bound and time-specific[8]; and subjectivists contend that our ethical preferences are just that: preferences. They arise from our emotions and so can be discounted as "emotivist" predilections.[9]

This critique rejects religious perspectives, of course, including the provisions of the natural law as reflected, most notably, in the Ten Commandments; but it pertains, as well, to Aristotle's conception of virtue to the extent that the several virtues, i.e., prudence, justice, temperance, fortitude, etc., are grounded in and arise from our shared nature as human beings. The sophists—against whom Aristotle positioned much of his ethical reasoning—were the first subjectivists to organize as a school of sorts, arguing that "there is no criterion of virtue, as such, apart from success, and no criterion of justice, as such, apart from the dominant practice of each particular city."[10] Others would follow in their wake.

For some, this supposed lack of immutable standards is something to be celebrated. According to Friedrich Nietzsche, Christian moral teaching, in particular, is nothing less than a repression of a natural "will to power" that lies dormant in most of us. And postmodernists tend to reject all such standards of behavior as ideological and hegemonic. For others, however, the supposed lack of an "Archimedean lever" by which to regulate behavior is something to be lamented. This included Thomas Hobbes who bemoaned life unbounded by any ethical standards of any kind as "solitary, poor, nasty, brutish, and short."[11] Hobbes and other Enlightenment philosophers advanced social contracts as a remedy for this "natural state of affairs." See section 415.

Extreme determinists go even further. They reject the idea of free will altogether, without which, in fact, no conceptions of the moral and the just make sense. According to this view, no "degrees of freedom" exist for anyone or anything in the material world. Everything is

---

8. The relativist critique is a serious one. Alasdair MacIntyre thus asks: "Are we not doomed to historical and social relativism? The answer to this is complex . . . There are certain features of human life which are necessarily or almost inevitably the same in all societies, and that, as a consequence of this, there are certain evaluative truths which cannot be escaped . . . " For instance, "it is almost inconceivable that certain qualities such as friendliness, courage, and truthfulness will not be valued . . . " Further, "human society presupposes language; language presupposes rule following; and such rule following presupposes a norm of truth telling." See MacIntyre, *A Short History of Ethics*, 95–96.

9. Hepburn, "Emotive Theories of Ethics," 225–226.

10. MacIntyre, *A Short History of Ethics*, 14.

11. Hobbes, *Leviathan*.

predetermined by that which preceded it. As described by Roy C. Weatherford, "all events without exception are effects—events necessitated by earlier events. Hence any event of any kind is an effect of a prior series of effects, a causal chain with every link solid."[12]

The stoics were determinists. They reduced virtue to a disciplined acquiescence to the immutable laws of the universe. According to Zeno, Epictetus, Seneca, and Marcus Aurelius, and the other stoics of ancient Greece and Rome, "men as rational beings can become conscious of the laws to which they necessarily conform, and virtue consists of conscious assent to, vice in dissent from, the inevitable order of things."[13] Given their understanding of efficient causation, the materialists of the Enlightenment also tended to this view. In pursuing it, however, they reached far beyond questions of physical motion and change, key foci in Aristotle's metaphysics. Indeed, extreme determinists question many of the most basic assumptions upon which any society is built, including love, friendship, duty, loyalty, merit, and just punishment for one's anti-social behaviors.

Those who follow Aristotle more closely tend to hold more moderate views in this regard. Although he did not employ the term as such, it is clear that Aristotle restricted his understanding of "free will" to deliberative choices, i.e., *prohaireses*: "The agent must be in a certain condition when he [acts virtuously]; in the first place, he must have knowledge, secondly, he must choose the acts, and choose them for their own sakes, and thirdly, his action must proceed from a firm and unchangeable character."[14] Thomas Aquinas endorsed this view: "The term *choice* expresses something belonging to the reason or intellect, and something belonging to the will."[15] More to the point, "in moral matters, the reason holds the place of commander and mover, while the appetitive power is commanded and moved."[16] The conviction that a robust

---

12. Weatherford, "Determinism," 194.

13. MacIntyre, *After Virtue*, 105–106. The stoics's outlook on life was not moderated by any concept of grace and could be unremittingly dour as a result. "Desire, hope, and fear, pleasure and pain are against reason and nature," they argued; "one should cultivate a passionless absence of desire and disregard of pleasure and pain. They called this principled stance *apathy*." See MacIntyre, *After Virtue*, 106.

14. Aristotle, *Nicomachean Ethics*, 30–31. See also Kenny, "Introduction," xvii. See also Aristotle, *The Eudemian Ethics*, 24.

15. Aquinas, *The Summa Theologica and The Summa Contra Gentiles*, 514.

16. Aquinas, *The Summa Theologica and The Summa Contra Gentiles*, 584.

conception of causation can be harmonized with free will is referred to as compatibilism.[17]

A third view stands in opposition to ethical realism: fideism.[18] At first glance, fideism may seem to lie beyond the scope of this text. It is, after all, a religious perspective rather than a philosophy *per se*. That said, fideism arose—in part—out of nominalism, a philosophical rejection of the metaphysics of the Aristotelian-Thomist Tradition. See section 205. Again, nominalism dismisses all non-sensible metaphysical concepts, e.g., being, substance, essence, nature, etc., as superfluous. This includes moral standards discerned or devised by human beings. According to Servais Pinckaers, William of Ockham "established the idea of obligation at the center of his moral theory . . . Ockham went so far as to maintain that God could, without impunity, annihilate a person or condemn to damnation one who loved him above all things and tried with all his heart to please him. The reason given was that God could do whatever he willed with his creatures and was answerable to no one."[19]

According to fideists, the good, the moral, and the just cannot be accessed by way of reason. *Contra* ethical realists, there is no such thing as virtue beyond the strict obedience owed to God as the supreme lawmaker. Further, no law is "written on our hearts," i.e., natural law, and so knowable as such. The only thing that counts is obedience to God's commands, the reasons for which lie far beyond our ability to comprehend. Indeed, these commands may even be arbitrary and/or capricious in nature.[20]

17. Weatherford, "Compatibilism and Incompatibilism," 144.

18. *Faith Connection*: Fideism is incompatible, in fact, both with philosophy and theological inquiry, a concern well expressed by Pope John Paul II in *Fides et Ratio*: "There are signs of a resurgence in *fideism*, which fails to recognize the importance of rational knowledge and philosophical discourse for the understanding of faith, indeed for the very possibility of belief in God. One currently widespread symptom of this fideistic tendency is a 'biblicism' which tends to make the reading and exegesis of Sacred Scripture the sole criterion of truth. In consequence, the word of God is identified with Sacred Scripture alone, thus eliminating the doctrine of the church . . . " See John Paul II, *Fides et Ratio*, no. 55. Alasdair MacIntyre goes so far as to describe fideism as a kind of "Christian irrationalism." See MacIntyre, *A Short History of Ethics*, 120.

19. Pinckaers, *The Sources of Christian Ethics*, 248.

20. *Faith Connection*: This perspective is reflected in God's response—better described, perhaps, as a rant—to Job's bitter complaint about his suffering in chapters 38 and 39 of the Book of Job. Indeed, Job's response epitomizes fideism's point of view: "Look, I am of little account; what shall I answer you? I put my hand over my mouth. I have spoken once, I will not reply; twice, but I will do so no more" (Job 40:4–5). It is not difficult, in fact, to see a direct line that connects Ockham's nominalism and the Reformed Tradition's doctrine of double predestination.

407. HUMAN NATURE IN THE ARISTOTELIAN-THOMIST TRADITION

According to Aristotle, Thomas Aquinas, and other ethical realists, ethical and moral reasoning begins with human nature, i.e., human anthropology or ontology. Unless we have some conception of what we are, i.e., our essence, and the purpose for which we exist, i.e., our nature, we cannot know what the good is or what the good life means.

Aristotle defined human beings as reasoning beings. Our ability to reason—indeed, to choose between this and that option in what we think, say, and do—separates us from other animals. As noted in chapter 2, Aristotle viewed human beings as actual real beings whose being can be examined from two complementary perspectives: our essence *qua* human beings and our nature *qua* human beings. Again, our essence is that which separates us from other species and that which distinguishes us as individuals, too; and our nature is our way of "being in the world" and includes the final cause or causes to which we are oriented, i.e., our purpose or reason to exist, our ultimate end, or teleology. See sections 213 and 214.

Thomas Aquinas endorsed this view, but went further. We must remember, of course, that Aquinas was a synthesizer. He hoped to harmonize Aristotle's metaphysical, epistemological, and ethical realism with Judeo-Christian thought. It is not surprising, therefore, that Aquinas defined human beings, not just as reasoning beings, but as children of a loving God who have been created to know and love him and each other, too.

408. ALTERNATIVE VIEWS OF HUMAN NATURE

Over the centuries, various philosophies have espoused other understandings of human nature. As we shall see, these alternative views beget very different understandings of the good and the good life, and, hence, the moral and the just.

- Plato portrayed human beings as preexistent but now embodied souls who should orient themselves to the ethereal Forms with which they were once acquainted.

- The ancient stoics understood human beings to be but one of many types of material entities in the natural world and so fully subject to its unfolding in time in a fully-determined fashion.
- Although the rationalists of the Enlightenment joined Aristotle and Aquinas in describing human beings as reasoning beings, their understanding of what we can know about ourselves—and the sensible world, too—was severely circumscribed. In their view, we are embodied minds that have little or no sure access to the sensible world. See section 305.
- In contrast, the empiricists of the Enlightenment eschewed a robust understanding of the mind and so portrayed human beings—for the most part—as pleasure-seeking and pain-minimizing creatures who are, nonetheless, subject to the social conventions of their own time and place. See section 305.
- This understanding of human nature was embraced by the utilitarians of the late eighteenth and early nineteenth centuries and by the pragmatists of the twentieth century as well.
- John Locke and Karl Marx—as different as their philosophies certainly are—both described human beings in economic terms oriented to property ownership, in the case of Locke, and to wage-earning and capital accumulation, in the case of Marx.
- As noted above, Friedrich Nietzsche ascribed our deepest human yearnings to a will to power.
- The language theorists of the nineteenth and twentieth centuries described human beings as meaning-making creatures, as did the existentialists of the last two centuries, albeit to very different effect.
- More recently, constructivists and postmodernists have disavowed any single understanding of human essence and nature. According to constructivists, our understanding of ourselves is negotiated in social settings. Postmodernists agree, but disavow any perceived need to articulate a shared or common understanding of human nature as "totalizing."

The point is that philosophy has moved a long way from the understanding of human beings, i.e., our essence and nature, espoused in the Aristotelian-Thomist Tradition, which had long held pride of place in philosophy and was thought to be in harmony with Christian theology.

As we shall see, these developments—particularly over the course of the last 400 years—go a long way toward explaining the cacophony of views pertaining to the meaning of the good or the good life now extant in our culture.

409. THE GOOD IN THE ARISTOTELIAN-THOMIST TRADITION

Aristotle described the good in four overlapping and complementary ways. First, the good life is a life lived in the contemplation of truth.[21] This is not surprising, given Aristotle's privileging of our capacity to reason.

Second, he defined the good as a life lived virtuously. See section 412. In Aristotle's view, the habitual exercise of prudence, justice, temperance, and fortitude, in particular, can be an end in and of itself and so constitute the good. The moral virtues are properly ordered or oriented to particular ends. Moral virtues are traditionally thought of as habits oriented to the good. Conversely, a vice can be described as a habit oriented to that which is evil or to that which could impede our realization of the good.[22]

Third, Aristotle described the goal of virtuous living as *eudaimonia*,[23] a term that refers, not to happiness *per se*, as is sometimes suggested, but to the concept of human flourishing or fulfillment. *Eudaimonia* thus speaks to a larger human purpose or *telos*. It concerns more than a particular good or an ephemeral experience of one kind or another. According to Aristotle, "happiness is the activity of a complete life . . . "[24] The relationship of his conception of the virtues to this more broadly conceived *telos* is explained by Paul J. Wadell: "A virtue is a characteristic way of behavior which makes both actions and persons good and which also enables one to fulfill the purpose of life."[25]

Finally, Aristotle described a life lived virtuously as "noble" or "honorable." Surprisingly, he did not explain what he meant by this.[26] Given

21. Aristotle, *Nicomachean Ethics*, 166, 169.

22. Like virtue, vice is a matter of choice. As noted by Aristotle, "wickedness *is* voluntary." See Aristotle, *Nicomachean Ethics*, 45.

23. *Eudaimonia* can be translated into Latin as either *felicitas* or *beatitudo*. See Ten Klooster. *Thomas Aquinas on the Beatitudes*, 75.

24. Aristotle, *The Eudemian Ethics*, 15.

25. Wadell, "Virtue," 998.

26. Aristotle, *The Eudemian Ethics*, 42, 146–147.

this, some dismiss Aristotle's concern for honor as a mere "byproduct" of his ethics,[27] and others regard him as hyper-conservative or conventional.[28] A fairer reading, perhaps, would locate Aristotle's understanding of nobility or honor in his metaphysics. In this view, a life lived virtuously is a life lived in harmony with our nature, i.e., our received or appropriated teleology, as human beings. As described by Paul J. Wadell, "when anyone both possesses and exercises the virtues, that person is brought to the wholeness proper to human nature; conversely, a lack of virtue constitutes a depraved nature and a diminished self."[29] Thomas Aquinas seems to have interpreted Aristotle's conception of nobility and honor in this way: "Habit implies a disposition in relation to a thing's nature."[30] Further, "there is a certain natural disposition demanded by the human species, so that no man can be without it. And this disposition is natural in respect of the specific nature."[31]

Like Aristotle, Aquinas privileged contemplation. Not surprisingly, however, he filtered his understanding of contemplation through a Christian lens and so declared its proper focus to be God rather than truth *per se*: "Man's ultimate happiness consists in the contemplation of truth. For this operation alone is proper to man . . . " That said, "man's happiness consists solely in the contemplation of God."[32] And like Aristotle, Aquinas promoted virtuous living as an end in itself: "Habits are perfections . . . And perfection is of the greatest necessity to a thing, since it is the nature of an end."[33] Finally, Aquinas endorsed Aristotle's understanding of *eudaimonia*, i.e., fulfillment or happiness, as essential to the good life.[34] At the same time, Aquinas argued that the prospect of death precludes true happiness in this plane of existence.[35]

There remains, nonetheless, a certain tension between Aquinas's understanding of virtue and honor, on the one hand, and Aristotle's

---

27. MacIntyre, *A Short History of Ethics*, 60.

28. See, for instance, Kenny, "Introduction," xxv. See also MacIntyre, *A Short History of Ethics*, 68, 79, 83.

29. Wadell, "Virtue," 998.

30. Aquinas, *The Summa Theologica and The Summa Contra Gentiles*, 545.

31. Aquinas, *The Summa Theologica and The Summa Contra Gentiles*, 548.

32. Aquinas, *The Summa Theologica and The Summa Contra Gentiles*, 453–454.

33. Aquinas, *The Summa Theologica and The Summa Contra Gentiles*, 545. See also Kerr, *After Aquinas*, 118.

34. Aquinas, *The Summa Theologica and The Summa Contra Gentiles*, 448.

35. Aquinas, *The Summa Theologica and The Summa Contra Gentiles*, 465.

understanding of virtue and honor, on the other. Indeed, it is unlikely that Aristotle would have recognized certain Christian virtues as noble or worthy of praise, including, for instance, two virtues prominently featured in Matthew's version of the beatitudes: poverty of spirit and meekness. As noted by Alasdair MacIntyre, "it would be purely unhistorical to look in (Aristotle's) *Ethics* for a moral virtue such as meekness, which enters only with the Christian gospels . . . "[36]

Aquinas resolved this tension by positing a third set of virtues. Aristotle had followed tradition in privileging four moral virtues, i.e., prudence, justice, temperance, and fortitude, and three intellectual virtues, i.e., wisdom, science, and understanding. In order to harmonize Aristotle's ethical realism with Christian belief and practice, Aquinas added three theological virtues long celebrated in Christian theology: faith, hope, and charity. This addition gave him access to a number of defining Christian virtues, including, most notably, humility. As Anthony Kenny notes, Aquinas thereby "Christianized" Aristotle's understanding of the virtues.[37]

410. ALTERNATIVE VIEWS OF THE GOOD

Again, a conception of the good or the good life should follow from one's understanding of human nature.

- As an idealist, Plato understood the knowledge of Forms achieved through contemplation as *the* good.
- Given their espoused determinism, the ancient stoics aspired to *apatheia*, i.e., a stance of dispassionate indifference.[38]
- Consistent with their near-exclusive focus on epistemology, the rationalists of the Enlightenment embraced rational certainty as the good, as narrow and unimaginative as this *telos* might seem.
- Their empiricist contemporaries also celebrated knowledge. That said, the materialist underpinnings of their philosophy would morph over time into a narrow conception of the good as the experience of pleasure and the minimization of pain, i.e., hedonism.

---

36. MacIntyre, *A Short History of Ethics*, 67.
37. Kenny, "Introduction," xxvii.
38. MacIntyre, *A Short History of Ethics*, 105–106.

- As we shall see, duty served as the ultimate good in Immanuel Kant's ethical system. See section 413.

- In time, John Locke's economic liberalism would engender an agnostic position with respect to the good. Classic liberalism and its contemporary manifestation, libertarianism, hold individual rights to be sacrosanct and so, too, the atomistic aspirations of individuals. Tradition, culture, and duty count for little in these philosophies.

- Friedrich Nietzsche celebrated the self-realized exercise of individual and group power.[39]

- Marxists view material equality as the singular goal of the social order and politics.

- Having defined human beings as meaning-seeking beings, existentialists celebrate the personal experience of meaning as the ultimate good.

- Like libertarians, postmodernists eschew any particular understanding of the good. According to these philosophers, distinct goods have to be "constructed" and negotiated in particular communities.

Indeed, many different understandings of the good or the good life are now extant in our culture. We should not think of these alternative "goods" as arbitrary in nature, however. Each of them follows from a particular understanding of what it means to be a human being. This is why metaphysics—or whatever ontology or anthropology might substitute for metaphysics in any given philosophy or worldview—precedes or should precede its ethical and moral prescriptions.

411. A DISJUNCTION IN ETHICAL AND MORAL THINKING

As a result of these developments, a crisis in moral thinking followed in the West during the time of the Enlightenment.[40] Having gradually

---

39. This explains why Nietzsche was so celebrated by Adolph Hitler and many of his fellow Nazis.

40. *Faith Connection*: Religion played a role in this regard as well. *Sola gratia*, i.e., by grace alone, was adopted as a rallying cry in the sixteenth century in both the Lutheran Tradition and the Reformed Tradition. In embracing this principle, the Protestant reformers rejected the idea that human beings can in any sense earn or merit salvation. The very idea that human beings can play any role in developing or forming virtue was

dislodged a belief in God from any role in moral thinking, it became more and more difficult for philosophers to link their conceptions of human nature and the good, on the one hand, to their conceptions of the moral and the just, on the other. As explained by Charles Taylor, the links between and among these four elements in our moral thinking have become increasingly attenuated by deism, utilitarianism, romanticism, and other modern philosophies.[41] In effect, our human anthropologies and ontologies and our understandings of the good, too, have been delinked from our conceptions of moral behavior and justice.

---

dismissed out of hand. Virtue is entirely God's work, the reformers argued. What we perceive to be virtues are gifts that cannot be earned or merited. The Reformed Tradition's understanding of "sanctification," in particular, holds that any apparent growth in "godliness" is entirely attributable to the store of grace accumulated by Jesus in his death and resurrection. John Calvin (1509–1564) further argued that virtues are gifted out of this store of grace even to those who are predestined to damnation in order to ensure the right ordering of society. Virtue lies entirely beyond the influence or control of any human being. Remarkably, Roman Catholicism also pivoted away from virtue ethics in the wake of the Reformation. A two-tiered understanding of discipleship emerged in the post-Tridentine church: on the one hand, a path of rigorous formation designed exclusively for priests and members of religious communities; on the other, a nominal Christianity oriented more explicitly to the Ten Commandments than to the virtues. Virtue was thereafter deemed supererogatory, i.e., as something "good," but certainly not expected of the laity. According to Servais Pinckaers, "we thus find Protestant thought in agreement with post-Tridentine Catholic tradition, at least on this point: the relegation of the Sermon on the Mount to a marginal position with respect to [our] central teachings. The Decalogue now claimed first position with respect to [Catholic] moral teaching and in Protestant morality..." See Pinckaers, *The Sources of Christian Ethics*, 139. This new moral regime was embraced in short order. According to Charles Taylor, "it was perhaps more than understandable that, after the terrible struggles around deep theological issues to do with grace, free will, and predestination, many people should hunger for a less theologically elaborate faith which would guide them toward holy living . . . What is significant is that the plea for a holy life came to be reductively seen as a call to center on morality, and morality, in turn, as a matter of conduct . . . Religion is narrowed to moralism." See Taylor, *A Secular Age*, 225. This tendency was prominently featured in the Catholic Jansenism of seventeenth- and eighteenth-century France and in the Reformed Tradition as well.

41. Taylor, *A Secular Age*, 306–320.

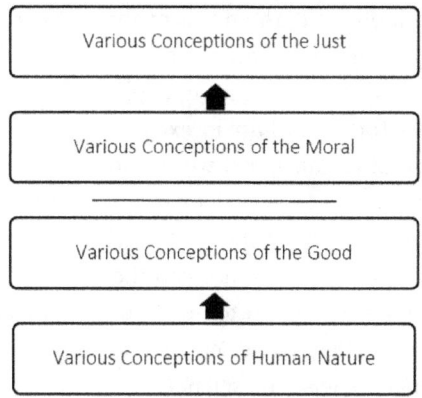

Figure 4

As Alasdair MacIntyre notes, the moral philosophies now available to us are "emotivist" in nature. They are not grounded in any meaningful way on a common understanding of human nature or on a clear conception of the good. They are little more than preferences or opinions. According to MacIntyre, the anthropological roots and the assertions of the good in these philosophies are little more than personal and group preferences. As a result, we have been left with a tepid form of "civil religion" in our public life, weak tea that is unreflectively accepted by some, but, nonetheless, suspect.

Is this a problem? Some philosophers think it is. Charles Taylor expressed this concern in the form of two questions: "Are (we) living beyond our moral means in continuing allegiance to our standards of justice and benevolence? Do we have ways of seeing good which are still credible to us, which are powerful enough to sustain these standards?"[42] Clearly, he thought the answer to the first question was "yes" and the answer to the second "no."

412. THE MORAL IN THE ARISTOTELIAN-THOMIST TRADITION

We have defined the "moral" as the way in which one thinks about and treats oneself and others. This is an Aristotelian understanding of the

---

42. Taylor, *A Secular Age*, 517. Some others, including Deirdre N. McCloskey, are more sanguine in this regard. See McCloskey, *The Bourgeois Virtues*, 23, 28–29.

moral to the extent that it focuses more on the individual and his or her relationships with others than on this or that act *per se*, the primary object of interest in some other conceptions of the moral.

Aristotle relied on the virtues in explicating moral behavior. A virtue can be understood as a human excellence or *arete*. Following Aristotle, but with a Christian gloss, we traditionally categorize individual virtues as theological, intellectual, or moral in nature. Again, the theological virtues include faith, hope, and charity. One cannot be trained in the theological virtues, as such, nor can they be developed by habit. The theological virtues are believed to be "infused" in us as gifts. According to Thomas Aquinas, they come "entirely from the outside."[43] The intellectual virtues include wisdom, science, and understanding,[44] all three of which can be developed through explicit instruction and the disciplined application of certain decision rules or through the affirmation of certain intellectual commitments. In contrast, the moral virtues can only be developed by habit or sustained practice. Our primary concern here is the moral virtues.

Although there are competing taxonomies, four moral virtues, i.e., prudence, justice, temperance, and fortitude or courage, are traditionally thought of as all-encompassing in nature and hence as cardinal or "hinge" virtues.[45] Reflecting this view, Deirdre N. McCloskey contends that prudence encompasses "know-how, foresight, *phronesis*, self-interest, and contextual rationality." Justice implies both "social balance and honesty." Temperance manifests as "individual balance and restraint, chastity, sobriety, and humility." And "autonomy, daring, endurance, and steadfastness" are part and parcel of the cardinal virtue of fortitude or courage.[46] McCloskey argues persuasively that structuring any discussion of the virtues around the three theological virtues and the four cardinal

---

43. Aquinas, *The Summa Theologica and The Summa Contra Gentiles*, 599.

44. Aquinas, *The Summa Theologica and The Summa Contra Gentile*, 568–577. See also Aristotle, *Nicomachean Ethics*, 27.

45. As a practical matter, prudence or right judgment is often thought of as the most important of the cardinal virtues. Thomas Aquinas certainly believed so: "Prudence is absolutely the principal of all the virtues." See Aquinas, *The Summa Theologica and The Summa Contra Gentiles*, 589. As noted by Paul J. Wadell, "prudence connects the everyday with the ultimate." In turn, "justice is doing what needs to be done in the way it needs to be done"; and temperance and fortitude or courage "both pertain . . . to impediments to action. Their focus is the emotions, particularly when they make doing good more difficult instead of facilitating the doing of good." See Wadell, "Virtue," 1005–1006.

46. McCloskey, *The Bourgeois Virtues*, 66.

or hinge virtues is advisable since these taxonomies enable us to tap into the West's rich patrimony of moral thinking.[47]

Aristotle believed that the underlying "truth" of the virtues can be objectively demonstrated by way of the "mean": "Virtue is a state of character concerned with choice, lying in a mean, i.e., the mean relative to us, this being determined by a rational principle, and by that principle by which the man of practical wisdom would determine it. Now it is a mean between two vices, that which depends on excess and that which depends on defect . . . "[48] The virtue of courage, for instance, lies between two vices. According to Aristotle, "the coward, the rash man, and the brave man are concerned with the same objects but are differently disposed toward them; for the first two exceed and fall short, while the third holds the middle, which is the right position . . . "[49] Similarly, modesty is the virtue or mean that lies between the vices of shamelessness and bashfulness; and dignity is the virtue or mean that lies between the vices of servility and churlishness.[50] As described by Alasdair MacIntyre, "a mean is a rule or principle of choice between two extremes."[51] Most importantly, because any given virtue can be rationally identified in this way, it is objective in nature and not just a matter of personal preference.

Christian ethics absorbed much of this thought. We see vestiges of Greek and Roman thought, for instance, in the wisdom of the early church fathers. Although a platonic framework tended to be favored during the church's first millennium, Aristotle's ethics were influential, too.

Thomas Aquinas embraced Aristotle's understanding of the cardinal virtues, attributing them, not only to "the Philosopher," but to Gregory the Great as well.[52] He also adopted Aristotle's conception of the mean as a way to objectively identify a virtue: "It is evident that the good of moral virtue consists in conformity with the rule of reason. Now it is clear that between excess and deficiency the mean is equality or conformity. Therefore, it is evident that moral virtue consists in a mean."[53]

Aquinas extended on Aristotle's conception of the moral in three ways, however, one of which has already been noted: Aquinas positioned

---

47. McCloskey, *The Bourgeois Virtues*, 361.
48. Aristotle, *Nicomachean Ethics*, 33.
49. Aristotle, *Nicomachean Ethics*, 49.
50. Aristotle, *The Eudemian Ethics*, 19.
51. MacIntyre, *A Short History of Ethics*, 65.
52. Aquinas, *The Summa Theologica and The Summa Contra Gentiles*, 588.
53. Aquinas, *The Summa Theologica and The Summa Contra Gentiles*, 606.

the theological virtues of faith, hope, and charity alongside Aristotle's taxonomies of the intellectual and moral virtues.

Further, Aquinas relied on the theological concept of grace—drawn largely from Augustine—to overcome the crippling prospect of sin.[54] In fact, Aquinas walked a fine line with respect to the question of moral efficacy.[55] On the one hand, he maintained—*contra* the reformers of the sixteenth century—that human beings retained some degree of moral efficacy following the fall of Adam and Eve. On the other, he argued that God's grace is essential to virtuous living: "Because human nature is not altogether corrupted by sin, namely, so as to be shorn of every good of nature, even in the state of corrupted nature it can, by virtue of its natural endowments, perform some particular good, such as to build dwellings, plant vineyards, and the like; yet it cannot do all the good natural to it, so as to fall short in nothing. In the same way, a sick man can of himself make some movements, yet he cannot be perfectly moved with the movement of one in health, unless by the help of medicine he be cured. Hence in the state of the integrity of nature, man needs a gratuitous strength superadded to natural strength for one reason, *viz.*, in order to do and will supernatural good . . . "[56] Indeed, "in the state of corrupted nature, man cannot fulfill all the divine commandments without healing grace."[57]

Still further, Aquinas advanced a traditional understanding of the natural law—again, drawn largely from Augustine[58]—as a sure foundation for moral thinking: "All things partake in some way in the eternal law in so far as, namely, from its being imprinted on them, they derive their respective inclinations to their proper acts and to divine providence in a more excellent way, in so far as it itself partakes of a share of providence, by being provident both for itself and for others. There, it has a share of

---

54. Aristotle certainly wrestled with the concept of vice. In his view, vices, i.e., morally suspect habits, inhibit our natural orientation to the virtues, i.e., the mean. "Vice" differs, however, from the Christian concepts of original sin, mortal sin, and concupiscence, the impediments to virtuous living uniquely recognized by Christians with which Thomas Aquinas had to contend.

55. Alasdair MacIntyre thus locates Thomas Aquinas between two poles: Aristotle's relative optimism and the pessimism of Augustine and the reformers of the sixteenth century: "Because he has neither the earlier Augustinian nor the later Protestant belief in the wholesale corruption of human desires and choices, he can treat human nature as it is, as a tolerably reliable guide to human nature as it ought to be." See MacIntyre, *A Short History of Ethics*, 118.

56. Aquinas, *The Summa Theologica and The Summa Contra Gentiles*, 655.

57. Aquinas, *The Summa Theologica and The Summa Contra Gentiles*, 659.

58. Augustine, *The City of God*, 870.

the eternal reason whereby it has a natural inclination to its proper act and end; and the participation of the eternal law in the rational creature is called the natural law."[59]

Catholic moral teaching had, in fact, long affirmed the existence of the natural law, i.e., a variously articulated sets of moral principles[60] believed to be knowable by all right-thinking people of all times and places, including non-Christians.[61] Indeed, Paul had referred to the natural law in his Letter to the Romans: "When the Gentiles who do not have the law by nature observe the prescriptions of the law, they are a law for themselves even though they do not have the law. They show that the demands of the law are written in their hearts . . . " (Rom 2:14–15). According to Augustine and other proponents of natural law theory, God has instilled a certain orientation to moral behavior in every one of us.[62] And according to Thomas Aquinas, at least, "the common principles" embedded in the natural law "cannot be blotted out from men's hearts."[63]

That said, Thomas Aquinas's development of the natural law is regarded by some as more theological than philosophical in nature *per se*.[64]

59. Aquinas, *The Summa Theologica and The Summa Contra Gentiles*, 618. See also Kenny, "Introduction," xxvii. It is arguable that Aristotle was cognizant of something akin to the natural law. He notes, for instance, that "part of political justice is natural, part legal; natural, that which everywhere has the same force and does not exist by people's thinking this or that; legal, that which is originally indifferent, but when it has been laid down is not indifferent . . . That which is by nature is unchangeable . . . " See Aristotle, *Nicomachean Ethics*, 83. This concept is undeveloped in Aristotle's work, however.

60. *Faith Connection*: The Ten Commandments are typically advanced as *the* paradigmatic expression of the natural law. See Dent, "Moral Law," 144.

61. *Faith Connection*: Although Protestant theologians have tended to reject the very idea of the natural law as insufficiently cognizant of sin and its corroding influence on conscience, some, including Quakers, for instance, invoke the somewhat analogous concept of the "inner light." In this view, the perception of God's hopes and dreams for us is directly accessible to those among us who are properly attuned. In this view, ready access to God's expectations can be attributed, less to human nature and less to virtue honed by habit, than to prayer and to a personal relationship with God.

62. *Faith Connection*: A sharp distinction should be drawn between the portrayal of the Ten Commandments in natural law theory and in fideism's understanding of the Decalogue. In natural law theory—as espoused by Christian thinkers, at least—the Ten Commandments are innate in us. The Decalogue represents the codified version of the law that is written—first and foremost—on our hearts. The objective truth of the Ten Commandments is knowable for this reason. In contrast, fideism views the Ten Commandments as God's dictates from above. As such, they are not subject to reasoning on our part or comprehensible in any real sense. They are simply given.

63. Aquinas, *The Summa Theologica and The Summa Contra Gentiles*, 645.

64. Kerr, *After Aquinas*, 103.

Further, it lacks the precision of his teachings pertaining to the virtues. According to Fergus Kerr, "Thomas is so unclear about which of the natural law precepts are primary and which are secondary, and, anyway, allows so much variability at the level of detailed choices, that his position seems little different from any other relativism."[65]

413. ALTERNATIVE VIEWS OF THE MORAL

As noted above, virtue ethics had been abandoned for the most part in the wake of the sectarian rivalries of the sixteenth and seventeenth centuries, and this development has accelerated since the Enlightenment and persists to this day. This does not mean, however, that Enlightenment philosophers did not recognize the need for at least some standards of social behavior. David Hume, for instance, anchored his moral thinking in the complex emotional lives of human beings. Jeremy Bentham, the father of utilitarianism, touted the twin poles of pleasure and pain. And G. W. F. Hegel defined moral behavior expansively as that which is in conformance with the "world spirit" or *zeitgeist*.

Because of its singular importance in the West—most notably its association with the United Nations's Universal Declaration of Human Rights (1948)—we would do well to linger a bit over Immanuel Kant's understanding of moral behavior, however. In fact, Kant's *Groundwork for the Metaphysics of Morals* (1785) is widely recognized as one of the most influential texts of all time. A methodological idealist, Kant believed that we can reason our way to certain rules that can ensure moral behavior. We do not need God, Kant argued, to reveal the universal laws in accord with which we should conduct our lives. To this end, he postulated three decision rules: one, any maxim can acquire the status of a universal law to the extent that it promotes or circumscribes an activity or action in a manner to which we could all be expected to agree; two, people should not be treated as means, but as ends in and of themselves; and three, we should categorically honor any ethical principle that we think should apply to everyone. The word "categorical" is important here. It means that results do not matter. A categorical imperative should be followed regardless of any particular outcome that might follow from its adoption.

Although Kant's scheme is haled by many as a remarkable achievement, it fails in four distinct ways. First, Kant's conception of categorical

---

65. Kerr, *After Aquinas*, 98.

imperatives is better described as an intellectual virtue than a moral virtue *per se*. Kant did little more than proffer a method for articulating decision rules. Habit and formation play no role in Kant's ethics.[66] Second, lacking an ontological foundation, Kant's assertion of an innate human dignity—and so our need to treat every human being as an end rather than as a means—is just that, an assertion, hence Alasdair MacIntyre's dismissal of Kantian ethics as emotivist. Third, Kant's moral prescriptions are rigid to say the least. He goes to great lengths—tortuous lengths, in fact—in describing how a man should respond to an angry ax murderer demanding to know the whereabouts of the poor man's son! The problem with categorial imperatives is that they are just that: categorical. They demand a "yes" or "no" response. Nuance plays no role. "Situational sensitivity"[67] counts for little. There is no gray in a categorical imperative, only black and white. Prudence and *phronesis* play no role in a binary moral framework of this kind.[68] Finally, Kant was raised as a Pietist and was clearly imbued with a deep religious sensibility.[69] Indeed, he has been rightly criticized for appropriating religious virtues and values in order to stave off an existence Thomas Hobbes more forthrightly portrayed—in the absence of any perceived standards of behavior—as "solitary, poor, nasty, brutish, and short." Alasdair MacIntyre uses the word "parasitic," in fact, in describing Kant's ethics.[70]

---

66. Aristotle would likely have dismissed the idea of the "categorical imperative" out of hand. As noted by R. W. Browne, "the moral philosopher can only lay down general principles for man's guidance and each individual man must do the rest. The casuist may profess to be more particular, he may profess to lay down accurate special rules of conduct, which will meet every individual case, but his professions will be unfulfilled ... If in this case, or in any other, you deal with men this way, you are dealing with them as children; and, therefore, according to Aristotle's views, as being incapable of perfect moral action." See Browne, "Introduction," 6–7.

67. Slote, "Problems of Moral Philosophy," 593.

68. *Faith Connection*: This is a far cry from *The Rule of Benedict*, for instance, a governing document oriented to the virtues that resembles more a procedure for the prudent granting of dispensations or exceptions than a rigid set of categorical decrees. See Benedict, *The Rule of Saint Benedict*.

69. MacIntyre, *After Virtue*, 44. See also MacIntyre, *A Short History of Ethics*, 192.

70. MacIntyre, *A Short History of Ethics*, 197.

414. THE JUST IN THE ARISTOTELIAN-THOMIST TRADITION

The just can be understood as a particular kind of moral behavior. Whereas the moral pertains to how we think about and treat ourselves and others, the just focuses on the needs of the broader community or society as a whole. More specifically, distributive justice addresses the extent to which and the manner in which we share life's benefits and burdens.[71]

We tend to associate justice with particular acts or think of the just in terms of criteria or distributive schemes of one sort or another. This was not how Aristotle approached justice, however. It is important to note that his two books on ethics, i.e., *Eudemian Ethics* and *Nicomachean Ethics*, preceded his *Politics*.[72] In Aristotle's view, there are no just acts *per se*, only moral people who act, not only in the spheres of the intrapersonal and the interpersonal, but in the public arena, too.[73]

This explains why Aristotle focused so intently on the topic of friendship in both of his books on ethics.[74] Indeed, he approached the challenge of distributive justice through the lens of friendship and all that true friendship entails.[75] According to Aristotle, "when men are friends, they have no need of justice . . . "[76] Further, "all justice is about relations towards a friend."[77] He even described "the promotion of friendship" as a "political skill" and "concord" among citizens as a kind of friendship.[78] That said, Aristotle dismissed friendship based on utility or pleasure in

---

71. Goldman and Bender, "Justice," 433.

72. It is likely that both the *Eudemian Ethics* and the *Nicomachean Ethics* were drawn either from Aristotle's own lecture notes or from his students's notes.

73. MacIntyre, *A Short History of Ethics*, 57.

74. *Faith Connection*: Like Aristotle, Jesus's moral teachings had little to do with governmental structures or public distribution schemes *per se*: "Repay to Caesar what belongs to Caesar and to God what belongs to God" (Matthew 22:21). And like Aristotle, Jesus celebrated friendship: "This is my commandment: love one another as I love you . . . I no longer call you slaves, because a slave does not know what his master is doing. I have called you friends, because I have told you everything I have heard from my Father" (John 15:12–15). Aristotle and Jesus differed, however, in their respective conceptions of those whom we should seek to befriend. Whereas Aristotle recommended no more than a small circle of compatible friends, Jesus commanded that we love even our "enemies" (Matthew 5:44) and that we do so even if this requires that we forgive, "not seven times, but seventy-seven times" (Matthew 18:22).

75. Kenny, "Introduction," xxvi.

76. Aristotle, *Nicomachean Ethics*, 125.

77. Aristotle, *The Eudemian Ethics*, 131.

78. Aristotle, *The Eudemian Ethics*, 112, 128.

favor of "perfect friendship" based—as we might expect—on the full realization of the virtues: "Perfect friendship is the friendship of men who are good, and alike in virtue; for these wish well alike to each other *qua* good, and they are good themselves."[79]

Aristotle recognized, nonetheless, that certain material, social, and formational prerequisites are essential to virtuous living. He acknowledged, for instance, that "friendship depends on community."[80] Further, "there are some things the lack of which takes the lustre from happiness, as good birth, goodly children, beauty... Happiness seems to require this kind of prosperity..."[81] Not surprisingly, Aristotle filtered this incipient understanding of the common good through the lens of virtue: "If *all* were to strive towards what is noble and strain every nerve to do the noblest deeds, everything would be as it should be for the common weal, and everyone would secure for himself the goods that are the greatest, since virtue is the greatest good."[82]

Aristotle also looked to the city-state to ensure the education and formation of children, for "it is difficult to get from youth up a right training for virtue if one has not been brought up under the right laws... Their nurture and occupation should be fixed by law... The man who is to be good must be well trained and habituated."[83] That said, Aristotle located justice—and the other virtues as well—in individual persons rather than in the city-state *per se*.

With respect to distributive justice, Thomas Aquinas followed Aristotle to a considerable extent. Aquinas focused less on friendship, however, and more on the common good and the role of the state. *Contra* today's libertarians, Thomas Aquinas affirmed the primacy of the common good: "A law, properly speaking, regards first and foremost the order of the common good..."[84]

Aquinas also followed Aristotle in assigning the state a surprisingly robust role with respect to human purpose or *telos*: "Since every part is

---

79. Aristotle, *Nicomachean Ethics*, 127.

80. Aristotle, *Nicomachean Ethics*, 133.

81. Aristotle, *Nicomachean Ethics*, 20. Aristotle thus disdained the stoic virtue of *apatheia*: "Those who say that the victim on the rack or the man who falls into great misfortune is happy if he is good, are, whether they mean to or not, talking nonsense." See Aristotle, *Nicomachean Ethics*, 122. See also MacIntyre, *A Short History of Ethics*, 101.

82. MacIntyre, *A Short History of Ethics*, 151.

83. Aristotle, *Nicomachean Ethics*, 157, 171.

84. Aquinas, *The Summa Theologica and The Summa Contra Gentiles*, 614.

ordained to the whole as the imperfect to the perfect, and since one man is a part of the perfect community, law must needs concern itself properly with the order directed to universal happiness. Therefore, the Philosopher (Aristotle) mentions both happiness and the body politic, since he says that we call those legal matters *just which are adapted to produce and preserve happiness and its parts for the body politic*. For the state is a perfect community,[85] as he says in his *Politics*."[86] Further, "just as the good of one man is not the last end, but is ordained to the common good, so too the good of one household is ordained to the good of a single state . . . "[87]

Aquinas went further, however, in endorsing the Christian virtue of charity. In doing so, he followed the early church fathers in anchoring our responsibilities to each other in Scripture. Indeed, Christians have long located the proper exercise of the virtues in the Old Testament prophets's condemnation of idolatry and the indifference exhibited by Israel's leaders to the plight of those who live on the margins of life, i.e., the *anawim*, in the beatitudes delineated in chapter 5 of Matthew's Gospel, in the parable of the sheep and the goats in chapter 25 of Matthew's Gospel, and in the commandment to love one another in chapter 13 of John's Gospel.[88] According to Servais Pinckaers, Thomas Aquinas thought these and other "evangelical principles" function much like the natural law; like the natural law, they are "inscribed in human hearts by the action of the Holy Spirit."[89]

415. ALTERNATIVE VIEWS OF THE JUST

The disjunction in moral thinking that followed the Enlightenment was described in section 411. Lacking a common conception of human nature and the good, some had wondered if it would ever be possible to embrace once again a shared understanding of the moral and the just. Indeed, can we hope to forestall a descent into the kind of life described by Thomas Hobbes as a war of all against all?

Various solutions have been proposed. Some are deontological in nature, i.e., rules-based and, hence, independent of any outcomes that

---

85. The word "perfect" in this context refers to the autonomy of the state. The state is deemed "perfect" in the sense that it does not answer to a higher authority.

86. Aquinas, *The Summa Theologica and The Summa Contra Gentiles*, 612.

87. Aquinas, *The Summa Theologica and The Summa Contra Gentiles*, 614.

88. It is unlikely, in fact, that the values embedded in these and other stories from Scripture would have made much sense to Aristotle.

89. Pinckaers, *The Sources of Christian Ethics*, 364.

could result; and some are teleological in design, i.e., dependent solely on any outcomes or results that could accrue and, hence, unconstrained by any "real" boundaries. Several of these schemes are examined here: social contracts, i.e., a deontological strategy; utilitarianism, i.e., a teleological scheme; two varieties of libertarianism, one deontological and the other teleological; and pragmatism, i.e., a teleological approach.

Thomas Hobbes, John Locke, and Jean-Jacque Rousseau promoted the use of written or implied constitutions codifying the rules by which any given people should govern themselves. The starting points for their analyses, i.e., their respective understandings of human nature, differed considerably, however. As noted above, Hobbes's view in this regard was bleak in the extreme. John Locke was somewhat less dour than Hobbes, and Jean-Jacques Rousseau was downright giddy with respect to our potential to collaborate with one another. Further, whereas Hobbes understood the purpose of government to be law and order, Locke hoped to protect the people who are governed from those who govern; and, ever the optimist, Rousseau promoted a framework through which the collective aspirations of the people, i.e., the "general will," can be realized.[90]

90. In the United States, we have benefited greatly from our written Constitution. We owe a great debt to John Locke, in particular, for its inspiration. The body of this seminal document and the Bill of Rights provide a framework for collective decision-making and a bulwark against oppression. Nevertheless, written and implied social contracts are not unproblematic. By definition, constitutional protections are limited to citizens. There is no conception in our Constitution of a universal brotherhood or sisterhood based on a shared relationship with God. This limitation is playing out today in our ongoing debate about undocumented immigrants. Viewed as sisters and brothers in Christ, undocumented immigrants have certain rights, and committed Christians have certain obligations with respect to them as fellow sons and daughters of God the Father. Our religious views are not controlling in our current political context, however. Undocumented immigrants are not citizens, and few legal rights in the United States extend to them. Further, the precise meaning of the phrase "the common consent of the governed" is unclear. No one alive today was present when the Constitution was signed. Our consent is implied. It is increasingly clear in our politics, however, that some among us feel less than fully embraced as fellow citizens who are entitled to equal protection under the law. This is why—in part—we are experiencing public protests and incidents of domestic terrorism; and this is why—no doubt—certain movements such as *Black Lives Matter*, *Occupy Wall Street*, and the *Tea Party* find support. Today, many are clearly disillusioned with our national politics. Finally, written and implied social contracts tend to be defensive in nature and hence minimalist in their aspirations. As noted by Alasdair MacIntyre, "gross inequality in property is consistent with Locke's doctrine of a natural right to property," for instance. See MacIntyre, *A Short History of Ethics*, 158. The rights articulated in our Bill of Rights focus on prohibited governmental actions. Positive rights, e.g., the right to health care, the right to affordable housing, the right to an education, etc., fall outside the scope of our enumerated rights. Indeed, the rights, privileges, and obligations articulated in written and implied

A more recent rules-based construct has been proposed by John Rawls, whose *Theory of Justice* (1971) has drawn considerable attention in recent years. Moving beyond Kant, Rawls threw off all vestiges of Christian morality. Instead of reasoning his way to an understanding of distributive justice that mimics the objectives of Christian moral and ethical thinking, Rawls promoted self-interest as a starting point. He began with a thought experiment. Imagine your "original position," he proposed. Imagine your original position before you knew when and where you would be born, before you knew your gender, before you knew your religion or the culture into which you would be born. Imagine your original position before you knew if you would be born into a slave family or a free family or a poor family or a wealthy family. Assume that a "veil of ignorance" has been draped over you, a veil of ignorance through which you cannot see or even imagine the various contingencies that make you who you are. Then, once you have fully embraced this original position, ask yourself the following question: "Into what kind of society would I choose to be born?"[91]

Rawls assumed that most of us would adopt a risk averse position. We would hope to avoid being born into abject poverty in a slave economy that might discriminate against our gender, our religion, or our perceived abilities or lack thereof. Given this, we would opt for certain protections that would ensure a minimal level of security—a minimal level of justice, in fact—for all. Rawls then proposed three rules that should inform our political decision-making: one, each person should enjoy an equal right to the most extensive basic liberties compatible with a similar degree of freedom for all others; two, political decisions should be rendered in such a way that the economic and social circumstances of the least-advantaged among us are improved in some minimal way, at least, as each and every public policy decision is rendered, i.e., Rawls's "difference principle"; and three, all "offices and positions" should be open to everyone under conditions of fair equality of opportunity. Considered as a whole, Rawls's theory of justice argues for a society that respects individual rights, a society that ensures that its least advantaged members benefit in some

---

social contracts tend to be formal and procedural in nature. They do not underwrite anything like *eudaimonia* or human flourishing as such.

91. Rawls, *A Theory of Justice*. The astute reader may notice a passing resemblance between Rawls's concept of the "original position" and Aristotle's metaphysical description of "being," on the one hand, and Rawls's concept of "contingencies" and Aristotle's understanding of "accidents" or "attributes," on the other.

way—even if it is only minimally so—from every public policy and social practice adopted over time, and a society that distributes positions of authority on the basis of competence rather than rank or privilege.[92]

Eschewing rules-based schemes altogether, the utilitarians of the late eighteenth and nineteenth centuries focused exclusively on results. Their approach was teleological in nature. According to utilitarians, a decision about the justice of any particular political or social policy should be based solely on the consequences resulting from that policy. Note the adverb "solely" in this definition. According to utilitarians, only the consequences of any given action matter. In a utilitarian scheme of distributive justice, nothing is right or wrong *per se*. There is no rule to check against. According to utilitarians, only one principle should be employed in deciding if a particular decision is just or unjust: the results it produces, both positive and negative, *vis-à-vis* any alternative that might be proposed.

Two Englishmen are recognized as the architects of utilitarian thought: Jeremy Bentham and John Stuart Mill.[93] Bentham argued that public and social policies should be oriented to happiness, which he narrowly defined as the experience of pleasure and the avoidance of pain: "Nature has placed mankind under the governance of two sovereign masters, pain and pleasure. They alone point out what we ought to do and determine what we shall do; the standard of right and wrong, and the chain of causes and effects, are both fastened to their throne. They govern us in all we do, all we say, all we think; every effort we can make to throw off our subjection to pain and pleasure will only serve to demonstrate and confirm it. A man may claim to reject their rule, but in reality, he will

---

92. The problem with Rawls's theory of justice is that it is entirely theoretical. Its critics charge that no one can truly imagine anything like an "original position." Further, risk aversion as a universal disposition is assumed. In this sense, Rawls's theory of justice, too, can be viewed as an emotivist construct. It is a society that John Rawls very much longed for, it seems.

93. Jeremy Bentham was a thoroughgoing materialist. He did not believe in God, in heaven or hell, or in sin or virtue. This does not mean that Bentham was a wanton sop, however. In fact, he accomplished much over the course of his lifetime that is considered praiseworthy. Bentham contributed significantly to the development of public education in Great Britain and to prison reform, for instance. John Stuart Mill, the son of one of Bentham's friends and the author of *On Liberty* (1859), attempted to rescue utilitarian thinking from some of its more obvious flaws. Most importantly, Mill maintained that the state has no right to interfere in the private lives of individuals. Like Bentham, Mill was a social reformer. He was, for instance, an early advocate for the right of women to vote.

remain subject to it."[94] Bentham's approach was truly hedonistic. In his view, nothing can be considered intrinsically good or bad. As physical beings living in a material world, we cannot know good or bad *per se*; we can only know pleasure and pain.

Further, all pleasures and pains can be quantified as positive or negative "utiles," a term coined by Bentham. And once the values of these pleasures and pains have been calculated for any particular pair of public policy or social alternatives, decision-makers should simply choose the one that maximizes the overall happiness of those whose interests are being considered.[95]

Contemporary utilitarians have generally avoided the kind of specificity that can lead to unacceptable outcomes in utilitarian thinking. Preference utilitarians, for instance, argue that we should calculate utiles associated with broad preferences rather than particular acts. To

---

94. Bentham, *An Introduction to the Principles of Morals and Legislation*.

95. There are obvious problems with utilitarianism. Most significantly, perhaps, it is difficult to balance pleasure and pain in a simple equation. How should the funding of a community orchestra, for instance, be balanced against street repairs? It is sometimes suggested that money can serve this function, but money can be a rather crude way to decide how we should allocate life's benefits and burdens, the primary purpose of any system of justice. Further, how should the intensity of any particular pleasure or pain be weighed? How should we proceed if three people are mildly opposed to a policy proposal, but a fourth thinks it is the greatest thing since sliced bread? There is no way to distinguish "extreme support" from "mild support" or "extreme opposition" from "mild opposition" in most voting systems. Still further, how should we go about ascertaining the perspectives of everyone who could possibly be affected by a proposed policy change? Timeframe can be a problem as well. Consider global warming. Fossil fuels are relatively cheap now, but their continued use is heating up the planet, thus spawning an array of public policy challenges. Further, global warming may not be reversible. Given this, how should we balance pleasures and pains that have yet to fully manifest against the pleasures and pains of the moment? Hedonistic utilitarianism cannot account for the problem of sustainability. Utilitarianism's cavalier approach to minority rights is generally recognized as its most serious flaw, however. It provides no conceptual space for human rights. Of the several non-realist political philosophies examined here, the very idea of human rights only makes sense, in fact, in a rules-based moral system. Utilitarianism is only concerned about happiness, which it defines in terms that are exclusively materialistic. Utilitarianism strives to produce the greatest quantity of happiness possible for the greatest number of people. The interests of racial minorities, religious minorities, the LGBTQ community, the mentally ill, etc., can be discounted all too easily in a calculation of "utiles" associated with any public or social policy of interest to these communities. Finally, hedonistic utilitarianism does not account for personal loyalties. Everyone's "utiles" are just as good as everyone else's. We know, however, that people hold particular allegiances in real life, affinities that inform their judgments about who should get what and who should bear what. There is no room for this kind of thinking in utilitarianism. There is no room, for instance, for patriotism or religion—particular kinds of affinities—in a utilitarian moral framework.

protect minority rights, rule utilitarians hypothesize that we would all want to live in a society in which minority perspectives and lifestyles are protected. Following this logic, they recommend that we apply the concept of utiles to the development of certain rules rather than to particular decisions or to particular policies. To ensure sustainability, some suggest that we replace the utilitarian commitment to the "maximization" of utility with a lesser standard: "optimization," perhaps.[96]

Broadly speaking, libertarianism affirms the rights of individuals to acquire, hold, and exchange their property with minimal interference from the state. From the libertarian point of view, the individual rather than the community or the state is the primary object of concern.

Although John Locke is thought to be the father of libertarianism, F. A. Hayek and Milton Friedman are credited with breathing life into this contemporary manifestation of classical liberalism. Hayek and Friedman opposed the interventionist fiscal policies promoted by John Maynard Keynes (1883–1946) and advocated, instead, for the restrained use of monetary policy, governmental deregulation, and the privatization of certain public services. In the latter half of the twentieth century, Ayn Rand fired the libertarian imagination with two best-selling novels, *The Fountainhead* (1943) and *Atlas Shrugged* (1957). And Robert Nozick is credited with having made the case for libertarianism as a political philosophy. In *Anarchy, State, and Utopia* (1974), he argued that nothing more than a minimal state "limited to the narrow functions of protection against force, theft, fraud, enforcement of contracts, and so on" can be justified without violating an individual's rights.[97]

In fact, two very different "language games" fall under the rubric of libertarianism. Ayn Rand and Robert Nozick are associated with the deontological version of this resurgent political philosophy. They viewed property rights as sacrosanct and argued that taxation is best understood as a kind of forced labor or slavery. "Self-ownership" is a key principle in this strain of libertarian thought. In contrast, Milton Friedman and others have argued that the private sector simply produces better results, i.e., more wealth and better social outcomes, when left to its own devices. Their claims are teleological in nature and, hence, subject to verification.[98]

---

96. Slote, "Utilitarianism," 892.

97. Nozick, *Anarchy, State, and Utopia*, xix.

98. Like the rules-based and utilitarian political philosophies examined above, libertarianism is not without its problems. First, libertarians generally espouse a negative conception of rights. This is clearly evident in the first ten amendments to the United

Pragmatism—a teleological approach to distributive justice and government, more generally—is a uniquely American philosophy. It features a practical perspective, an ethic of individualism, confidence in the scientific method, and optimism, four ideas associated by some with the American character. Pragmatism's first generation of theorists included Charles Sanders Peirce, William James, and John Dewey. As a political philosophy, it was held in high regard from the turn of the prior century through the 1940s, but was then eclipsed to a considerable extent by other views. This changed in the 1970s with the work of two philosophers, Jürgen Habermas, whose understanding of truth claims was briefly examined in section 317, and Richard Rorty, both of whom have acknowledged a substantial debt to John Dewey.

Several elements in the thinking of pragmatism's first generation of scholars persist in the work of today's pragmatists. One, the community should be approached through the individual, rather than vice-versa. The value of autonomous choice recurs as a priority in their work. Two, the

---

States Constitution, which is based, to a significant degree, on the political philosophy of John Locke. The Bill of Rights affirms, for instance, that a citizen's speech cannot be abridged, that his or her home cannot be searched, and that he or she cannot be jailed without formal charges being filed. These are "freedoms from." "Freedoms to" or "freedom for" are anathema to most libertarians. They are hard pressed to acknowledge a right to an education, a right to medical care, or a right to adequate housing. Second, the concept of "self-ownership," which is asserted in no uncertain terms in the deontological version of libertarianism, is anything but self-evident. Libertarianism can thus be dismissed as but one of several "language games," to use Wittgenstein's terminology, or emotivist political philosophies, to use MacIntyre's terminology, all of which are essentially unmoored in any anthropological or ontological sense. Third, libertarians struggle to explain why inherited wealth should be excluded from taxation. This is particularly so in the case of wealth originally acquired through the exploitation of workers or the "unjust" confiscation, at some point in time, of another person's property. Robert Nozick devised three rules pertaining to private holdings to address this concern: first, a person who initially acquires a holding in accordance with the principle of justice is entitled to that holding; second, a person to whom a holding is transferred in accordance with the principle of justice is entitled to that holding; and third, no one, including the state, is entitled to a holding except by the repeated applications of rules one and two." See Nozick, *Anarchy, State, and Utopia*, 3. Nozick then described the circumstances under which the original acquisition and the subsequent transfer of an acquisition can be considered just. Although his reasoning is logical enough, critics contend that the practical application of Nozick's theory of distributive justice in the real world would be unwieldy to the point of impossibility. Reparations for slavery is often suggested as a test case in this regard. Where to begin? And where to end? Fourth, there is an implicit assumption in the teleological version of libertarianism that everyone has the capacity and the wherewithal to pull themselves up by their own bootstraps. This is not necessarily so in the case of deeply impoverished communities, i.e., communities with few financial, social, or cultural resources with which to work.

world should be understood in natural terms. There is no appeal in pragmatism to metaphysics or to spiritual or ideal beliefs. Three, the experimental attitude is embraced. This is evident among today's pragmatists, less in the celebration of science, a recurring theme in the contributions of Peirce, James, and Dewey, than in their consistent appeal to the need for discursive engagement. Four, many of today's pragmatists share the optimistic outlook for which Peirce, James, and Dewey were celebrated.

In the absence of any external standard by which to adjudicate claims in the public arena, Jürgen Habermas recommends that we focus, instead, on certain rules of engagement, i.e., the conditions that would set the stage for an "ideal speech situation." It was Richard Rorty, however, who has contributed more than anyone else to the resurgence of pragmatism in recent decades. According to Rorty, there are no external standards against which any idea, fact, or claim can be assessed. There is no foundation, as such, on which to build a metaphysics, an epistemology, or an ethical system. In fact, "there is nothing to people except what has been socialized into them—their ability to use language, and thereby to exchange beliefs and desires with other people."[99] There is "no deep down there," according to Rorty.[100] Indeed, he defined pragmatism as "anti-essentialism applied to notions like 'truth,' 'knowledge,' 'language,' 'morality,' and similar objects of philosophical theorizing."[101] According to Rorty, the only standards we have access to are those that we arrive at discursively. Rorty argued that human nature is malleable or contingent. We engage in "sentence uttering" in order to cope with our environment and nothing more.[102] We "muddle through."[103] Rorty was not interested in pursuing the question of human motivation any more deeply than this.

The understanding of the good that follows from Rorty's critique is less clear, however. At one point, he identified the good as success, thereby echoing Dewey's circular argument on behalf of growth: the goal of success is simply continued success.[104] At another point, Rorty extolled freedom as an important value, but pointedly backed away from any suggestion

---

99. Rorty, *Contingency, Irony, and Solidarity*, 177.
100. Rorty, *Consequences of Pragmatism*, xxxviii.
101. Rorty, *Consequences of Pragmatism*, 162.
102. Rorty, *Philosophy and the Mirror of Nature*, 11.
103. Rorty, *Philosophy and the Mirror of Nature*, 11.
104. Rorty, *Consequences of Pragmatism*, 172.

that liberty might be a preeminent good. *Contra* deontological libertarians, liberty is but one value among many others for pragmatists.[105]

Rorty had little to say about moral behavior, since he did not believe that there are any standards, as such, against which to assess human interactions. According to Rorty, there is simply no getting around the fact that all human interactions require discursive engagement. He had more to say about the just, however. Rorty's understanding of justice was culture-bound, however; indeed, he restricted the parties with whom we can expect to engage in meaningful discourse to the industrialized West.[106] Rorty thus joined John Rawls in discounting our ability to overcome the formidable barriers of geography, culture, and religion in our pursuit of justice.[107]

What should we make of these several alternatives to the ethical realism of the Aristotelian-Thomist Tradition? The walling off of a shared conception of human nature and a shared understanding of the good from our conception of moral behavior, i.e., how we think about and treat ourselves and others, on the one hand, and justice, i.e., how life's benefits and burdens should be shared, on the other, has been costly. The various understandings of the human person that undergird the systems of distributive justice developed since the Enlightenment are undeniably anemic. This is particularly so in the case of the various rules-based constructs examined above and utilitarianism, which views human beings as little more than pleasure-seeking and pain-minimizing animals. Libertarianism assumes an agnostic position on the question of human nature

---

105. Rorty, *Contingency, Irony, and Solidarity*, 50, 53.

106. Rorty, *Consequences of Pragmatism*, 173.

107. The Achilles heel of Rorty's thesis lies in the expectation that individuals will respond positively to the abandonment of any and all external standards of judgment. The claim that an individual will be more interested in, more committed to, or more loyal to a community because he or she is no longer weighed down by culturally transmitted ideas of the good, the moral, and the just is suspect, however. It reflects a blind belief in progress that seems entirely out of place given the history of the twentieth century. Absent an underlying belief in progress, however, Rorty's optimism is problematic. He derided Jürgen Habermas because "he is more afraid of the sort of 'romantic' overthrow of established institutions, personified by Hitler and Mao, than of the suffocating effects of what Dewey called the 'crust of convention.'" See Rorty, *Contingency, Irony, and Solidarity*, 66. The desire to find shelter that is more secure than that which Rorty offers makes a great deal more sense after the flimsy foundation of his optimism is exposed, however. Habermas's ongoing search for an Archimedean lever, i.e., his theory of "communicative action," seems more than justified and so, too, the ethical realism of the Aristotelian-Thomist Tradition. In the end, Rorty's "easygoing liberalism" amounts to little more than whistling in the dark. See Klingwell, *A Civil Tongue*, 37.

or ontology, and pragmatists tend to view human beings as culture-bound and culturally determined. Anything deeper or more respectful of the human person[108] is simply beyond the reach of these several political philosophies. The secular moral systems developed over the course of the last several centuries claim to fill a gap left by the abandonment of a Christian worldview, but they do so poorly if at all.

Further, these various alternatives to ethical realism promise little beyond law and order, i.e., social contract theory; the maximization of pleasure and the minimization of pain, i.e., utilitarianism; a jealous regard for privacy and property, i.e., libertarianism; and more and more conversation, i.e., pragmatism. Lacking a fulsome understanding of human nature and a shared conception of the good, none of them offers much in terms of decision-making that can be considered just. Moreover, they provide thin purchase for those who seek meaningful change in the way life's benefits and burdens are shared.

Still further, the motives for pursuing change from within any of these several alternatives are off-putting, to say the least. A fear of chaos and risk aversion are assumed in the case of the several rules-based constructs examined above. Motivation is explained exclusively in terms of pleasure and pain in the case of utilitarianism. Antipathy to interference serves this same purpose for libertarians. And communicative competence and cultural affinity are assumed respectively by Habermas and Rorty to be entirely sufficient or, at least, nearly so to satisfy our felt need for norms and a measure of social stability.

Is this enough: fear, the promise of pleasure, the forestalling of pain, and value-free competence? Assessing these options from within the Aristotelian-Thomist tradition, the answer is "no." To participate in civic discourse, one must first be formed in virtue, e.g., prudence, justice, temperance, and fortitude or courage, understood as a habitual disposition oriented to moral and just behavior.

Where does this leave us? Some, including Alasdair MacIntyre, have expressed great concern, in fact: "In our society, the acids of individualism have for four centuries eaten into our moral structures, for both good and ill. But not only this: we live with the inheritance of not only one,

---

108. *Faith Connection*: This explains why the Catholic Church's recent embrace of Thomist personalism has served to reinforce its traditional privileging of ethical realism. Indeed, "the human being is a person, not just an individual. The term 'person' indicates 'a nature endowed with intelligence and free will': he is therefore a reality that is far superior to that of a subject defined by the needs arising solely from his material dimension." See Pontifical Council for Justice and Peace, *Compendium* no. 391.

but of a number of well-integrated moralities. Aristotelianism, primitive Christian simplicity, the puritan ethic, the aristocratic ethic of consumption, and the traditions of democracy and socialism have all left their mark upon our moral vocabulary. With each of these moralities there is a proposed end or ends, a set of rules, a list of virtues. But the ends, the rules, the virtues, differ . . . It follows that we are liable to find two kinds of people in our society: those who speak from within one of these surviving moralities and those who stand outside all of them . . . There exists no court of appeals, no impersonal neutral standard . . . To those who speak from without, those who speak from within appear merely to be uttering imperatives which express their own liking and their private choices. The controversy between emotivism and prescriptivism, on the one hand, and their critics, on the other, thus expresses the fundamental moral situation of our own society."[109]

---

109. MacIntyre, *A Short History of Ethics*, 266.

5

More Recent Expressions of Thomism

501. NEW DIRECTIONS

As noted in chapter 1, interest in the realism embodied in the Aristotelian-Thomist Tradition had substantially faded by the seventeenth century. Metaphysics had simply gone out of fashion in the academy. In its place, epistemology would emerge as the most important concern of Enlightenment philosophers, including, most notably, René Descartes and Immanuel Kant. Linguistics and language conceived more broadly would assume preeminence among scholars in the nineteenth century. Questions pertaining to personhood, identity, and the experience of meaning would predominate through much of the twentieth century. And late in the twentieth century, a "postmodern" concern for culture and the power of competing narratives would emerge as key foci.

Unfortunately, this decline in interest in the Aristotelian-Thomist Tradition was evident not just in the academy. As noted in section 104, Thomas Aquinas's teachings went out of vogue in the church, too. Indeed, the church had entered into an extended period of intellectual dormancy in the seventeenth century. Thomas Aquinas's closely-argued reasoning in *Summa Theologica* and *Summa Contra Gentiles* was distilled into bare summaries that could be learned by rote in seminary classes. And as noted in section 405, Aquinas's extensive reflections on the virtues were abandoned in favor of the Decalogue as the surest foundation for moral thinking.

The perennial tradition again attained salience in the intellectual life of the church in the late nineteenth century. Indeed, the

Aristotelian-Thomist Tradition would prove remarkably adept in engaging the philosophical concerns of the twentieth and twenty-first centuries. As we shall see, "transcendental Thomists" have appropriated the thought of Immanuel Kant. "Existential Thomists"—including, most notably, Karl Rahner (1904–2004) and Pope John Paul II—have taken up key questions pertaining to human purpose, authenticity, and the experience of meaning. "Analytic Thomists" have engaged the thought of Ludwig Wittgenstein and others. Key topics in these dialogues have included Wittgenstein's concept of "language games," the nature and use of signs and symbols, the pragmatics of discourse, and structural linguistics. And Charles Taylor has forthrightly addressed the implications of constructivism for those who uphold the ongoing viability of the Aristotelian-Thomist Tradition.[1]

That said, some caution should be exercised in addressing these still developing streams of thought. Some "Thomists" address concerns that would not have occurred to Aristotle or to Thomas Aquinas. As a result, some extrapolation of Aristotelian and Thomist thought is required in order to bring the realism of the perennial tradition into dialogue with contemporary philosophies. According to F. C. Copleston, "in some cases, at least, Thomists have the rather disconcerting habit of finding texts in Aquinas to justify them in presenting as developments of his philosophy ideas which have certainly come to them via contemporary non-Thomist thinkers."[2] Fergus Kerr is even more critical in this regard: "Current readings of Thomas' work are so conflicting, and even incommensurable, that integrating them into a single interpretation seems impossible. Some readings are deeply misguided; but even these, since they issue from respectable theological and philosophical presuppositions, demand and deserve attention."[3]

With this caveat in mind, synopses of recent iterations in Thomist thought follow. In each instance, the underlying concerns of the "Thomism" under investigation will be described. Linkages to the realism

---

1. In *Fides et Ratio*, Pope John Paul II decried modern philosophy's abandonments of a foundational concern for being and metaphysics more generally. See John Paul II, *Fides et Ratio*, nos. 5 and 97. At the same time, he exhibited a remarkable sensitivity to the concerns of existential philosophers and to the cultural and other contextual concerns of postmodernists and others as well. See John Paul II, *Fides et Ratio*, nos. 2 and 71.

2. Copleston, *Aquinas*, 251.

3. Kerr, *After Aquinas*, 15–16.

of the Aristotelian-Thomist Tradition will then be noted. And this will be followed by one or more critiques advanced by others.

Reference to "Thomism" rather than to the Aristotelian-Thomist Tradition will be intentional from this point forward. The several "Thomisms" addressed here proceed forthrightly—for the most part—from a Christian perspective. They are unabashedly Catholic in their outlook. Thomas Aquinas is thus invoked, not just as a philosopher, but as a Catholic philosopher. The designation "Thomist" attests to this foundational commitment.

502. NEO-THOMISM

As detailed in section 104, Thomism—under the moniker "neo-Thomism"—emerged in the church in the late nineteenth century as an intellectual anchor of sorts. Key developments in this regard included the publication of Leo XIII's encyclical *Aeterni Patris* (1879), Pius X's encyclical *Pascendi Dominici Gregis* (1907), and his 24 theses pertaining to "authentic Thomism" and "authentic Catholic philosophy." Jacques Maritain (1882–1973), Étienne Gilson, and Mortimer Adler (1902–2001) are among the most highly esteemed of the neo-Thomists of the twentieth century.

Neo-Thomism is of marginal interest in today's academy.[4] During its zenith, however, neo-Thomist thought served two purposes. First, it was mounted as an explicit—albeit belated—response to the Enlightenment, most notably to the rationalist philosophies of René Descartes, Baruch Spinoza, and Gottfried Leibniz and the empiricism of Francis Bacon, Thomas Hobbes, John Locke, and George Berkeley. Indeed, the church had become increasingly alarmed by the extent to which Enlightenment thought had taken hold among social elites and the degree to which it had engendered both widespread skepticism and a materialist understanding of the cosmos in the broader culture. To a considerable extent, this first purpose was polemical in nature.[5] The second purpose

---

4. Hart, "Neothomism in America," 357.

5. Two books cited in this text reflect this polemical stance, in fact: *An Introduction to Philosophy* by Paul I. Glenn, which was originally published in 1943, and *An Introduction to Catholic Philosophy* by A. C. Cotter, which was originally published in 1949. They are both entirely faithful to Thomist thought and were considered excellent primers in their day. That said, they disparage Enlightenment thought and fail to engage in any meaningful way.

was pedagogical. In the place of the abbreviated manuals of the seventeenth and eighteenth centuries, Aquinas's unabridged works—most notably, his *Summa Theologica* and *Summa Contra Gentiles*—were again employed in forming future priests and in undergraduate courses in Catholic colleges and universities as well.[6]

Some argue that neo-Thomist thought represents the use of Aquinas's metaphysics for a purpose for which it was not intended. In this view, the neo-Thomists of the late nineteenth and twentieth centuries employed it—to a substantial extent—in opposition to the several epistemologies, i.e., rationalism, empiricism, and transcendental idealism, of the Enlightenment. In Fergus Kerr's view, "Thomas became the answer to Descartes."[7] Further, "the mid-nineteenth-century revival of interest [in Thomism], primarily in his supposedly Aristotelian philosophy, was intended to put it to use in containing and eradicating the supposedly Cartesian/Kantian subjectivist individualism to which Roman Catholic thinkers were then attracted."[8] According to some, including Étienne Gilson, this had the unfortunate effect of distorting Thomism to a considerable extent.[9]

503. TRANSCENDENTAL THOMISM

The transcendental Thomists of the twentieth century advanced well beyond the thought of Thomas Aquinas *per se*. In doing so, they hoped to bring Thomas Aquinas into conversation with Enlightenment thought, most notably the transcendental idealism of Immanuel Kant. The most prominent transcendental Thomists of the last century included Joseph Maréchal (1878–1944), Bernard Lonergan (1904–1984), Karl Rahner, and Cornelio Fabro (1911–1995). (Karl Rahner was deeply influenced by existentialism, as well, most notably the work of Martin Heidegger, under whom he studied, and so is identified below as an existential Thomist.)

Recall from section 112, that Kant had tried to reconcile the epistemologies of the rationalists and the empiricists of the Enlightenment. To this end, Kant's transcendental idealism questioned our ability to know things we encounter in the real world as they truly are, i.e., their noumena.

---

6. Peterson and Pugh, "Introduction to Analytic Thomism," xviii.
7. Kerr, *After Aquinas*, 18.
8. Kerr, *After Aquinas*, 208.
9. Gilson, *Methodological Realism*, 52.

He argued, instead, that certain innate structures in our minds—our understanding of causation, for instance—enable us to organize our perceptions of the phenomena we encounter in the sensible world.[10]

On the surface, Kant's distinction between apprehensible phenomena and their corresponding noumena bears a resemblance to the distinction Thomas Aquinas—drawing on Aristotle—makes between accidents and substance. See sections 211 and 215. Like Kant's phenomena, accidents are knowable through our senses; and like his noumena, substances—as the term is understood in the Aristotelian-Thomist Tradition—are not.[11] That said, there are significant differences between Kant's epistemology and the metaphysics of the perennial tradition. Kant did not define noumena in terms of existence. According to Kant, noumena are material in nature. Noumena are simply things in the world that are not knowable in and of themselves. They are only knowable to the extent that the innate categories in our minds make them available to us.[12] Further, Kant did not address the status of potential beings or mind-dependent beings.

Some transcendental Thomists go well beyond Kant, however, in appropriating his epistemology. Joseph Maréchal, for instance, associated Kant's noumena with things as they are known in the mind of God: "It is only in the mind of God that the known objects have their full interiority, the interiority of the effect in its adequate cause."[13] In doing so, he essentially affirmed Kant's understanding of the way in which our minds structure the phenomena we encounter in the sensible world: "By its very nature, our intellect possesses the transcendental principles which allow us to reconstruct a unity that is 'intelligible in act' on the model of representation that is only intelligible in potency. In modern terminology, this amounts to saying it contains a '*synthetic a priori* condition,' which is not quantitative and sensible, but which starts operating only with the effective cooperation of the senses."[14]

---

10. Recall from section 413 that Kant had eschewed virtue ethics in favor of a set of rationally-devised "categorical imperatives" that can be used to discern one's moral duty. That said, transcendental Thomists of the twentieth century were more concerned with Kant's epistemology than his ethics.

11. Gilson, *Methodological Realism*, 21.

12. Gilson, *Methodological Realism*, 44.

13. Maréchal, "Transcendental Thomism," 320.

14. Maréchal, "Transcendental Thomism," 322.

Bernard Lonergan similarly affirmed the essential role that our minds play in parlaying any encounter with phenomena in the sensible world into true knowledge: "Human knowing is a compound of many operations of different kinds . . . The process of inquiry, investigation, reflection, coming to judge is governed throughout by the exigencies of human intelligence and human reasonableness . . . "[15] And it is not just about knowledge *per se*. According to Lonergan, an individual comes to know himself or herself as a self or as a person in these processes. Indeed, Lonergan follows Aquinas in focusing his analysis on understanding, judging, and deciding, operations that are *essentially* personal in the sense that, whenever they are performed, the self is aware of, is present to, or experiences itself operating. "Such operations not only intend objects, then, but also render the operating self-conscious. Thus, by their intentionality, personal operations make objects present to the self and in the same act, by their consciousness, they simultaneously make the operating person present to itself—makes it a self."[16]

504. EXISTENTIAL THOMISM

Recall from section 114 that existentialism represented one of the twentieth century's most prominent streams of continental philosophy. In fact, the secular existentialism of Jean-Paul Sartre and Martin Heidegger, most notably, would exert a substantial influence on the work of a number of existential Thomists, including Karl Jaspers (1883–1969), a non-Catholic; Gabriel Marcel (1889–1973); Karol Wojtyla, later Pope John Paul II; and Jean-Luc Marion (b. 1946). (Although Wojtyla's philosophical work was clearly informed by existential thought, it is even more closely associated with the phenomenalism of Edmund Husserl, Max Scheler (1874–1928), and Maurice Merleau-Ponty. For this reason, the philosophy to which Wojtyla adhered throughout his

---

15. Lonergan, "The Subject," 383. Lonergan also invoked existential thought and the hermeneutics espoused by Hans-Georg George Gadamer and Paul Ricoeur—see section 114—in arguing that a subject can be fundamentally changed by an encounter with phenomena: "Our reflections on the subject have been concerned with him as a knower, as one that experiences, understands, and judges. We have now to think of him as a doer, as one that deliberates, evaluates, chooses, acts. Such doing, at first sight, affects, modifies, changes the world of objects. But even more, it affects the subject himself. For human doing is free and responsible . . . By his own acts the human subject makes himself what he is to be . . . " See Lonergan, "The Subject," 385.

16. Conn and Conn, "Self," 872.

papacy—personalism—is addressed separately in section 506.) The religious existentialism of Søren Kierkegaard, a Lutheran; Paul Tillich, a Lutheran; Martin Buber (1878–1965), a Jew; and Miguel de Unamuno (1864–1936), a Catholic, also influenced the development of existential Thomism in the twentieth century.

Two aspects of existential thought have proven attractive to some Thomists: first, the concept of *Dasein* in Martin Heidegger's work; and second, the inexorable drive in all of us to experience some sense of meaning in our lives. Heidegger's account of *Dasein* in his seminal work, *Being and Time* (1927), bears a striking resemblance, in fact, to the concept of being in the realist metaphysics of the Aristotelian-Thomist Tradition. See section 208. Heidegger argued that an interest in being should precede all other interests. He identified being as *Dasein*[17] and argued that the philosophical study of *Dasein* should come before any other approach to the study of mankind. "'What is a human being?' is to be discussed philosophically. The existential analytic of *Dasein* is *prior* to any psychology, anthropology, and especially biology."[18] Further, *Dasein* can only be discovered in existence. It has no determinative essence as such. Indeed, existence comes before essence. As noted by Fergus Kerr, however, "Heidegger is very insistent that Being is not in any sense an entity or god. On the contrary, no worse error can be imagined than the reification of *Dasein*. There is no Being except in the existence of beings; and beings do not show up except in the light of Being."[19]

Other existentialists would shy away from Heidegger's understanding of *Dasein*. Karl Jaspers preferred the term "*Existenz*," which he defined as the will to be authentic.[20] Jean-Paul Sartre characterized man's ontological predicament as the flight of an unachievable "for itself" from an "in-itself." Further, a true sense of authenticity cannot be achieved because the "in-itself" is mired in its "facticity," that is, the contingencies of everyday existence.[21] And Paul Tillich dismissed the concept of *Dasein* as

17. This term, which is unique to Heidegger, is drawn from the German words *da*, i.e., here, and *sein*, i.e., to be. See Heidegger, *Being and Time*, 6.

18. Heidegger, *Being and Time*, 42.

19. Kerr, *After Aquinas*, 87.

20. Jaspers, *Reason and Existenz*, 62.

21. Sartre defines the for-itself "as the being which comes to itself in terms of its future, the being which makes itself exist as having its being outside itself in the future." See Sartre, *Being and Nothingness*, 181. In contrast, the in-itself reflects an unconscious engagement or entanglement in the everyday world. The in-itself lacks presence to itself. This concept of "presence" reflects the influence of Edmund Husserl's phenomenology

excessively metaphysical or even "mystical."[22] Like Heidegger, however, Jaspers, Sartre, and Tillich located existence at the center of philosophy.

The experience of "meaning" in one's life is an overarching concern in existential thought. Indeed, existentialists contend that meaning is an inexorable and universal drive. It can be understood as a personal sense of unity and purpose that is distinct from the satisfaction of any physical or psychological need. According to existentialists, this drive is prompted by five realities that together circumscribe the human condition.

- The prospect of suffering and death and the nagging sense of life's absurdity prompt a degree of dread or *angst* in reflective human beings.
- The creation or discovery of meaning is fundamental to who we are as persons. It is universal in nature. The felt need for a sense of meaning demands satisfaction.[23] The experience of meaning cannot be achieved in the satisfaction of an ephemeral disposition or need.
- The experience of meaning entails the whole person, not just a particular aspect or dimension of a life, e.g., work life, a defining relationship, identity as a member of a particular community, etc.. Meaning cannot be compartmentalized. It must be experienced as a natural unity.
- The experience of meaning must be appropriated at the personal level. It cannot be imposed from outside.
- Finally, meaning is oriented to the future. This explains why it is experienced as a purposeful drive.

Viktor Frankl's thought is helpful in this regard. In *Man's Search for Meaning* (1946), Frankl drew on his experiences in two Nazi concentration camps in defining human beings as meaning-seeking beings. He further argued that meaning can be experienced in one, two, or three ways: first, in work and in the execution of other kinds of creative tasks; second,

---

on existential thought.

22. Tillich, *The Courage to Be*, 149.

23. Clifford Geertz argued in this vein that "the drive to make sense out of experience, to give it form and order, is evidently as real and as pressing as the more familiar biological needs." See Geertz, *The Interpretation of Cultures*, 140.

in the relationships that are central to our lives; and third, in the attitude one assumes in the face of an unavoidable circumstance.[24]

When the pursuit of meaning is frustrated, discomfort, dissonance, and/or conflict can follow.[25] According to some existentialists, life is most authentically experienced as a question that demands an answer. In this sense, life is inherently "empty." We are challenged to "fill it," it seems, with that which can engender a sense of meaning.[26]

At first glance, this may seem to extend far beyond Thomas Aquinas's understanding of essence. As noted in section 214, essence is typically understood in a twofold way: first, it distinguishes one species from another and, second, it distinguishes one individual in a species from every other member of that species. In effect, existential Thomists posit a third way in which we can distinguish ourselves as persons. According to this view, men and women do more than simply participate in or exemplify the essence of humanity or human nature, and they do more than make their way in the world as human beings are wont to do. Individual human beings are unique. They are "persons." As such, they are challenged to proactively discover or create identities that uniquely define them and distinguish them from all others. In other words, they are driven to discover or create meaning. Referencing Gregory of Nyssa, John Paul II advanced this view in his encyclical letter *Veritatis Splendor*:

---

24. *Faith Connection*: According to Frankl, "life can be meaningful in a three-fold way: one, through *what we give* to life (in terms of our creative acts); two, by *what we take* from the world (in terms of our experiencing values); and three, through *the stand we take* toward a fate we no longer can change . . . " See Frankl, *Psychotherapy and Existentialism*, 115. All three of these possibilities lend themselves to a Christian interpretation, of course. The journey of discipleship, growth in the virtues, and the exercise of servant leadership can all be experienced as profoundly creative. An ever-deepening relationship with God and with other human beings—now recognized as brothers and sisters in Christ—can be deeply meaningful as well. And as we shall see, even the faithful stance we assume *vis-à-vis* dysfunction we experience in our families, in our workplaces, and in the public square, too, can be intensely meaningful as well. Indeed, we can come to see these kinds of troubling experiences as a call to Christian witness or even as a "way of the cross."

25. Gabriel Marcel—for one—certainly believed this to be the case for most people today. See Marcel, "Ontological Mystery," 345.

26. *Faith Connection*: The problem occurs when we attempt to fill the ontological emptiness that is part and parcel of human existence with something that fails to engender an authentic experience of meaning. Too often, we seek to "medicate" this experience of life as a "question that demands an answer" or to counsel it into silence in succumbing to one or more temptations to unhealthy materialism or sensuality, unhealthy vanity, or unhealthy pride. Viewed from a Christian perspective, these root sins forestall the authentic experience of life into which we are all invited by God.

"We are in a certain way our own parents, creating ourselves as we will by our own decisions."[27] The self-directed nature of this developmental drive does, indeed, extend beyond the understanding of essence as the concept has traditionally been understood in the perennial tradition.[28]

Consider the insights of Karl Rahner in this regard. Rahner did not believe that our understanding of human purpose is pre-determined. It must be selected or developed from among an available set of options. "There are no ultimate basic attitudes, no absolute standards of value or systems of co-ordinates for determining the meaning of existence . . ."[29] In this sense, freedom lies at the root of Rahner's existential analysis. His understanding of freedom differed, however, from the anemic notions with which most of us are familiar. In Rahner's view, freedom touches upon the very core of human existence. "Freedom is first of all 'freedom of being.' It is not merely a quality of an act and capacity exercised at some time, but a transcendental mark of human existence itself."[30] Indeed, human beings "determine,"[31] "realize,"[32] or "form"[33] themselves. In Rahner's view, a human being can be understood as a "mystery,"[34] as a "question" with no self-evident "answer."[35]

Like other existentialists, Rahner believed that human beings define themselves in the context of an uncertain future. "Man is *par excellence* the being which is *in fieri*, the being which in virtue of its very nature (in virtue of nature and grace alike) is bound to keep itself open to an ever-greater future."[36] Life is thus experienced as "a venturing, planning, devising anticipation of the future."[37] Indeed, the past is constantly re-worked in the light of an emerging future.[38]

27. John Paul II, *Veritatis Splendor*, no. 71.

28 *Faith Connection*: In advancing their arguments in this regard, existential Thomists tend to rely on two passages from the Jewish Scripture, in particular: "I am who am," God's self-identification as pure existence in Exodus 3:14; and the account of God's creation of men and women "in his own likeness" in Genesis 1:27.

29. Rahner, "Intellectual Honesty and Christian Faith," 262.

30. Rahner, "Theology of Freedom," 287.

31. Rahner, The Experiment with Man," 212.

32. Rahner, "Theology of Freedom," 195.

33. Rahner, "On Christian Dying," 287.

34. Rahner, "Proving Oneself in Time of Sickness," 278.

35. Rahner, "Thoughts on the Possibility of Belief Today," 14.

36. Rahner, "Being Open to God as Ever Greater," 27.

37. Rahner, "The Dignity and Freedom of Man," 237.

38. Rahner, "The Sin of Adam," 253.

Some Thomists are dismissive of existentialism's potential to complement or inform the Aristotelian-Thomist Tradition. Jacque Maritain's *Existence and the Existent* (1947) is a case in point. (Maritain is often interpreted as a neo-Thomist, but preferred to be identified as a "paleo-Thomist."[39] He had little interest in existential Thomism or in any other alternative to the teachings found in Thomas Aquinas's original texts.) Maritain's argument was threefold. First, he took umbrage with Heidegger's appropriation of a term of art that was essentially spiritual or theological in nature, i.e., *Dasein* or existence, in support of a non-religious and baldly atheistic philosophy of being. After all, Thomas Aquinas—the preeminent philosopher of being of the scholastic era—was a theologian as well as a Christian philosopher; and even Aristotle posited the existence of God, albeit a God narrowly construed as an "unmoved mover." Although this concern is understated in Maritain's work, it clearly fueled the animus that pervades *Existence and the Existent*. Second, Maritain was convinced that existentialism discounts the critical importance of essence and nature in the Aristotelian-Thomist Tradition. See sections 213 and 214. To the extent that Aquinas put existence before substance in his ontology of being, Maritain thought of him as an authentic existentialist. At the same time, Aquinas balanced his concept of being with robust understandings of essence and nature. Maritain argued that this critical balance is missing in the versions of existentialism espoused by Martin Heidegger and Jean-Paul Sartre: "It is the same form of existentialism—in which the primacy of existence is asserted, but paid for by the abolition of intelligible nature or essence—that we find again in the atheistic existentialism of today ... The notion of 'project' is an ambiguous substitute for the notion of essence or quiddity."[40] In Maritain's view, a search for meaning delinked from robust understandings of essence and nature is a recipe for sheer acts of will, such as the kind espoused by Friedrich Nietzsche. Third, Maritain followed Thomas Aquinas in affirming the efficacy of the natural law. See section 412. Any consideration of the natural law as a moral constraint is absent in the atheistic versions of existentialism proffered by Heidegger and Sartre.

---

39. Maritain, *Existence and the Existent*, 1.
40. Maritain, *Existence and the Existent*, 4–5.

505. ANALYTIC THOMISM

At first glance, analytic philosophy may seem to have little in common with the realism of the Aristotelian-Thomist Tradition. Recall from section 114 that analytic philosophy is viewed by many as an Anglo-American rival to the various continental philosophies, i.e., phenomenalism, existentialism, hermeneutics, and postmodernism, that achieved standing in the twentieth century. Again, it arose from the logical positivism of the Vienna Circle, but focused more on language—more specifically, on propositions—than science *per se*. Its early exemplars included Gottlob Frege, Bertrand Russell, Alfred North Whitehead, and Ludwig Wittgenstein.

In truth, an interest in mutual dialogue is more evident among some analytic philosophers than among Thomists. Peter Geach (1916–2013), Elizabeth Anscombe, and John Haldane (b. 1954) have played significant roles, nonetheless, in advancing this conversation. An effort to bridge the gap—the many gaps, in fact—between the realism of the Aristotelian-Thomist Tradition and analytic philosophy began in earnest with a 1997 issue of *The Monist*, a highly esteemed journal, that was entirely devoted to this topic.

The reason for this interest is quite clear, in fact. Having achieved their first goal, i.e., the vanquishing of idealism, analytic philosophers quickly encountered two problems. First, their parsing of propositions in order to reveal non-sensical truth claims does not constitute a positive philosophy as such. Analytic philosophy has no truth claims of its own to assert. It only has a method or set of methods for use in critiquing others's truth claims. More to the point, "there is no particular method of doing analytic philosophy [as such] apart from giving high priority to rigorous argumentation and clarity of expression."[41] The second problem stems from the first. In terms of content, analytic philosophy lacks coherence. The topics addressed by analytic philosophers are so broad that it is difficult—if not impossible—to isolate its core interests. For instance, the formulaic critique of propositions espoused by the early Wittgenstein seems to have little in common with the "form of life" or "expression of culture" critique advanced by the later Wittgenstein. Analytic philosophy lacks a metaphysical platform from which to advance its epistemology and so is left with little more than a critical method. This explains the appeal that Thomism holds for some analytic philosophers. The realism

---

41. Peterson and Pugh, "Introduction to Analytic Thomism," xiii.

that lies at the root of the Aristotelian-Thomist Tradition includes a robust metaphysics and a corresponding epistemology and ethics, too. Thomism has that which analytic philosophy clearly lacks.

The most promising work in this embryonic dialogue pertains to metaphysics. (Again, these developments are attributable—for the most part—to those who labor in the camp of analytic philosophy.) This is not surprising. Observers have long noted that Ludwig Wittgenstein—in both his early and later iterations—affirmed the reality and knowability of the sensible world. He thus concurred—at some level, at least—with Aristotle and Thomas Aquinas regarding the ontological status of actual real beings. See section 209. That said, the ontological status of mind-dependent beings represents a more formidable challenge. See section 210. The latter Wittgenstein affirmed Aquinas's view, however, that "conceptual awareness, and hence linguistically expressible awareness, has as its first (and causally foundational) goal, communication about things that exist independently in our mental states."[42] And drawing on a distinction noted by Jacques Maritain, a neo-Thomist, John Cahalan has further articulated the kind of existence—or subsistence—enjoyed by mind-dependent beings: "Entitative existence is what we call 'real' existence, when we contrast a real existent with something that is merely an object of imagination or conception. However, Maritain is saying that to be an object of consciousness is a real mode of existence, where 'real' is in contrast to what is apparent or fictitious but not genuine. Intentional existence is a secondary and diminished sense of 'existence,' but it is a genuine mode of existence, since the relation of awareness of an object could not be what it is were awareness not an existence of the object."[43] A fair minded reading suggests that these twin acknowledgments fit quite comfortably under the rubric of metaphysical realism.

Modest progress has also been achieved, it seems, in the philosophical sub-discipline of epistemology. Referencing the work of Jonathan Jacobs and John Zeis, Brian J. Shanley notes that analytic philosophy's epistemological assumptions are not inconsistent with a realist epistemology *per se*. The challenge for analytic philosophers—in the view of Jacobs and Zeis, at least—is where to locate the epistemology of the Aristotelian-Thomist Tradition "on the contemporary epistemological map. They argue that it is primarily externalist, non-evidentialist and natural, but that

---

42. Cahalan, "Wittgenstein as a Gateway to Analytical Thomism," 197.
43. Cahalan, "Wittgenstein as a Gateway to Analytical Thomism," 205.

it also incorporates elements of foundationalist, coherence, internalist and normative theories of cognition. This leads to a simple but important conclusion: "The standard dichotomies of the justification of belief do not apply to the Aristotelian-Thomistic theory of knowledge."[44] Again, this view—if endorsed—could signal something of a reproachment.

Less progress is evident with respect to moral behavior and ethics. As noted in chapter 1, meta-ethics, i.e., the logical meaning of ethical claims, is of interest to analytical philosophers. They have little to say, however, about the implications of particular ethical claims *per se*, which they tend to view as expressions of psychological states, emotive dispositions, or personal intuitions. That said, some analytic philosophers have described the contemporary version of virtue ethics as an extension of analytic philosophy, presumably because scholars now working in this sub-discipline employ rigorous analysis in their work. This is clearly a case of intellectual poaching, however, given virtue ethics's long association with the Aristotelian-Thomist Tradition.

That said, this dialogue is quite tentative in nature and one-sided, too. For their part, Thomists seem to question what—if anything—they might have to gain from this cross-pollination of ideas. And Brian J. Shanley, for his part, has expressed concern about "a tendency in analytic philosophy to domesticate Aquinas metaphysically so that he fits neatly into analytic categories."[45]

506. PERSONALISM

Personalism represents a rather broad movement that first emerged in France in the 1930s. It was deeply influenced by both phenomenalism and existential thought.[46] As noted by Thomas D. Williams, Karol Wojtyla—later Pope John Paul II—embraced Thomist personalism in response to "his experience of Hegelian totalitarianism in his native Poland, both the Nietzschean (National Socialism) and Marxist (Leninist Communism) stamp."[47] Thomist personalism has also been referred to as a kind or Christian humanism and as a distinctly Catholic philosophy.[48]

    44. Shanley, "On Analytical Thomism," 221.
    45. Shanley, "On Analytical Thomism," 220.
    46. Acosta and Reimers, *Karol Wojtyla's Personalist Philosophy*, 23.
    47. Williams, "What is Thomistic Personalism," 172.
    48. *Faith Connection*: Wojtyla, for example, pointed to the documents of the Second Vatican Council "in which Christ is presented as a revealer of the full mystery of man

Proponents of Thomist personalism locate the human person at the center of philosophical discourse. That said, today's proponents of personalism address certain concerns and employ language that would have been unfamiliar to Thomas Aquinas. Nevertheless, Aquinas's anchoring of Aristotle's moral framework to distinctive Christian values and intellectual commitments underwrites today's Thomist personalism.

The fullest explication of philosophical personalism is found in Karol Wojtyla's *Person and Act* (1959), a text in which the future pontiff tried to integrate the phenomenalism of Max Scheler, in particular, and existential philosophy, too, into the metaphysics, epistemology, and ethics of the perennial tradition. Wojtyla's second philosophical work, *Love and Responsibility* (1960), applied the several principles Wojtyla associated with personalism to the human relationship of love. And this latter work would provide a philosophical foundation for the development of Pope John Paul II's theology of the body, which unfolded in a series of lectures delivered between 1979 and 1984.

Key principles in Karol Wojtyla's version of personalism include the following.[49]

- The future pontiff affirmed the independent reality of the sensible world and our ability as reasoning beings to know the objective truth about things in the material world. Wojtyla thus positioned himself as a metaphysical and epistemological realist in the Aristotelian-Thomist Tradition.

- Wojtyla's human anthropology built on the hylomorphic theory—see section 212—endorsed by both Aristotle and Thomas Aquinas. As described in section 211, a human being is best understood as a "suppositum" or fully individuated and concreated substance comprised of both form and matter. Wojtyla thus rejected the mind-body dualism espoused by Enlightenment philosophers. This understanding underlies his theology of the body, in fact.

---

and of human dignity... The dignity proper to man, the dignity that is held out to him both as a gift and as something to be striven for, is inextricably bound up with the truth. Truthful thinking and truthful living are the indispensable and essential components of that dignity." See Wojtyla, *Sign of Contradiction*, 118–119.

49. This synopsis of Karol Wojtyla's personalist philosophy is largely drawn from an excellent analysis found in Miguel Acosta and Adrian J. Rimers, *Karol Wojtyla's Personalist Philosophy: Understanding Person & Act*, 2016.

- Wojtyla endorsed Thomas Aquinas's understanding of essence as that which distinguishes one species from another and as that which distinguishes one member of a species from every other member of that species. Nevertheless, he embraced the existential belief that each of us is responsible for forming ourselves into true persons. In Wojtyla's view, our essence is not entirely given to us as such.

- He also embraced existentialism's understanding of meaning as an inherent drive in all human beings. According to Miguel Acosta, the following questions were uppermost in Wojtyla's mind: "Who are we? Where do we come from? Why are we partially alike and partly different? Why am I a thinking being? What is going on inside of me? What will happen when I die?" According to Wojtyla, "these are the questions that every human being poses to himself throughout his life?"[50] These kinds of critical questions are addressed in key church documents as well.[51]

- Reflecting his appropriation of certain existential themes, Wojtyla argued that conscious choice, the dispositions and stances we adopt *vis-à-vis* the world, and—even more importantly—the actions we take on the basis of our conscious choices, i.e., our "operativity," reveal who we are to ourselves as we observe ourselves in action. This self-observation in action reflects the influence of phenomenalism in Wojtyla's work and aligns the future pontiff with the understanding of purposive choice or *prohaireses* espoused by Aristotle and Aquinas as the proper domain in which free will can be exercised. See section 406.

- According to Wojtyla, engaging in action and objectifying these actions in reflection results in two kinds of transcendence: "vertical

---

50. Acosta and Reimers, *Karol Wojtyla's Personalist Philosophy*, 110.

51. *Faith Connection*: This includes the Second Vatican Council's *Gaudium et Spes*: "In the face of modern developments there is a growing body of people who are asking the most fundamental of all questions or are glimpsing them with keener insight: What is humanity? What is the meaning of suffering, evil, death, which have not been eliminated by all of this progress? What is the purpose of these achievements, purchased at so high a price? What can people contribute to society? What can they expect from it? What happens after this earthly life has ended?" See Second Vatican Council, "Gaudium et Spes," no. 18. See also Second Vatican Council, "Nostra Aetate," no. 1. This view is reflected in the *Catechism of the Catholic Church* as well: "By love, God has revealed himself and given himself to man. He has thus provided the definitive, superabundant answer to the questions man asks himself about the meaning and purpose of his life." See *Catechism*, nos. 68. See also nos. 282 and 1006.

transcendence," i.e., self-determination which leads, in turn, to self-possession and self-dominion, and "horizontal transcendence," which orients us to the truth of the external world, thereby obviating both solipsism and the kind of "autonomous subjectivism" reflected, for instance, in Nietzsche's "will to power."

- Wojtyla described the experience of transcendence as "felicity," the sense of grateful fullness to which we are all called as human beings. This rarely used term is similar in meaning to the Greek word *eudaimonia*. In fact, *felicitatis* is the Latin equivalent of the Greek word *eudaimonia*. Wojtyla employed the term "felicity" rather than *eudaimonia*, however, in order to emphasis the role grace must necessarily play if we are to achieve our ultimate happiness.[52]

- The kinds of emotions celebrated by phenomenalists and romantics, too, are part and parcel of our makeup as human beings. Indeed, emotions are "deeply rooted" in our spiritual lives.[53] Wojtyla thus rejected the reduction of all knowledge to sense-experience and/or intellectual reasoning. That said, emotions need to be oriented to values that are objectively knowable. This reflects a realist understanding of moral behavior. Like the moral virtues, this "education of affectivity" is a kind of disciplined habituation.

- Wojtyla rejected the skepticism of the seventeenth and eighteenth century rationalists and the relativism of today's postmodernists, too. According to the future pontiff, we are not isolated in our own minds. Drawing on certain phenomenological insights, Wojtyla argued that it is natural for us to recognize others as persons and that this fact alone provides common ground on the basis of which we can discern collective action in the world.

- Finally, we can only know ourselves in the context of community. After all, community is the domain in which we act. With this in mind, Wojtyla affirmed the need to recognize and treat all other persons as "neighbors." This universal designation extends beyond Aristotle's more narrow understanding of friendship. See section 414. The two concepts bear a resemblance, nonetheless.

---

52. Acosta and Reimers, *Karol Wojtyla's Personalist Philosophy*, 178.

53. Like other phenomenologists, including Max Scheler, Wojtyla argued against the stoic teaching that the emotions should be suppressed. Affectivity is part and parcel of our identity as human beings.

507. VIRTUE ETHICS

As noted in section 412, Aristotle and Thomas Aquinas both affirmed our need to develop the moral virtues, e.g., prudence, justice, temperance, fortitude, etc., as ingrained habits. Following the disjunction in moral thinking described in section 411, various alternatives to the virtues have been advanced by secular philosophers over the last 400 years, including, most notably, positive laws promulgated by governments legitimated by social contracts of one sort or another, i.e., laws that are not anchored, as such, in the natural law or in any other overarching moral construct, including Immanuel Kant's concept of reasoned duty and the twin poles of pleasure and pain proposed by Jeremy Bentham. See section 413.

According to some who promote these kinds of prescriptive constructs, "prudence-based ethics, i.e., virtue ethics, seems much too likely to succumb to subjectivism."[54] This is the fault line, in fact, that separates the moral thinking of the Aristotelian-Thomist Tradition from the formulaic moral schemes advanced in the seventeenth and eighteenth centuries, in particular. Virtue ethics is oriented to the formation of individuals. It holds that that which is moral can be known, and it is confident that moral behavior is possible. Again, Aristotle and Thomas Aquinas were both optimists in this regard.

Following centuries of disinterest, virtue ethics has made something of a comeback over the course of the last 40 years. Led by Alasdair MacIntyre, Philippa Foot, Deirdra N. McCloskey, and others, virtue ethics is experiencing a revival of sorts. Still, the resurgence of virtue ethics faces formidable opposition in the academy. Postmodernists, in particular, are skeptical of virtue ethics. In their view, the traditional virtues can reinforce certain power structures that are deeply embedded in our culture.

508. CATHOLIC SOCIAL TEACHING

We would be remiss in failing to note the philosophical underpinnings of Catholic social teaching, which has achieved increasing prominence over the course of the last century. Today's expression of this tradition was launched in 1891 in an encyclical written by Pope Leo XIII, *Rerum Novarum* (*Of New Things*), which addressed a number of social problems caused by the industrial revolution and the political upheavals that had

---

54. Kerr, *After Aquinas*, 123.

swept across Europe in the latter half of the nineteenth century. Promulgated some 40 years before the labor reforms of the New Deal, *Rerum Novarum* affirmed the God-given dignity of workers and their families and championed the rights of workers.[55] *Rerum Novarum* spawned a series of social justice encyclicals over the course of the next century, each of which built on the letters that had preceded it. Over time, they codified a coherent, comprehensive, and philosophically-tethered understanding of social justice. In the 55 years since the close of the Second Vatican Council, the several themes developed in these encyclicals have been gathered under seven broad headings: the life and dignity of the human person; the call to family, community, and participation; rights and responsibilities; the preferential option for the poor; the dignity and rights of workers; solidarity; and care for God's creation.[56]

Of these several principles, the first stands out: the affirmation of the sacredness of life and the inherent dignity of the human person. This seminal teaching is grounded in Scripture, of course. Thomas Aquinas thus cited Genesis 1:26 in insisting on the inviolability of human dignity: "Let us make man in our own image and likeness." He asserted, too, the universal destination of all goods in God. These twin foci explain why human flourishing, i.e., *eudaimonia* or happiness, is privileged over property rights in Thomist thought and in Catholic social teaching.

With respect to epistemology, the apprehension-judgment-reasoning triad espoused by Thomas Aquinas[57] bears a strong resemblance to the see-judge-act method associated with theological reflection. See appendix 2.

---

55. *Faith Connection*: It is difficult to overestimate what a sea change this document represents. At the Second Vatican Council, the overall trajectory of *Rerum Novarum* and the social justice encyclicals that followed it was explicitly embraced. In lengthy sessions convened in 1962, 1963, 1964, and 1965, the council fathers abandoned the church's centuries-long opposition to modernity and democracy. To use Pope John XXIII's celebrated terms for this remarkable turnabout, the church "opened its windows to the world," i.e., *aggiornamento*, and it did so by "returning to the sources," i.e., *ressourcement*, most notably, the patrimony of the Jewish and Christian Scriptures and the work of the early church fathers. Catholic bishops and scholars were thus invited to reclaim the powerful prophetic voice of the Jewish Scriptures and the prophetic voice of Jesus as well.

56. Pontifical Council for Justice and Peace, *Compendium*.

57. Cotter, *An Introduction to Catholic Philosophy*, 273.

Appendix 1

Reflection Questions

CHAPTER 1: INTRODUCTION TO PHILOSOPHY IN THE ARISTOTELIAN-THOMIST TRADITION

1. What is philosophy?
2. What are the most important subdisciplines in philosophy? How are they related?
3. How does the Catholic Church understand philosophy and its relationship with theology?
4. Has this always been so?
5. What is realism?
6. What do we mean when we refer to the "Aristotelian-Thomist Tradition"?
7. Can history and culture explain certain developments in philosophy? What might this mean for us today?
8. What is the relationship between myth and philosophy?
9. What concerns were foremost in the minds of the presocratics?
10. What do we mean when we refer to the "golden age" of Greek philosophy?
11. What distinguished Socrates's philosophy from Plato's and Plato's philosophy from Aristotle's?

12. What explains the lack of original philosophical work in the waning days of the Roman Empire?
13. What distinguished medieval philosophy from the various philosophies of the ancients?
14. What accounts for the decline of the Aristotelian-Thomist Tradition in the early modern period?
15. Why is Renaissance philosophy important?
16. How did Enlightenment philosophy differ from medieval philosophy?
17. In what sense, are we all "children of the Enlightenment"?
18. How would you describe the various philosophies of the nineteenth century, i.e., their key interests, their worldview, etc.?
19. What philosophies achieved prominence in the nineteenth century?
20. How would you describe the various philosophies of the twentieth century, i.e., their key interests, their worldview, etc.?
21. What philosophies achieved prominence in the twentieth century?
22. What accounts for the revival of Thomist thought in the late nineteenth century?

CHAPTER 2: METAPHYSICS

1. What is metaphysics?
2. What are its key concerns?
3. What do we mean when we refer to metaphysical realism?
4. What views does the Catholic Church harbor with respect to metaphysical realism?
5. How would you describe other perspectives that are opposed to metaphysical realism? What are the pros and cons of these other views?
6. What does the Aristotelian-Thomist Tradition mean when it refers to "existence"?
7. How does our understanding of "existence" inform our understanding of God?
8. What is "being"?

9. How should we distinguish between "nonbeing" and "potential being"?
10. What do we mean when we refer to "mind-dependent beings"? In what sense are they "real"?
11. Why is the concept of "universals" problematic in epistemology?
12. Why is the concept of "substance" important in metaphysics? How does the metaphysical concept of "substance" relate to the "things" we encounter in the sensible world?
13. What do "form" and "matter" refer to in the Aristotelian-Thomist Tradition?
14. How do "form" and "matter" relate to our understanding of the soul?
15. What do we mean when we refer to a "suppositum"?
16. How should we distinguish between the concepts of "essence" and "nature"? What do they have to do with "being"?
17. What do we mean when we refer to "accidents" in the Aristotelian-Thomist Tradition?
18. What do we mean when we refer to "predicamentals"?
19. What do we mean when we refer to "transcendental properties"?
20. In what sense does the Aristotelian-Thomist Tradition continue to wrestle with the same questions with which the presocratics wrestled?
21. What explains the decline in interest in metaphysics in the early modern period?
22. What explains the renewed interest in metaphysics in the late nineteenth century?
23. What implications does the Aristotelian-Thomist Tradition hold for our faith commitments as Catholic Christians?

CHAPTER 3: EPISTEMOLOGY

1. What is epistemology?
2. What are its key concerns?

3. What do we mean when we refer to epistemological realism?
4. What views does the Catholic Church harbor with respect to epistemological realism?
5. How would you describe other perspectives that stand in opposition to epistemological realism?
6. What are the pros and cons of these other views?
7. What is knowledge? How is knowledge related to truth?
8. How do different epistemologies account for the acquisition of knowledge?
9. What is the chief impediment to the acquisition of knowledge according to critics of epistemological realism? How do realists in the Aristotelian-Thomist Tradition respond to these criticisms?
10. What is skepticism? Is it a serious problem in philosophy?
11. How should we distinguish between and among *a posteriori* truths, *a priori* truths, and *synthetic a priori* truths?
12. What do we mean when we refer to "certitude"?
13. What kinds of evidence do epistemological realists privilege? Do you agree with their view in this regard?
14. What methods of investigation are privileged by epistemological realists?
15. How would you describe the epistemology promoted by Plato, e.g., his understanding of what can be known, the kinds of truths to which he subscribed, the kinds of impediments with which he had to contend, the kinds of evidence he privileged, and his preferred methods of investigation?
16. How would you describe the epistemology promoted by the rationalists of the seventeenth and eighteenth centuries, e.g., their understanding of what can be known, the kinds of truths to which they subscribed, the kinds of impediments with which they had to contend, the kinds of evidence they privileged, and their preferred methods of investigation?
17. How would you describe the epistemology promoted by the empiricists of the seventeenth and eighteenth centuries, e.g., their understanding of what can be known, the kinds of truths to which

they subscribed, the kinds of impediments with which they had to contend, the kinds of evidence they privileged, and their preferred methods of investigation?

18. How would you describe Immanuel Kant's epistemology, e.g., his understanding of what can be known, the kinds of truths to which he subscribed, the kinds of impediments with which he had to contend, the kinds of evidence he privileged, and his preferred methods of investigation?

19. What is a proposition? What role do propositions play in philosophical inquiry?

20. What role do the predicamentals play in the development of propositions?

21. Are the predicamentals the only kind of "truth claims" that are relevant in epistemology?

22. What epistemologies do you think are most valued in our culture?

23. What implications do these alternative epistemologies hold for our faith?

CHAPTER 4: ETHICS, MORALITY, AND JUSTICE

1. What do we mean when we refer to an "articulated moral framework"?
2. What do we mean when we refer to the "good" or the "good life"?
3. What do we mean when we refer to the "moral" or "moral behavior"?
4. What do we mean when we refer to the "just" or to "justice"?
5. What is ethical realism?
6. What are the key concerns of ethical realists?
7. How do their views differ from other ethical and moral perspectives?
8. What views does the Catholic Church harbor with respect to ethical and moral realism?
9. How can we understand or justify the concept of "free will"?
10. How does the Aristotelian-Thomist Tradition understand human nature?

11. How do other ethical and moral systems understand human nature?
12. How does the Aristotelian-Thomist Tradition understand the "good" or the "good life"?
13. How do other ethical and moral systems understand the "good" or the "good life"?
14. How does the Aristotelian-Thomist Tradition understand moral behavior?
15. How do other ethical and moral systems understand moral behavior?
16. How does the Aristotelian-Thomist Tradition understand the "just" or "justice"?
17. How do other ethical and moral systems understand the "just" or "justice"?
18. How would you describe the moral thinking embedded in social contract theory?
19. How would you describe the moral thinking embedded in utilitarian thought?
20. How would you describe the moral thinking embedded in libertarianism?
21. How would you describe the moral thinking embedded in pragmatism?
22. In your view, is a common understanding of the "good," the "moral," and the "just" now possible in our world?
23. What implications does this hold for Christians?
24. What implications does it hold for ministry?

CHAPTER 5: MORE RECENT EXPRESSIONS OF THOMISM

1. What happened to Thomism after Thomas Aquinas?
2. What is neo-Thomism and what are its primary concerns?
3. What explains the sudden emergence of neo-Thomism at the end of the nineteenth century?

4. What is transcendental Thomism?
5. Who are its primary "conversation partners"?
6. What are its pros and cons? In your view, does transcendental Thomism have merit?
7. What is existential Thomism?
8. Who are its primary "conversation partners"?
9. What are its pros and cons? In your view, does existential Thomism have merit?
10. What is analytic Thomism?
11. Who are its primary "conversation partners"?
12. What are its pros and cons? In your view, does analytic Thomism have merit?
13. What is personalism?
14. Who are its primary "conversation partners"?
15. What are its most important assumptions?
16. What are its pros and cons? In your view, does personalism have merit?
17. What is virtue ethics?
18. How does it reflect the ethical and moral teachings associated with the Aristotelian-Thomist Tradition?
19. What accounts for the resurgence of virtue ethics in contemporary moral and ethical thinking?
20. What are its pros and cons? In your view, does virtue ethics have merit?
21. How would you describe Catholic social teaching?
22. How is it related to the Aristotelian-Thomist Tradition?

Appendix 2

Methods

It is helpful to have some sense of the methods developed and employed by philosophers over the centuries. That said, philosophers have rarely agreed about what constitutes a legitimate or useful method or line of argument in any given instance. Brief summaries of some of the more notably methods, strategies, and techniques employed by philosophers over time are provided here. These descriptions are based—for the most part—on the well-respected *Oxford Companion to Philosophy*. The online *Stanford Encyclopedia of Philosophy* can be a useful reference as well.

- Abduction: Abductive reasoning can be differentiated from deductive and inductive reasoning. Abduction "explains the available evidence."[1] It is thought to approximate the truth without asserting certainty or probability.

- Abstraction: In abstracting from any particular x, a philosophy isolates predicamentals that a set of x's hold in common. See section 215.

- Analogy: Analogies draw on similarities involving two items of interest in order to assert a truth claim about one of them. In Plato's famous analogy of the cave, the image of moving shadows projected on a wall is used to describe the nature of the ethereal Forms that provided a foundation for Plato's strong realism.

---

1. Hookway, "Abduction," 1.

Thomas Aquinas's descriptions of God in the first part of his *Summa Theologica* draw on analogies, most notably, to human beings who, "were made in the image and likeness of God," and to the world as we experience it as human beings. According to Fergus Kerr, "though we never mean anything of God and ourselves in exactly the same sense, it does not follow that what we say is simply ambiguous. There is a way we use words which is neither univocal nor equivocal. We often speak analogically. Thomas Aquinas does not seem to think there is anything remarkable about this, or that it requires any explanation in terms of a 'theory' of analogy. Using words analogically, he clearly thinks, is a perfectly familiar procedure."[2] This view reflects, in fact, the church's understanding of the analogic language we use in referencing God.[3]

- Analytic Reasoning: In the analytic philosophies of the nineteenth and twentieth centuries, analysis pertains to the breaking down of referential words and phrases in propositions into their most basic units so that they can be individually mapped against known phenomena or established truths. See section 114.

- Anamnesis: In Plato's theory of recollection, *anamnesis* is a contemplative method used to recall the ethereal Forms with which he believed we were acquainted before our births.[4] See section 305.

- Apperception: A particular kind of introspection posited by Gottfried Leibniz, apperception is unconscious inner awareness.

---

2. Kerr, *After Aquinas*, 60.

3. *Faith Connection*: As noted in the *Catechism of the Catholic Church*, "since our knowledge of God is limited, our language about him is equally so. We can name God only by taking creatures as our starting point, and in accordance with our limited human ways of knowing and thinking." See *Catechism of the Catholic Church*, no. 40. This approach to understanding God is sometimes referred to as "negative theology." "Thomas thinks that the middle way [between natural theology and fideism] is mandated by Scripture—Romans 1:20: 'the hidden things of God can be clearly understood from the things that He has made.'" See Kerr, *After Aquinas*, 60.

4. *Faith Connection*: In a very different sense, the term of "*anamnesis*" has been adopted by the church as a way of explaining the real presence of the Risen Christ in the Eucharist and his significance in salvation history. According to the Catechism of the Catholic Church, "in all the Eucharistic prayers, we find after the words of institution a prayer called the *anamnesis* or memorial . . . In the liturgical celebration of these events," i.e., the passion, death, and resurrection of Jesus, "they become in a certain way present and real." Indeed, they become a memory so powerful that they make present that which is remembered. See *Catechism*, nos. 1353 and 1364.

"Bracketing" is recommended by phenomenalists as a way to isolate opaque perceptions of this kind in order to bring them into consciousness.

- Argument: In everyday use, the word "argument" pertains to quarrels. In philosophy, an argument refers, instead, to "a complex consisting of a set of propositions—called premises—and a conclusion . . ."[5] Types of arguments include *deductively-based arguments*; *inductively-based arguments*; *arguments from signs*, i.e., a conclusion that some feature of a situation is present based on some other observed feature that generally indicates its presence; *argument from utility or usefulness*; *arguments from expert opinion*; *arguments from ethos*, i.e., a proposition advanced by a respected source; *argumentum ad ignorantia*, i.e., an assertion of truth based on its not having been disproven; *argumentum ad populum*, i.e., an appeal to popular opinion; and *argumentum ad misericordiam*, i.e., an appeal to pity,[6] the latter three of which are generally recognized as fallacies.

- Axiom: Axioms are propositions that are assumed to be true in a school of thought, in an academic discipline, or within a community of practice.

- Bootstrapping: In philosophy, the informal term "bootstrapping" is used to describe a line of reasoning that builds on an established premise and proceeds without the benefit of further input, evidence, or support.

- Bracketing: This technique is associated, in particular, with the phenomenalism of Edmund Husserl. It involves the conscious distillation or isolation of the subjective apprehension of an encounter with a phenomenon, e.g., a thing in the world, a relationship, an emotion, etc., from any background knowledge, e.g., scientific, conceptual, traditional, cultural, contextual, etc., with which it could be associated so that it can be subjected to introspective analysis. See section 114.

- Brain in a Vat: This often-used conjecture that we are nothing more than brains in vats is posited by Cartesians and other rationalists to call into question the reliability of all that we take for granted in our daily lives. See section 312.

---

5. Kirwan, "Argument," 48.
6. Walton, "Types of Arguments," 48–49.

- Brute Facts: This term is used in philosophy to describe the terminus of a line of argument for which no further explanation or cause can or could be provided or should be required.

- Casuistry: Casuistry is a kind of moral reasoning that examines the extent to which any given act of conscience is consistent with or contrary to particular stipulations in the positive or natural law. Because they tend to be largely case-based, legal and medical ethics often employ casuistic reasoning. That said, casuistry represents a controversial type of reasoning in the academic discipline of philosophy.

- Common Sense: In realism, our everyday understanding of the sensible world, relationships, ourselves, and our obligations in the world is highly valued as a starting point for philosophical reasoning. The potential of common sense to mislead us tends to be asserted more forthrightly by certain philosophers, including rationalists, logical positivists, and postmodernists.

- Counterfactuals: "A counterfactual is a 'conditional' whose antecedent is known to be false."[7]

- Deconstruction: An analytic technique associated with Jacques Derrida and other postmodernists, deconstruction is used to analyze a circumstance of interest in the cultural or social environment so that certain unacknowledged ideologies and inequities that may underlie it or may be associated with it can be named and then resisted or confronted.

- Deduction: A deduction is a type of argument in which a conclusion is drawn from one or more premises. Formally described by Aristotle, deductions have long been valued in philosophy because they purport to demonstrate certainty.

- Defeasibility: Defeasibility addresses the extent to which a truth claim is susceptible to defeat, i.e., nullification, termination, or substantial revision.

- Definition or the Clarification of Terms: Since Aristotle, the specification of terms has proven essential in philosophical discourse. That said, some "definitions 'dubbed' persuasive may generally purport

---

7. MacIntosh, "Counterfactuals," 169.

to describe the true or 'real' existing meaning of a term while in fact stipulating a particular or altered use."⁸

- Demonstration: This generic term pertains to a proof for a particular proposition or truth claim.

- Deontological Argument: In moral reasoning, a deontological argument is one that relies solely on a pre-established standard of judgment. Any outcomes that could possibly accrue play no role in making a decision or taking an action on deontological grounds.

- Dialectic: In a general sense, the term "dialectic" or *elenchus* pertains to any form of reasoning that proceeds through the skillful use of questions and answers in order to reveal inconsistencies and other deficiencies in thinking. "By dialectic, Plato understands a process of rational argument which is a development from the dialogue of the Socratic interrogation. Beginning from some proposition which has been advanced for consideration, one ascends in one's search for justifications up a deductive ladder until one reaches the indubitable certainties of the Forms."⁹ The Socratic method and the *quodlibetical* disputations of the scholastics are both examples of the dialectic method. In the nineteenth century, G. W. F. Hegel posited a dialectic process involving the interplay of thesis, antithesis, and synthesis over time. Karl Marx would later employ this threefold process in his materialist interpretation of history.

- Doctrine of Double Effect: This principle is often evoked in ethical reasoning about particular cases. As explained by Nicolas Dent, "in many actions, we may identify the central, directly intended goal or objective for the principal sake of which the action is selected and done. However, there will normally also be side effects for the process of achieving that objective or of its accomplishment, which may be known prior to taking the action. The doctrine of double effect maintains that it may be permissible to perform a good act with the knowledge that bad consequence will ensue, but that it is always wrong intentionally to do a bad act for the sake of good consequences that will ensue."¹⁰

---

8. Stevenson, "Definition," 181–182.
9. MacIntyre, *A Short History of Ethics*, 42.
10. Dent, "Double Effect," 204–205.

- Doubt: Methodological doubt pertains to a disciplined reservation concerning the truth of any given proposition until sufficient proof has been marshaled.

- Eidetic Reflection: A method associated with Edmund Husserl's version of phenomenalism, eidetic reflection involves a shift in our focus or attention away from a particular instance of an entity to its abstract properties or essence. See section 114.

- Existential Recollection: This term of art pertains to the individual's responsibility to transcend the contingency of his or her life so that an authentic experience of meaning can be created or discovered. Existential reflection is thought to involve a two-stage process. In the first stage, "I become capable of taking up my position in regard to my life . . . In the second, I recollect in the measure of which recollection can be self-conscious."[11] See section 504.

- Explanation: In a general sense, an explanation is a convincing or compelling account for the truth of a proposition or truth claim.

- Fallacies: Argumentation fallacies are commonly recognized errors in reasoning, for instance: *ad hominem attacks*, i.e., attacking the individual instead of the argument; *appeals to pity*, i.e., urging the hearer to accept the argument based upon an appeal to emotions, sympathy, etc.; *appeals to the popular*, i.e., urging the hearer to accept a position because a majority of people hold to it; *appeals to tradition*, i.e., encouraging someone to accept something because it has been done or believed for a long time; *begging the question*, i.e., assuming the truth of a proposition you are trying to prove; *faulty assertions of cause and effect*, i.e., assuming that a presumed effect is related to a particular cause because the events occurred in proximity to each another in space and/or time; *unjustified divisions*, i.e., assuming that what is true of the whole is true for the parts; *equivocations*, i.e., using the same term in an argument in different places even though the meanings implied differ; *false dilemmas*, i.e., giving only two choices even though more options are available; *genetic fallacies*, i.e., attempting to endorse or disqualify a claim because of the origin or because of irrelevant aspects of the claim's history; *guilt by association*, i.e., rejecting an argument or claim because the person who is proposing it likes someone who is disliked by another

---

11. Marcel, "Ontological Mystery," 348.

person; *circular reasoning*, i.e., the use of a premise in a syllogism that is the equivalent of the syllogism's conclusion; *non-sequiturs*, i.e., a conclusion that does not follow logically from a premise; *poisoning the well*, i.e., presenting negative information about a person before he or she speaks in order to discredit the person's argument; *red herrings*, i.e., introducing a topic not related to the subject at hand; *special pleadings* or the use of double standards, i.e., applying a standard in one situation that is different from a standard applied in a comparable situation; *straw man arguments*, i.e., producing an argument about a weaker representation of the truth and attacking it; and *category mistakes*, i.e., attributing a property to something that could not possibly have that property.

- Hermeneutics: This term of art invokes the image of the Greek god Hermes who carried messages from one god to another. Hermeneutics pertains to the interpretation of texts and other kinds of artifacts. See section 114.

- Heuristic: A heuristic is a "rule of thumb" that is used in deciding a question or in making a judgment. A heuristic can be understood as a kind of informal axiom that is adhered to and invoked by members of particular communities in familiar circumstances.

- Hypothesis: According to Larry Laudan, a hypothesis is a "hunch, speculation, or conjecture proposed as a possible solution to a problem and requiring further investigation of its acceptability by argument or observation and experiment."[12]

- Imagination: Although imagination is often derided as a poor substitute for reasoning, some philosophers "assign it to a central role in explaining the mind's ability to represent any reality,"[13] that is, to its capacity to bring to mind that which is not taken to exist in space and time.

- Inductive Reasoning: Inductive reasoning draws on a study of two or more particulars in advancing a truth claim about a class of particulars. Although induction is generally held in high esteem by philosophers and scientists, too, the rationalists of the seventeenth and eighteenth centuries questioned its validity since causation involving future events should not be assumed and because of the

---

12. Laudan, "Hypothesis," 385.
13. Martin, "Imagination," 395.

near impossibility of testing all occurrences of most events in nature. Statistical analysis is a particularly powerful tool in advancing inductive proofs. See section 316.

- Inference: To infer is to draw a conclusion from a proof or from data. Three types of inference are employed in philosophical reasoning. "In deductive theories, an inference is justified if it conforms to a principle of logic or to an argument validated by the principles of logic . . . Inductive inferences are those that project beyond the known data . . . And abduction is recognized in two varieties. In one sense, it is inference to the 'best explanation,' which is a means of justifying the postulation of unobservable phenomena on the strength of explanations they afford of observable phenomena. In its other variety, abduction is the process of forming generic beliefs from known data."[14]

- Inner Sense: John Locke and Immanuel Kant both referred to our "inner sense" as a kind of introspection in which we apprehend the contents of our thinking in a way that is analogous to our perception of things in the external world.

- Intuition: Some Enlightenment philosophers argued that intuition is analogous to sense perception. It pertains to truths we know that cannot be accessed by way of our five physical senses, including certain abstract concepts such as numbers, tautological claims, and—according to Immanuel Kant—certain concepts that are innate to the structures of our minds, including causation and time. See section 305.

- Judgment: Judgment can be understood as an assertion of truth that may or may not be true or constitute true knowledge. See section 309.

- Language: The analysis of language has long been of interest to philosophers. Aristotle, in particular, devoted a great deal of attention to the precise meaning of terms used in everyday speech. More recently, the logical positivists of the nineteenth century hoped to separate propositions pertaining to material things from the kinds of truth claims they believed to be nonsensical. For their part, the analytic philosophers of the twentieth century hoped to reduce the meaning of propositions to logical formulae for analysis. This included Frenge, Russell, and the early Wittgenstein. Others,

14. White, "Inference," 407.

including the later Wittgenstein, constructivists, and postmodernists, have since tended to analyze language from the perspectives of the cultural contexts and power structures in which the use of language is embedded.

- Legal Reasoning: Legal reasoning makes use of positive law and—in some instances—the natural law. Casuistic reasoning is a type of legal reasoning.

- Logic: Logic lies at the heart of philosophical reasoning and is considered a distinct sub-discipline within the academic discipline of philosophy. Aristotle was the first to articulate a fully developed system of logic. Peter Abelard developed his own treatise on logic, which was widely used in the West over the course of the Middle Ages. In the Modern Era, Gottfried Leibniz aspired to the development of a universal language that could be employed with mathematical precision, a task that was taken up by the analytic philosophers of the twentieth century.

    Two principles, in particular, provide a foundation for Aristotelian logic and for all subsequent systems of logic, too: the principle of non-contradiction and the principle of sufficient reason. Both are believed to be self-evident. The principle of non-contradiction holds that something cannot be and not-be in the same way at the same time. And the principle of sufficient reason holds that there is a knowable cause for every effect in nature.

    Systems of logic can be deployed in different ways and in different contexts. Deontic logic, for instance, pertains specifically to propositions or truth claims involving "obligations, permissions, prohibition, moral commitments, and other normative matters."[15] And modal logic distinguishes that which must be true, e.g., $2 + 2 = 4$, from contingent truths.

- Models: Models are physical or conceptual representations of structures, processes, and theories that are used to formally display the interrelationships of their component parts. Models can streamline analysis by reducing the number of factors or variables presented for consideration or critique.

- Ockham's Razor or the Principle of Parsimony: According to Marilyn McCord Adams, Ockham's razor, is a "methodological principle

---

15. Kuhn, "Deontic Logic," 186.

dictating a bias toward simplicity in theory construction, where the parameters of simplicity vary from the kinds of entities to the number of presupposed axioms to characteristics of curves drawn between data points. Although noted by Aristotle, the principle of parsimony became associated in time with William of Ockham because it captures the spirit of his philosophical conclusions."[16] See section 205.

- Other Disciplinary Fields: More so than some other fields of inquiry, philosophy has a rich history of relying on insights drawn from other academic disciplines for new perspectives. This includes mathematics, physics, biology, history, economics, psychology, linguistics, social anthropology, computer science, and—more recently—the emerging science of artificial intelligence.[17]

- Possible Worlds: "Possible worlds" are used by philosophers as a way to distinguish that which is necessarily true from that which is merely contingent. Possible worlds provide a lens through which we can explore possibilities that may not have manifested in our own world due to certain contingencies. "Possibly p' is thus rendered "there is a world in which p', and necessarily p' becomes 'At all worlds, p'. Modality is explained away!"[18] That said, the concept of "possible worlds" is a controversial one in the academic discipline of philosophy. Although most metaphysicians are content to treat possible worlds as a kind of thought experiment, others, drawing on multiverse theory, argue that all possible worlds are real, in fact, albeit separated from us in space and time.

- Ratiocination: This particular type of reasoning was posited by Thomas Aquinas. It involves the "direct, non-inferential apprehension of truth possessed by God and angels."[19] This kind of knowledge can only be acquired by way of revelation or contemplation.

- Reduction: A philosophical reduction asserts that all that needs to be said about any given event or phenomenon is entirely explainable in terms of a single concept, variable, or context. Three types of reduction are generally acknowledged. "*Ontological reductionism*

16. Adams, "Ockham's Razor," 663.
17. Williamson, *Philosophical Method*, 100–113.
18. Crane, "Possible Worlds," 707.
19. Mele, "Ratiocination," 741.

refers to the belief that the whole of reality consists of a minimal number of entities or substances . . . *Methodological reductionism* claims that, in science, 'small is beautiful.' Thus the best scientific strategy is always to attempt explanation in terms of ever more minute entities . . . And *theory reductionism* raises the question of the relation between successive theories in a field, as between Newton's theory and that of Einstein."[20] The monistic claim, for instance, that all thinking can be reduced to physical or material phenomena is an example of ontological reduction and so, too, the assertion that there is no such thing as free will since every action we take as human beings is fully determined.

- Regressive Argumentation: In a regressive argument "a stronger conclusion must be (determined to be true) if an indubitable fact about experience is to be possible."[21] René Descartes's *cogito, ergo sum*, i.e., "I think, therefore I am," is an example of a regressive argument. Existence is deemed a "stronger conclusion" than thinking *per se*.

- Reasoning: As described by Christopher Kirwan, reasoning is a "mental state or state of holding reasons for or against believing something or doing (or choosing or aiming at) something or feeling somehow. The word 'reasoning' describes two associated *processes*: searching for such reasons (often co-operatively), and giving them when you or somebody else has found them. A third process, gaining understanding of a reason that somebody else has given, is similar."[22]

- Rhetoric: Much derided in the history of philosophy, rhetoric is the art of crafting compelling arguments in a speech. Whereas truth is the goal of philosophical inquiry, winning is the objective in rhetoric.

- Scientific Method: The now well-developed process of hypothesis formation and subsequent testing that relies on induction and employs scientific tools and techniques was first described by Francis Bacon. See section 316.

- Scientism: This pejorative terms is applied to reasoning that displays any one or more of three assumptions: "that the sciences are more important than the arts for an understanding of the world in which

20. Ruse, "Reductionism," 750–751.
21. Taylor, "Transcendental Arguments," 472.
22. Kirwan, "Reasoning," 748.

we live, or, even, all we need to understand it; that only a scientific methodology is intellectually acceptable; therefore, if the arts are to be a genuine part of human knowledge, they must adopt it; and that philosophical problems are scientific problems and should only be dealt with as such."[23]

- See-Judge-Act: Some trace the origins of this method to the Second Vatican Council. Pope John XXIII's belief that the church needed to better "read the signs of the times" (Matthew 24) found expression in the see-judge-act method recommended by Bernard Lonergan and Belgian Cardinal Joseph Cardijn (1882–1967). In the context of theological reflection, "seeing" involves seeing, hearing, and experiencing the lived reality of an individual or a community. This kind of analysis requires both social data and insights, on the one hand, and theological and religious insights, on the other. "Judging" refers to an analysis of the situation under investigation and the formulation of an informed judgment. Finally, "acting" requires planning and the execution of concrete steps aimed at transforming the social structures determined to have contributed to the phenomenon under investigation.

- Semiotics: Although not addressed in this text, semantics represents an important extension in philosophy's "linguistic turn" in the late twentieth century and in the twenty-first century. As noted by C. W. Morris, "the general study of signs (semiotics) can be divided into three branches. These are syntactics, or the study of the relation of signs to other signs; semantics, or the study of the relation of sign to the things they represent; and pragmatics, or the study of the relation of signs to their users."[24]

- Set theory: Drawn from mathematics, set theory plays an important role in metaphysical discourse. It is advanced as an alternative to the understanding of universals in the Aristotelian-Thomist Tradition. Set theory is a key concept in logic as well.

- Slippery Slope: This term of art is often used in moral reasoning to describe "a practice that may be unobjectionable in one type of case,

---

23. Noordhof, "Scientism," 814.
24. Lowe, "Semantics," 820.

- if it is once permitted, but which will inevitably be extended to other more dubious cases."[25]
- Stochastic Process: This term pertains to statistical analyses involving multiple trials that produce probabilistic outcomes.
- Stories and Narrative Accounts: In the twentieth and twenty-first centuries, an increasing number of philosophers—including, most notably, Charles Taylor and Alasdair MacIntryre—have come to understand human beings—using MacIntyre's term—as "story-telling animals." We make sense of our lives in the stories we tell of ourselves and the communities of which we are members. According to MacIntyre, life can be understood as a "narrative quest" in which we craft our own unique stories, stories that are invariably oriented to the experience of meaning. "I am the subject of a history that is my own and no one else's, that has its own peculiar meaning. When someone complains—as do some of those who attempt to commit suicide—that his or her life is meaningless, he or she is often and perhaps characteristically complaining that the narrative of their life has become unintelligible to them, that it lacks any point, any movement toward a climax or a telos."[26] Servais Pinckaers concurred using language that is explicitly Christian: "The problem of life's meaning and goal is primordial . . . Since the question of life's goal or ultimate end is so important, we might define Christian ethics as the science that teaches us the meaning of life. It shows us the supreme end toward which all our actions should be directed, the end that gives them meaning, value, and wholeness."[27]
- Syllogisms: Aristotle commended syllogisms as the ideal form of deductive argumentation. A syllogism is an inference made up of three propositions, in a perfect syllogism, two premises and one conclusion. Three terms are distributed in the three propositions as follows: a middle term is common to the two premises, the second term is common to the conclusion and one of the premises, and the third term is common to the conclusion and the other premise. Consider the classic syllogism: "All men are mortal; Greeks are men; therefore, Greeks are mortal." The first two phrases are premises and the third is the conclusion the follows from them. The middle term,

---

25. Warnock, "Slippery Slope," 828.
26. MacIntyre, *After Virtue*, 217.
27. Pinckaers, *The Sources of Christian Ethics*, 23.

which is common to the two premises, is "men." The second term, which is common to the first premise and the conclusion, is "mortal." And the third term, which is common to the second premise and the conclusion, is "Greeks." An imperfect syllogism involves more than two premises. Additional premises are sometimes added in dialectic discourse as a question is refined—sometime over and over again—in the iterative search for truth. An "enthymeme" is a syllogism in which one or more premises are unspecified.

Thomas Aquinas and others in the Aristotelian-Thomist Tradition have offered a number of syllogisms to prove God's existence philosophically, including the following.

- "God is a being which has every perfection. (This is true as a matter of definition.) Existence is a perfection. Hence God exists.

- "I conceive of a being than which no greater can be conceived. If a being than which no greater can be conceived does not exist, then I can conceive of a being greater than a being than which no greater can be conceived—namely, a being than which no greater can be conceived that exists. I cannot conceive of a being greater than a being than which no greater can be conceived. Hence, a being than which no greater can be conceived exists.

- "It is possible that God exists. God is not a contingent being, i.e., either it is not possible that God exists, or it is necessary that God exists. Hence, it is necessary that God exists. Hence, God exists.

- "The word 'God' has a meaning that is revealed in religious experience. The word 'God' has a meaning only if God exists. Hence, God exists.

- "I exist. Therefore something exists. Whenever a bunch of things exist, their mereological sum also exists. Therefore the sum of all things exists. Therefore God—the sum of all things—exists.

- "Say that a God-property is a property that is possessed by God in all and only those worlds in which God exists. Not all properties are God properties. Any property entailed by a collection of God-properties is itself a God-property. The

God-properties include necessary existence, necessary omnipotence, necessary omniscience, and necessary perfect goodness. Hence, there is a necessarily existent, necessarily omnipotent, necessarily omniscient, and necessarily perfectly good being (namely, God)."[28]

- Tautology: A tautology is a kind of argument or proposition that has the form: A = A. See section 305.

- Teleological Argument: In moral reasoning, a teleological argument is one that relies solely on the outcome(s) that accrue from a decision that is adopted or an action that is taken. See section 415.

- Testimony: Although testimony is often relied upon in our everyday lives, it is generally suspect in philosophical reasoning. See section 313.

- Thought experiments: Thought experiments have played an important role in the history of philosophy. In a thought experiment, a situation is described. In subsequent iterations, additional conditions or constraints are added in order to isolate the essential matter of concern. These conditions or constraints do not need to exist or even be possible in the real world. Descartes's "evil demon" and the postulation of "possible worlds" are examples of conditions and constraints imposed in thought experiments. Famous thought experiments include Theseus's Ship, the Prisoner's Dilemma, the Trolley Car, and Schrodinger's Cat.

- Utility: Utility is a measure of the pragmatic usefulness of an idea, a decision, or an action in the world. The concept of utility is employed by utilitarian and pragmatic philosophers and other consequentialists as well. Utility also serves as an important decision-making criterion in everyday life, in government, and in business operations as well. See section 113.

- Verisimilitude: This evaluative term is recognized by some as an aesthetic measure of truth. A proposition is said to have verisimilitude if it is believed to approximate the truth in a way that "rings true."

28. Graham, "Ontological Arguments."

Appendix 3

Syllabus

INTRODUCTION TO PHILOSOPHY SYLLABUS

Course Name: Introduction to Philosophy

Instructor: Deacon Daniel Lowery
B.A., Valparaiso University
M.S.B.A., Indiana University Northwest
Ph.D., University of Illinois at Chicago
M.A.P.S. Catholic Theological Union

Telephone: (219) 677-3160 (cellphone)

E-mail: dlowery@saintmeinrad.edu

Hours Available: The instructor can be available as needed via email or telephone.

Dates and Times:

Location:

Course Description: Students will be introduced to the discipline of philosophy through the lens of the Aristotelian-Thomist Tradition. Although the Catholic Church does not endorse any particular philosophical perspective, the Aristotelian-Thomist Tradition has enjoyed a fruitful dialogue with Catholic theology over the course of many centuries.

The first of two extended weekends of instruction will be devoted to the history of philosophy, metaphysics, epistemology, ethical and moral thinking, and the development of various Thomist perspectives in the twentieth and twenty-first centuries. The second weekend will be devoted to the critical reading of philosophical texts.

Because this course is designed as the equivalent of a 3-credit hour college-level course, a considerable amount of work will be required before, between, and after the two weekends of instruction.

- Prior to the first extended weekend, students will be asked to read a text written by the instructor specifically for this course: *Philosophy in the Aristotelian-Thomist Tradition: A Primer*. This is a relatively short but—nonetheless—challenging text. Students should be sufficiently familiar with this material to respond in class to the review questions associated with each chapter.
- The first extended weekend of instruction will be devoted to material in the text written by the instructor. Class discussions will be organized around the review questions in appendix 1 of the text.
- Between the extended weekend sessions, students will be asked to read the encyclical letter *Fides et Ratio* by Pope John Paul II and key selections drawn from *Anthology of Catholic Philosophy* as indicated below. They will each be asked to prepare presentations pertaining to one or more assigned selections.
- In the second weekend session, students will deliver oral reports in a prescribed format and lead class discussions on the selection or selections drawn from *Anthology of Catholic Philosophy* assigned to them.
- After the second extended weekend session, students will complete and submit a final examination organized around three questions. See below.

Textbooks:

Philosophy in the Aristotelian-Thomist Tradition (2023).

Fides et Ratio (*On the Relationship between Faith and Reason*) (1998) by Pope John Paul II, ISBN 0-8198-2669-3. *Fides et Ratio* is also available at Fides et Ratio (14 September 1998) | John Paul II (vatican.va).

Anthology of Catholic Philosophy (2005), edited by James C. Swindal and Harry J. Gensler, 978-0742531987.

Learning Strategies: The course will be organized around:

- In-class discussions that address assigned readings;
- One or more class presentations based on assigned readings; and
- A take-home examination.

Grading Weights:
Class participation	30% of grade
Class presentation	30% of grade
Final examination	40% of grade

With respect to class participation, students are expected to initiate conversations with questions and comments as well as to respond to questions and other prompts provided by the instructor.

The take-home examination will be forwarded electronically to the instructor within three weeks of the close of the second in-class session. Three essays will be drafted, each of which will address one of the following topics:

- Compare and contrast a philosophical position or perspective associated with the Aristotelian-Thomist Tradition and a rival position or perspective.
- Explain how your thinking has or has not been changed on a particular philosophical position or perspective examined in class or in one or more of our readings.
- Identify implications that follow or could follow for ministry in the Catholic Church from a philosophical position or perspective addressed in class discussions or in one or more of our assigned readings.

Grading Scale:

A:	92 – 100		C:	72 – 77
A-:	90 – 91		C-:	70 – 71
B+:	88 – 89		D+:	68 – 69
B:	82 – 87		D:	62 – 67
B-:	80 – 81		D-:	60 – 61
C+:	78 – 79		F:	59 and below

Learning Objectives:

Outcome	Bloom's Taxonomy Level	Formative and Summative Assessment Methods
The student will be able to define philosophy as a discipline and describe its major sub-disciplines.	To know	In-class discussions, a class presentation, and final examination
The student will be able to explain the significance of the Aristotelian-Thomist Tradition and its relationship to Catholic theology.	To comprehend	In-class discussions and final examination
In a broad sense, the student will understand the development of philosophy in the West over the course of the last 2,500 years.	To know	In-class discussions, a class presentation, and a final examination
The student will be able to define metaphysics and describe its key concerns from the perspective of the Aristotelian-Thomist Tradition.	To comprehend	In-class discussions, a class presentation, and a final examination
The student will be able to compare and contrast the metaphysics of the Aristotelian-Thomist Tradition and alternative perspectives.	To synthesize	In-class discussions, a class presentation, and a final examination
The student will be able to define epistemology and describe its key concerns from the perspective of the Aristotelian-Thomist Tradition.	To comprehend	In-class discussions, a class presentation, and a final examination
The student will be able to compare and contrast the epistemology of the Aristotelian-Thomist Tradition and alternative perspectives.	To synthesize	In-class discussions, a class presentation, and a final examination

The student will be able to define ethical and moral thinking and describe its key concerns from the perspective of the Aristotelian-Thomist Tradition.	To know	In-class discussions, a class presentation, and a final examination
The student will be able to compare and contrast the ethical and moral thinking associated with the Aristotelian-Thomist Tradition and alternative perspectives.	To synthesize	In-class discussions, a class presentation, and a final examination
The student will understand the development of Thomism in the twentieth and 21st centuries.	To know	In-class discussions, a class presentation, and a final examination
In a general way, the student will understand how to critically read original philosophical texts.	To know	In-class discussions, a class presentation, and a final examination
The student will be able to lead critical discussions pertaining to original philosophical texts.	To apply	Class presentation
The student will be able to explain the relationships of several philosophical perspectives or insights to ministry in the Catholic Church.	To synthesize	In-class discussions and a final examination

Course Outline:

1st In-class Weekend:
    Session 1: Introduction to the Course
              Introduction to Philosophy
              Overview to the History of Philosophy
    Session 2: Metaphysics
    Session 3: Epistemology
    Session 4: Ethical and Moral Thinking
    Session 5: Thomism in the twentieth and 21st Centuries
    Session 6: The Critical Reading of Philosophy: An Example

2nd In-class Weekend:
    Session 1: *Fides et Ratio* by John Paul II
    Session 2: The Patristic Era
            "Freedom and Evil" by Irenaeus in Swindal and Gensler
            "Athens and Jerusalem" by Tertullian in Swindal and Gensler
            "Confessions" by Augustine in Swindal and Gensler

"Foreknowledge and Freedom" by Boethius in Swindal and Gensler

Session 3: The Middle Ages
"The Ontological Argument" by Anselm in Swindal and Gensler
"The Mind's Journey to God" by Bonaventure in Swindal and Gensler
"The Natural Law" by Thomas Aquinas in Swindal and Gensler
"Against Theistic Proofs" by William of Ockham in Swindal and Gensler

Session 4: Renaissance through the nineteenth Century
"Essence and Existence" by Francisco Suárez in Swindal and Gensler
"I Think, Therefore I Am" by René Descartes in Swindal and Gensler
"The Wager" by Blaise Pascal in Swindal and Gensler
"The Revival of Thomism" by Pope Leo XIII in Swindal and Gensler

Session 5: The twentieth Century and Beyond
"Action" by Maurice Blondel in Swindal and Gensler
"The Problem of Eudaemonism" by Max Scheler in Swindal and Gensler
"Transcendental Thomism" by Joseph Maréchal in Swindal and Gensler

Session 6: The twentieth Century and Beyond (continued)
"The Ontological Mystery" by Gabriel Marcel in Swindal and Gensler
"Can We Still Believe?" by Karl Rahner in Swindal and Gensler
"Virtue and Dependence" by Alasdair MacIntyre in Swindal and Gensler

Preparation for the Final Examination

Appendix 4

Critical Thinking Questions

1. Who is/are the author(s)?
2. What do we know about him, her, or them, e.g., professional positions, other work, standing in the communities with which he, she, or they is/are associated, other publications, etc.?
3. To what subdiscipline in philosophy should we assign this text, e.g., the history of philosophy, metaphysics, epistemology, ethics and morality, a meta-critique, etc.?
4. When was the text written? Is this dating pertinent to our critical reading of the text? If so, in what way?
5. To whom was the text addressed?
6. For what purpose was it written? For instance, was the text written in support of or in opposition to a particular document, established position, or perspective?
7. In one sentence, what is the thesis of the text?
8. What key arguments are advanced in the text?
    a. _____
    b. _____
    c. _____

9. What evidence, reasoning, or warrants are presented in support of each of these arguments?
    a. _____
    b. _____
    c. _____
10. What stated or unstated assumptions—if any—underlie these arguments?
11. Are any fallacies evident in these arguments?
12. Are the arguments advanced sound? Are they convincing? If so, in what way? If not, why not?
13. In what way—if any—do the arguments advanced underwrite, challenge, or extend the philosophical realism embodied in the Aristotelian-Thomist Tradition?
14. What counterarguments to the text's thesis could be advanced?
15. What implications—in terms of belief or action—would follow if the arguments advanced in the text are accepted?
16. What is left unsaid in the text?

Bibliography

à Kempis, Thomas. *The Imitation of Christ*, edited by William C. Creasy. Notre Dame, IN: Ave Maria, 1989.
Acosta, Miguel and Reimers, Adrian J. *Karol Wojtyla's Personalist Philosophy: Understanding Person & Act*. Washington D.C.: The Catholic University of American Press, 2016.
Adams, Marilyn McCord. "Ockham's Razor." In *Oxford Companion to Philosophy*, edited by Ted Honderich, 663. New York, NY: Oxford University Press, 1995.
Allison, Henry E. "Transcendental Analytic." In *Oxford Companion to Philosophy*, edited by Ted Honderich, 878. New York, NY: Oxford University Press, 1995.
Aquinas, Thomas. *Introduction to Saint Thomas Aquinas: The Summa Theologica and The Summa Contra Gentiles*, edited by Anton C. Pegis. New York, NY: Random House, 1948.
———. *On Being and Essence*. Monee, IL: Aubiblio, 2023.
———. "On Being and Essence," In *Anthology of Catholic Philosophy*, edited by James C. Swindal and Harry J. Gensler, 192–200. Lanham, MD: Bowman and Littlefield, 2005.
———. "The Existence of God." In *Anthology of Catholic Philosophy*, edited by James C. Swindal and Harry J. Gensler, 156–163. Lanham, MD: Bowman and Littlefield, 2005.
———. "The Principles of Nature." In *Anthology of Catholic Philosophy*, edited by James C. Swindal and Harry J. Gensler, 179–191. Lanham, MD: Bowman and Littlefield, 2005.
Aristotle. *Metaphysics*. Translated by William Ross. Monee, IL: Aubiblio, 2020.
———. *The Eudemian Ethics*. Translated by Anthony Kenny. Oxford University Press: Oxford, UK, 2011.
———. *Nicomachean Ethics*. Translated by R. W. Browne. Oakland Park, KS: Digireads.com, 2016.
———. *Prior & Posterior Analytics*. Monee, IL: CreateSpace Independent Publishing Platform, 2012.
Augustine. *City of God*. Translated by Henry Bettenson. London, GB: Penguin Classics, 1984.
———. *The Confessions*. New York, NY: Vintage Books, 1998.
Aumann, John. *Christian Spirituality in the Catholic Tradition*. San Francisco, CA: Ignatius, 2001.

Benedict. *The Rule of Saint Benedict.* Translated by M. L. del Mastro. Doubleday: New York, NY, 1975.

Bentham, Jeremy. *An Introduction to the Principles of Morals and Legislation,* 1789. http://www.earlymoderntexts.com/assets/pdfs/bentham1780.pdf. Accessed on June 19, 2023 at 9:15 a.m.

Bernasconi, Robert. "Maurce Merleau-Ponty." In *Oxford Companion to Philosophy,* edited by Ted Honderich, 554–555. New York, NY: Oxford University Press, 1995.

Boadt, Lawrence. *Reading the Old Testament: An Introduction.* New York, NY: Paulist, 1984.

Bonaventure. "The Mind's Journey to God." In *Anthology of Catholic Philosophy,* edited by James C. Swindal and Harry J. Gensler, 165–171. Lanham, MD: Bowman and Littlefield, 2005.

Broackes, Justin. "David Hume." In *Oxford Companion to Philosophy,* edited by Ted Honderich, 377–381. New York, NY: Oxford University Press, 1995.

Brodie, Alexander. "Thomas Aquinas." In *Oxford Companion to Philosophy,* 43–47, edited by Ted Honderich. New York, NY: Oxford University Press, 1995.

Brown, Harold I. "Innate Ideas." In *Oxford Companion to Philosophy,* edited by Ted Honderich, 409–410. New York, NY: Oxford University Press, 1995.

Browne, R. W. In Aristotle. "Introduction." In *Nicomachean Ethics.* Translated by R. W. Browne. Oakland Park, KS: Digireads.com, 2016.

Brueggemann, Walter. *Genesis.* Atlanta, GA: John Knox, 1982.

Buber, Martin. *I and Thou.* New York, NY: Touchstone, 1970.

Cahalan, John C. "Wittgenstein as a Gateway to Analytical Thomism." In *Analytical Thomism: Traditions in Dialogue,* edited by Craig Peterson and Matthew Pugh, 195–214. New York, NY: Ashgate, 2006.

Catechism of the Catholic Church. Vatican: Libreria Editrice Vaticana, 1997.

Conn, Joann Wolski and Conn, Walter E. "Self." In *The New Dictionary of Catholic Spirituality,* 865–875. Edited by Michael Downey. Collegeville, MN: The Liturgical Press, 1993.

Copleston, F. C. *Aquinas.* New York, NY: Penguin, 1970.

Cotter, A. C. *An Introduction to Catholic Philosophy.* Scotts Valley, CA: CreateSpace, 2017.

Crane, Tim. "Possible Worlds." In *Oxford Companion to Philosophy,* edited by Ted Honderich, 707. New York, NY: Oxford University Press, 1995.

De Unamuno, Miguel. *Tragic Sense of Life.* Translated by J. E. Crawford Flitch. New York, NY: Dover, 1954.

Dent, Nicholas. "Double Effect." In *Oxford Companion to Philosophy,* edited by Ted Honderich, 204–205. New York, NY: Oxford University Press, 1995.

———. "Moral Law." In *Oxford Companion to Philosophy,* edited by Ted Honderich, 144. New York, NY: Oxford University Press, 1995.

Downie, R. S. "Evidence." In *Oxford Companion to Philosophy,* edited by Ted Honderich, 254. New York, NY: Oxford University Press, 1995.

Dretske, Fred. "Belief." In *Oxford Companion to Philosophy,* edited by Ted Honderich, 82–83. New York, NY: Oxford University Press, 1995.

———. "Sensation." In *Oxford Companion to Philosophy,* edited by Ted Honderich, 821–822. New York, NY: Oxford University Press, 1995.

Flanigan, Owen. "History of the Philosophy of Mind." In *Oxford Companion to Philosophy,* edited by Ted Honderich, 570–574. New York, NY: Oxford University Press, 1995.

Francis. *Evangelii Gaudium (The Joy of the Gospel)*. Vatican: Libreia Editrice Vaticana, 2013.

Frankl, Viktor E. *Psychotherapy and Existentialism*. New York, NY: Washington Square, 1967.

Gadamer, Hans-Georg. *Truth and Method*. New York, NY: Continuum, 1978.

Geertz, Clifford. *The Interpretation of Cultures*. New York, NY: Basic, 1973.

Gilson, Étienne. *Methodological Realism*. San Francisco, CA: Ignatius, 2011.

Glenn, Paul J. *An Introduction to Philosophy*. London, England: Catholic Way, 2014.

Glock, Hans-Johann and Kalhat, Javier. "Lingustic Turn." In *Routledge Encyclopedia of Philosophy*. Accessed July 7, 2023, 2:05 p.m.

Goldman, Alvin and Bender, John. "Justice." In *Oxford Companion to Philosophy*, edited by Ted Honderich, 433–434. New York, NY: Oxford University Press, 1995.

Graham, Oppy. "Ontological Arguments." The Stanford Encyclopedia of Philosophy (Fall 2023 Edition), Edward N. Zalta & Uri Nodelman (eds.), forthcoming URL = <https://plato.stanford.edu/archives/fall2023/entries/ ontological-arguments/>. Accessed on August 8, 2023 at 6:05 a.m.

Grayling, A. C. *The History of Philosophy*. London, GB: Penguin, 2019.

Habermas, Jürgen. *The Theory of Communicative Action: Reason and the Rationalization of Society*. Boston, MA: Beacon, 1984.

Hacker, Peter. "Ludwig Josef Johan Wittgenstein." In *Oxford Companion to Philosophy*, edited by Ted Honderich, 912–916. New York, NY: Oxford University Press, 1995.

Hamlyn, D. W. "Idealism." In *Oxford Companion to Philosophy*, edited by Ted Honderich, 386–388. New York, NY: Oxford University Press, 1995.

Harari, Yuval Noah. *Sapiens: A Brief History of Humankind*. New York, NY: HarperCollins, 2015,

Hart, Charles. "Neothomism in America." In *Anthology of Catholic Philosophy*, edited by James C. Swindal and Harry J. Gensler, 357–361. Lanham, MD: Bowman and Littlefield, 2005.

Heidegger, Martin. *Being and Time*. Albany, NY: State University of New York Press, 1996.

Hepburn, R. W. "Emotive Theories of Ethics." In *Oxford Companion to Philosophy*, edited by Ted Honderich, 225–226. New York, NY: Oxford University Press, 1995.

Hobbes, Thomas. *Leviathan*. https://oll.libertyfund.org/title/smith-leviathan-1909-ed. Accessed on June 19, 2023 at 9:00 a.m.

Hookway, C. J. "Skepticism." In *Oxford Companion to Philosophy*, edited by Ted Honderich, 794–796. New York, NY: Oxford University Press, 1995.

Hume, David. Quoted in Michael Cohen. "Induction." In *Oxford Companion to Philosophy*, edited by Ted Honderich, 405–406. New York, NY: Oxford University Press, 1995.

Jacobs, James M. *Seat of Wisdom: An Introduction to Philosophy in the Catholic Tradition*. Washington, DC: Catholic University of America Press, 2022.

Jaspers, Karl. *Reason and Existenz*. New York: NY: Noonday, 1955.

John Paul II. *Fides et Ratio (On the Relationship of Faith and Reason)*. Boston, MA: Pauline Books & Media, 1998.

———. *Veritatis Splendor (The Splendor of the Truth)*. Vatican: Libreria Editrice Vaticana, 1993.

Kant, Immanuel. Quoted in Henry E. Allison. "Immanuel Kant." In *Oxford Companion to Philosophy*, edited by Ted Honderich, 435–438. New York, NY: Oxford University Press, 1995.

Kenny, Anthony. "Introduction." In *The Eudemian Ethics*. Translated by Anthony Kenny. Oxford University Press: Oxford, UK, 2011.

Kerr, Fergus. *After Aquinas: Versions of Thomism*. Malden, MA: Blackwell, 2002.

Kirwan, Christopher. "Argument." In *Oxford Companion to Philosophy*, edited by Ted Honderich, 47–48. New York, NY: Oxford University Press, 1995.

———. "Reasoning." In *Oxford Companion to Philosophy*, edited by Ted Honderich, 748–749. New York, NY: Oxford University Press, 1995.

Klingwell, Mark. *A Civil Tongue: Justice, Dialogue, and the Politics of Pluralism*. University Park, PA: The Pennsylvania State University Press, 1995.

Kuhn, Stephen T. "Deontic Logic." In *Oxford Companion to Philosophy*, edited by Ted Honderich, 186–187. New York, NY: Oxford University Press, 1995.

Kuhn, Thomas. *The Structures of Scientific Revolutions*. Chicago, IL: The University of Chicago Press, 2012.

Lacey, Alan. "Empiricism." In *Oxford Companion to Philosophy*, edited by Ted Honderich, 226–229. New York, NY: Oxford University Press, 1995.

———. "Rationalism." In *Oxford Companion to Philosophy*, edited by Ted Honderich, 741–744. New York, NY: Oxford University Press, 1995.

Laudan, Larry. "Hypothesis." In *Oxford Companion to Philosophy*, edited by Ted Honderich, 385. New York, NY: Oxford University Press, 1995.

Leo XIII. "The Revival of Thomism." In *Anthology of Catholic Philosophy*, edited by James C. Swindal and Harry J. Gensler, 279–281. Lanham, MD: Bowman and Littlefield Publishers, Inc., 2005.

Littlejohn, Clayton and Carter. J. Adam. *This is Epistemology: An Introduction*. Hoboken, NJ: John Wilen & Sons, 2021.

Lonergan, Bernard. "The Subject." In *Anthology of Catholic Philosophy,* edited by James C. Swindal and Harry J. Gensler, 380–389. New Lanham, MD: Rowman & Littlefield, 2005.

Loux, Michael J. *Metaphysics: A Contemporary Introduction*. New York, NY: Routledge, 1998.

Lowe. E. J. "Opposition to Metaphysics." In *Oxford Companion to Philosophy*, edited by Ted Honderich, 559. New York, NY: Oxford University Press, 1995.

———. "Semantics." In *Oxford Companion to Philosophy*, edited by Ted Honderich, 820. New York, NY: Oxford University Press, 1995.

———. "Truth." In *Oxford Companion to Philosophy*, edited by Ted Honderich, 881–882. New York, NY: Oxford University Press, 1995.

Jack MacIntosh. "Counterfactuals." In *Oxford Companion to Philosophy*, edited by Ted Honderich, 169. New York, NY: Oxford University Press, 1995.

MacIntyre, Alasdair. *After Virtue*. Notre Dame, IN: University of Notre Dame Press, 2007.

———. *A Short History of Ethics*. Notre Dame, IN: University of Notre Dame Press, 1998.

Marcel, Gabriel. "Ontological Mystery." In *Anthology of Catholic Philosophy*, edited by James C. Swindal and Harry J. Gensler, 345–349. Lanham, MD: Bowman and Littlefield, 2005.

Maréchal, Joseph. "Transcendental Thomism." In *Anthology of Catholic Philosophy*, edited by James C. Swindal and Harry J. Gensler, 318–325. New Lanham, MD: Rowman & Littlefield, 2005.

Maritain, Jacques. *Existence and the Existent*. Mahwah, NJ: Paulist, 2015.
Martin, Michael. "Imagination." In *Oxford Companion to Philosophy*, edited by Ted Honderich, 395. New York, NY: Oxford University Press, 1995.
McCloskey, Deirdra N. *The Bourgeois Virtues: Ethics for an Age of Commerce*. Chicago, IL: The University of Chicago Press, 2006.
Mele, Alfred R. "Ratiocination." In *Oxford Companion to Philosophy*, edited by Ted Honderich, 741. New York, NY: Oxford University Press, 1995.
Noordhof, Paul. "Scientism." In *Oxford Companion to Philosophy*, edited by Ted Honderich, 814. New York, NY: Oxford University Press, 1995.
Nozick, Robert. *Anarchy, State, and Utopia*. New York, NY: Basic, 1974.
Peterson, Craig and Pugh, Matthew. "Introduction to Analytic Thomism." In *Analytical Thomism: Traditions in Dialogue*, edited by Craig Peterson and Matthew Pugh, xiii–xxiii. New York, NY: Ashgate, 2006.
Pinckaers, Servais. *The Sources of Christian Ethics*. Washington, D.C.: The Catholic University of America Press, 1995.
Pius IX. "Constitution on the Catholic Faith (*Dei Filius*)." In *Anthology of Catholic Philosophy*, edited by James C. Swindal and Harry J. Gensler, 275–278. Lanham, MD: Bowman and Littlefield, 2005.
Pius X. https://www.vatican.va/content/pius-x/en/encyclicals/documents/hf_p-x_enc_19070908_pascendi-dominici-gregis.html, no. 6. Accessed May 23, 2023 at 1:00 p.m.
———. "Twenty-four Thomistic Theses." In *Anthology of Catholic Philosophy*, edited by James C. Swindal and Harry J. Gensler, 293–296. Lanham, MD: Bowman and Littlefield, 2005.
Pontifical Biblical Commission. "The Interpretation of the Bible in the Church." In *The Bible Documents*, edited by David A. Lysik. Chicago, IL: Liturgical Training, 2001.
Pontifical Council for Justice and Peace. *Compendium of the Social Doctrine of the Catholic Church*. Vatican: Libreia Editrice Vaticana, 2004.
Quinton, Anthony. "Philosophy." In *Oxford Companion to Philosophy*, edited by Ted Honderich, 666–670. New York, NY: Oxford University Press, 1995.
Rahner, Karl. "Being Open to God as Ever Greater." In *Theological Investigations: Further Theology of the Spiritual Life*" (vol. VII), 25–46. Translated by David Bourke. New York, NY: Seabury, 1977.
———. "On Christian Dying." in *Theological Investigations: Further Theology of the Spiritual Life I* (vol. VII), 285–293. Translated by David Bourke. New York, NY: Seabury, 1977.
———. "The Dignity and Freedom of Man." In *Theological Investigations: Man in the Church* (vol. II), 235–264. Translated by Karl-H. Kruger. Baltimore, MD: Helicon, 1963.
———. "The Experiment with Man." In *Theological Investigations: Writings of 1965-67* (vol. IX), 1–13. Translated by Graham Harrison. New York, NY: Seabury, 1972.
———. "Intellectual Honesty and Christian Faith." In *Theological Investigations: Further Theology of the Spiritual Life I* (vol. VII), 3–16. Translated by David Bourke. New York, NY: Seabury, 1977.
———. "Proving Oneself in Time of Sickness." In *Theological Investigations: Further Theology of the Spiritual Life I* (vol. VII), 275–284. Translated by David Bourke. New York, NY: Seabury, 1977.

———. "The Sin of Adam." In *Theological Investigations: Confrontations I* (vol. XI), 247–262. Translated by David Bourke. New York, NY: Seabury, 1974.

———. "Theology of Freedom." In *Theological Investigations: Concerning Vatican Council II* (vol. VI), 178–196. Translated by Karl-H. Kruger and Boniface Kruger. New York, NY: Seabury, 1974.

———. "Thoughts on the Possibility of Belief Today." In *Theological Investigations: Later Writings* (vol. V), 3–22. Translated by Karl-H. Kruger. Baltimore, MD: Helicon, 1966.

Rawls, John. *A Theory of Justice*. Cambridge, MA: Harvard University Press, 1971.

Rescher, Nicholas. "The Limits of Knowledge." In *Oxford Companion to Philosophy*, edited by Ted Honderich, 448. New York, NY: Oxford University Press, 1995.

Rorty, Richard. *Consequences of Pragmatism*. Minneapolis, MN: University of Minnesota Press, 1982.

———. *Contingency, Irony, and Solidarity*. New York, NY: Cambridge University Press 1989.

———. *Philosophy and the Mirror of Nature*. Princeton, NJ: Princeton University Press, 1979.

Ruse, Michael. "Humanism." In *Oxford Companion to Philosophy*, edited by Ted Honderich, 375–277. New York, NY: Oxford University Press, 1995.

———. "Reductionism." In *Oxford Companion to Philosophy*, edited by Ted Honderich, 750–751. New York, NY: Oxford University Press, 1995.

Sartre, Jean-Paul. *Being and Nothingness: A Phenomenological Essay on Ontology*. New York: NY: Washington Square, 1984.

Second Vatican Council. "*Gaudium et Spes*: Pastoral Constitution on the Church in the Modern World." In *Vatican Council II: The Basic Sixteen Documents*, edited by Austin Flannery, O.P. Northport, NY: Costello, 2007.

———. "*Lumen Gentium*: Dogmatic Constitution on the Church." In *Vatican Council II: The Basic Sixteen Documents*, edited by Austin Flannery, 1–95. Northport, NY: Costello, 2007.

———. "*Nostra Aetate*: Declaration on the Relationship of the Church to Non-Christian Religions." In *Vatican Council II: The Basic Sixteen Documents*. Edited by Austin Flannery, O.P. Northport, NY: Costello, 2007.

Shanley, Brian J. "On Analytical Thomism." In *Analytical Thomism: Traditions in Dialogue*, edited by Craig Peterson and Matthew Pugh, 215–224. New York, NY: Ashgate, 2006.

Sleigh, Jr., R. C. "Gottfried Wilhelm Leibniz." In *Oxford Companion to Philosophy*, edited by Ted Honderich, 477–480. New York, NY: Oxford University Press, 1995.

Slote, Michael. "Problems of Moral Philosophy." In *Oxford Companion to Philosophy*, edited by Ted Honderich, 591–595. New York, NY: Oxford University Press, 1995.

———. "Utilitarianism." In *Oxford Companion to Philosophy*, edited by Ted Honderich, 890–892. New York, NY: Oxford University Press, 1995.

Sosa, Ernest. "Essence." In *Oxford Companion to Philosophy*, 250–251, edited by Ted Honderich. New York, NY: Oxford University Press, 1995.

———. "Problems of Metaphysics." In *Oxford Companion to Philosophy*, edited by Ted Honderich, 559–563. New York, NY: Oxford University Press, 1995.

Sprigge, T. L. S. "Arthur Schopenhauer." In *Oxford Companion to Philosophy*, edited by Ted Honderich, 802–805. New York, NY: Oxford University Press, 1995.

———. "Baruch Spinoza." In *Oxford Companion to Philosophy*, edited by Ted Honderich, 845–848. New York, NY: Oxford University Press, 1995.

Stevenson, C. L. Quoted by Sybil Wolfram in "Definition." In *Oxford Companion to Philosophy*, edited by Ted Honderich, 182. New York, NY: Oxford University Press, 1995.

Suarez, Francisco. "Essence and Existence." In *Anthology of Catholic Philosophy*, edited by James C. Swindal and Harry J. Gensler, 235–240. Lanham, MD: Bowman and Littlefield, 2005.

Taylor, Charles. *A Secular Age*. Cambridge, MA: Belknap, 2007.

———. "Transcendental Arguments." In *Anthology of Catholic Philosophy*, edited by James C. Swindal and Harry J. Gensler, 472–477. Lanham, MD: Bowman and Littlefield, 2005.

Ten Klooster. *Thomas Aquinas on the Beatitudes: Reading Matthew, Disputing Grace and Virtue, Preaching Happiness*. Leuven: BE: Peeters, 2018.

Tertullian. "The Prescription Against Heretics," ANF03. In *Nicene and Post-Nicene Fathers*, edited by Philip Schaff, translated by Peter Holmes, 3139–3183. London, UK: Catholic Way, 2014.

Tillich, Paul. *The Courage to Be*. New Haven. CT: Yale University Press, 1980.

von Wahlde, Urban C. "John." In *The Jerome Biblical Commentary for the Twenty-first Century*, edited by John J. Collins, Gina Hens-Piazza, Barbara Reid, and Donald Senior, 1378–1444. London, UK: Bloomsbury, 2022.

Wadell, Paul J. "Virtue." In *The New Dictionary of Christian Spirituality*, edited by Michael Downey, 997–1007. Collegeville, MN: Liturgical Press, 1993.

Walton, Douglas. "Types of Arguments." In *Oxford Companion to Philosophy*, edited by Ted Honderich, 48–49. New York, NY: Oxford University Press, 1995.

Warnock, Baroness. "Slippery Slope." In *Oxford Companion to Philosophy*, edited by Ted Honderich, 828. New York, NY: Oxford University Press, 1995.

Weatherford, Roy C. "Compatibilism and Incompatibilism." In *Oxford Companion to Philosophy*, edited by Ted Honderich, 144. New York, NY: Oxford University Press, 1995.

———. "Determinism." In *Oxford Companion to Philosophy*, edited by Ted Honderich, 194–195. New York, NY: Oxford University Press, 1995.

White, John. "Inference." In *Oxford Companion to Philosophy*, edited by Ted Honderich, 407. New York, NY: Oxford University Press, 1995.

Williams, Thomas D. "What is Thomistic Personalism." In *Alpha Omega* VII, 2004.

Williamson, Timothy. *Philosophical Method: A Very Short Introduction*. Oxford, UK.: Oxford University Press, 2020.

Wojtyla, Karol. *Sign of Contradiction*. New York, NY: Seabury, 1977.

Name Index

Abelard, Peter, xiv, 18, 168
Adler, Mortimer, 135
Albertus Magnus, 7
Alexander the Great, 6
Alighieri, Dante, 20
Ambrose, 17
Anaxagoras, 13
Anaximander, 13
Anaximenes, 13
Andronicus of Rhodes,
Angelic Doctor. See "Thomas Aquinas"
Anscombe, Elizabeth Margaret, 31, 144
Anselm, 4, 18
Antisthenes, 16
Aquinas, Thomas, xiv, 3–4, 6, 7, 8–9, 12–13, 15, 18, 19, 28, 34–35, 36, 40, 41, 42–43, 44, 45, 46, 48, 50, 52, 53–55, 57, 58, 59, 60–62, 64, 65–66, 69–69, 70–72, 74, 76, 81, 87, 91, 96, 100, 101–2, 104, 106, 107, 108, 109–10, 114, 115, 117, 121–22, 133, 134, 135, 136, 137, 138, 139, 141, 143, 145, 146, 147, 148, 150, 151, 161, 169, 174
Aristotle, xiv, xv, 3, 6–10, 12, 13, 14, 15, 18, 19, 20, 32, 33, 34–35, 37, 41, 42–43, 44, 47, 48, 50, 52–56, 58, 59, 60, 61, 63, 65, 66, 68–69, 70–72, 74, 76, 79, 81, 87, 89, 91, 92–93, 95–96, 99–101, 102, 103, 104, 106, 107, 108–10, 114, 115–17, 120–22, 124, 134, 137, 143, 145, 147, 148, 149, 150, 163, 167, 168, 169, 172
Augustine, 3, 7, 17, 18, 20, 62–63, 71–72, 88, 116–17
Aurelius, Marcus, 16, 20, 104
Austin, John, 29
Averroes, 6
Avicenna, 6

Bacon, Francis, 1, 21, 73, 94, 135, 170
Bacon, Roger, 19
Benedict of Nursia, 18
Bentham, Jeremy, 24, 118, 125–26
Berkeley, George, 16, 21, 36, 73, 135
Boethius, 18
Bonaventure, xiv, 7, 8, 19, 35, 42, 71–72
Bradley, F. H., 23
Buber, Martin, 30, 139

Calvin, John, 122
Carnap, Rudolf, 16
Cassian, John, 18
Chesterton, G. K., 100
Chrysostom, John, 17
Churchill, Winston, 21
Comte, Auguste, 24–25
Copernicus, Nicholas, 12
Crates, 13

Darwin, Charles, 22
De Unamuno, Michael, 30, 139

Democritus, 13
Derrida, Jacques, 31, 163
Descartes, René, 21, 72, 76, 83, 91, 133, 135, 136
Dewey, John, 31, 129–30
Diogenes, 16
Duns, Scotus, xiv, 19, 35

Einstein, Albert, 12
Empedocles, 14
Engels, Friedrich, 24,
Epictetus, 16, 104
Epicurus, 16
Erasmus, 20

Fabro, Cornelio, 136
Foot, Philippa, 31, 150
Foucault, Michael, 31
Frege, Gottlob, 27, 144
Freud, Sigmund, 24
Friedman, Milton, 31, 127

Gadamer, Hans-Georg, 30, 138
Geach, Peter, 144
Gilson, Étienne, 23, 36, 69–70, 135, 136–37
Green, T. H., 23
Gregory of Nazianzus, 17
Gregory the Great, 17, 135

Habermas, Jürgen, 24, 31, 96–97, 128–29, 130–31
Haldane, John, 144
Hayek, F. A., 31, 137
Hegel, G. W. F., 22–23, 24–25, 36, 118, 146, 164
Heidegger, Martin, 29, 136, 138–40, 143
Heraclitus, 13
Hobbes, Thomas, 21, 22, 73, 103, 119, 122–23, 135
Hume, David, 21, 73, 85–86, 91, 93–94, 118
Husserl, Edmund, 29, 31, 138–39, 162, 165

Iamblichus, 17

James, William, 28, 31, 128–29
Jaspers, Karl, 138, 139–40
Jerome, 17
Jesus Christ, 2, 89–90, 112, 120, 151, 161

Kant, Immanuel, 15, 21, 24, 28, 36, 37–38, 68, 73–74, 76, 79, 85–87, 91, 94, 111, 118–19, 124, 134, 136–37, 150, 167
Keynes, John Maynard, 127
Kierkegaard, Søren, 12, 25, 29, 139

Leibniz, Gottfried, 21, 27, 72, 83, 135, 161, 168
Locke, John, 10, 21, 22, 73, 107, 111, 127–28, 135, 167
Lonergan, Bernard, 136, 138, 171
Lyotard, Jean-François, 31

Machiavelli Niccolò, 10, 20
MacIntyre, Alasdair, 31, 71, 72, 103–5, 109–10, 113, 115, 116, 119, 120, 122, 123, 128, 131–32, 150, 164, 172
Maimonides, Moses, 7
Mani, 72
Marcel, Gabriel, 138, 141, 165
Maréchal, Joseph, 136, 137
Marion, Jean-Luc, 138
Maritain, Jacques, 135, 143, 145,
Marx, Karl, 10, 22, 24, 107, 146, 164
McCloskey, Deirdra, 101, 113, 114
McTaggart, J. M. E., 23
Merleau-Ponty, Maurice, 29, 138
Mill, John Stuart, 24, 125
Moore, G. E., 28, 84
More, Thomas, 20

Nietzsche, Fredrich, 10, 25, 103, 107, 111, 143
Nozick, Robert, 31, 127–28

Parmenides, 7, 14, 38
Paul, 117
Peirce, C. S., 31, 128–29
Plato, 2, 3, 5, 6, 10, 12, 13, 14–15, 16, 19, 20, 22, 25, 36, 48, 52–53, 58,

NAME INDEX

63, 72, 74–75, 76, 78, 86, 90, 91, 93, 106, 110, 160, 161, 164
Petrarch, 20
Plotinus, 3, 16–17, 72, 76
Pope John Paul II, xii, 2, 4, 9, 29, 31, 35, 61, 70, 71, 85, 105, 134, 141, 142, 146–49
Pope Leo XIII, 8, 150
Pope Pius IX, 8
Pope Pius X, 8–10, 42, 70, 135
Popper, Karl, 26
Porphyry, 17
Proclus, 17
Pyrrho, 14
Pythagoras, 13

Quine, W. V., 26

Rahner, Karl, 134, 136, 142
Rand, Ayn, 31, 127
Rawls, John, 31, 124–25, 130
Ricoeur, Paul, 30, 69, 138
Rorty, Richard, 31, 128–30, 131
Rousseau, Jean-Jacques, 22, 123
Russell, Bertrand, 26–27, 144, 167
Ryle, Gilbert, 28–29

Sartre, Jean-Paul, 29, 138, 139–40, 143
Scheler, Max, 138, 147, 149
Schleiermacher, Friedrich, 22, 25
Schlick, Moritz, 26
Schopenhauer, Arthur, 17, 22–23, 36
Seneca the Younger, 16, 19, 104
Socrates, xiv, 10, 13, 14–15, 16, 63
Spinoza, Baruch, 21, 72, 83, 89, 135
Suarez, Francisco, xiv, 41

Taylor, Charles, 10, 12, 20, 112, 113, 134, 170, 172
Tertullian, 2
Thales, 13
Thomas à Kempis, 3
Thomas of Vio (Cajetan), xiv
Tillich, Paul, 29–30, 139–40

Whitehead, Alfred North, 27, 144
William of Ockham, xiv, 12, 19, 35, 37, 105, 169
Wittgenstein, Ludwig, 27–28, 128, 134, 144, 145, 167–68
Wojtyla, Karol. See "Pope John Paul II"

Zeno, 14, 16, 104

Subject Index

a posteriori knowledge, 5, 78–79, 81
a priori knowledge, 5, 19, 21, 27, 36, 74, 77, 78–79, 81, 83–84, 86–87, 91, 128, 137, 144
abduction, 160, 167
absolute mind, 22, 23, 36
abstraction, 49, 160
absurdity, 140
Academy, 6
accidental change, 63–64
accidents, 15, 37, 43, 45, 47, 49–52, 55, 56, 57, 58–60, 61, 62, 64, 65, 74, 95–96, 124
action, 60, 95, 101, 104, 108, 114, 118–19, 148, 149
actus primus, 44
actu secondus, 44–45
actual real being, 39, 44–47, 49, 51, 54, 55, 56–57, 58, 63, 65, 76, 87, 95–96, 106, 145
ad hominem attacks, 165
aesthetic experiences, 28, 85, 97, 174
aesthetic truth claims, 96
affection, 62
affirmations, 95
aggiornamento, 51
agnosticism, 2, 70
allegory of the cave, 52, 160
alteration, 64
analogy, 160–61
analytic Thomism, 6, 144–46
analytic truths, 72

anamnesis. See "recollection"
anawim, 122
angst, 25, 140
annihilation. See "corruption"
anthropology. See "ontology"
antithesis, 24, 164
apatheia. See "apathy"
apathy, 16, 110, 121
apologetics, 8
Apostolic Tradition, 90
appeals to the popular, 162, 165
appeals to tradition, 165
apperception, 161
apprehension, 162, 169, 61, 71, 87, 91, 94, 151
arete. See "human excellence"
argumentation fallacies, 165
arguments, 14, 82, 92, 94, 162, 166, 170
Aristotelianism, 19, 132
Aristotelian-Thomist Tradition, xi, xii, xiv, xv, 3, 5, 6–10, 12–13, 15, 19, 24, 31, 23, 33–34, 37, 38, 39, 40, 41, 42, 43, 45, 49–52, 53, 56, 57, 61, 62, 63, 65, 67, 70, 74, 75, 79, 82, 85, 86, 87, 88, 92, 96–97, 100–101, 102, 105, 106, 107, 108–10, 113–18, 120–22, 130, 131, 133–35, 137, 139, 142, 143, 144–46, 147, 150, 171, 173
artifact, 30
artificial intelligence, 2, 169
aspects. See "categories of being"

195

assertions, 78, 91, 95–97, 113, 165
Ataraxia, 16
attributes. See "accidents"
austere nominalism, 37
authenticity, 96, 134, 139
authority, 90, 122, 125
axioms, 162, 166

beatitudes, xiv, 110, 122
beauty, 61–62, 96, 97, 121
becoming, 42, 43–44
begging the question, 165
begriffsschrift, 27
being, xii, 2, 5, 9, 15, 29, 30, 32–33, 34, 36, 37, 38–39, 40, 41–49, 50, 51, 52, 53, 54 ,55, 56–58, 61–63, 65, 66, 74, 75–76, 77, 78–79, 85, 87–88, 89, 95–97, 105, 106, 124, 134, 137, 139, 142, 143, 145, 173–74
beings of reason. See "mind-dependent beings"
beliefs, 1, 2, 68, 69, 72, 77–78, 83, 86, 91, 105, 146
biblicism, 105
biology, 55, 139, 105
blank slate, 71, 91
Bolshevism, 10
bootstrapping, 79, 162
bracketing, 29, 162
brute facts, 163
bundle theory, 49
Byzantium, 6

calculation, 27, 126
cardinal virtues, 114, 115
casuistry, 163
categorical imperatives, 21, 100, 118–19, 137
categories of being, 40, 42, 50, 62, 88
category mistakes, 166
Catholic Church, xi–xii, 2–4, 7–9, 11, 35, 44, 51, 61, 70–72, 82, 101–2, 131
Catholic philosophy, 9, 42, 135, 146
Catholic social teaching, 150–51

causation, 11, 13, 14, 51, 58, 63–66, 78, 79, 80, 81, 82, 83, 86, 92, 93, 104–5, 106, 132, 166, 167
causes. See "causation"
certainty, 4, 74, 76, 82, 92, 110, 160, 163
chain of justifiers, 80
change, 11, 13, 14, 16, 17, 18, 36, 38, 45, 46, 51, 55, 58, 63–66, 79–80, 81, 94, 104
chaos, 131
characteristica universalis, 27
charity, 4, 17, 110, 114, 116, 122
choices, 104, 116, 118, 148, 165
circular reasoning, 166
citizenship, 20, 23, 120, 123
civil religion, 123
classification, 69
closure principle, 92
cogito, ergo sum, 76, 78, 84, 170
cognitive psychology, 29
coherentism, 81–82
Cold War, 23
collective aspirations, 123, 149
common good, 101, 121–22
common sense, 28, 49, 84–85, 87, 163
communicative action, 96, 130
communicative competence, 131
community, 23, 24, 82, 96, 98, 102, 120, 121–22, 127, 128, 130, 140, 149, 151, 171
compassion, 23
compatibilism, 105
conceptualism, 34, 35, 37, 42, 47
conceptualized order. See "social imaginaries"
conclusions, 73, 92, 169
concreated matter and form, 52, 54, 55, 56, 58, 147
concupiscence, 116
confessors, 101
consciousness, 23, 25, 29, 44, 64, 138, 145, 162
consent, 123
consequentialism, 23, 31
consumption, 132
contemplation, 71, 102, 108, 109, 110, 169

continental philosophies, 26, 29, 30, 138, 144
continental revolutions of 1848, 102
contingency, 69, 165
contract theory, 21, 31, 131
Copernican revolution, 73
correspondence theory, 28, 77
corruption, 65
cosmos, 14, 17, 20, 135
cost-benefit analyses, 24
Council of Trent, 7, 51, 101
counterfactuals, 163
Counter-Reformation, 8, 18, 101
creation, 22, 35, 38, 39, 65, 66, 140, 142, 151
criteriology, 32
critical theory, 96, 24
critique, 12, 26, 28, 31 94, 103, 129, 135, 144, 168
culture studies, 1, 2, 9
culture, 9, 10, 26, 32, 48, 103, 108, 111, 124, 130–31, 133, 135, 150

death, 25, 46, 55, 109, 112, 140, 148, 161
decalogue. See "Ten Commandments"
decomposition, 27
deconstruction, 31, 163
deduction, 79, 92, 163
defeasibility, 81, 163
definitions, 163
deism, 3
democracy, 21, 132, 151
demonstration, 93, 164
deontology, 122–23, 127, 128, 130, 164
Descartes's evil demon, 84, 89, 91, 92, 174
desert fathers, 2
designated matter, 54
determinism, 18, 100, 102, 110
devotio moderna, 70
dialectic, 2, 14, 34, 93, 164, 173
dialogue, xi, 15, 47, 63, 93, 134, 144–45, 146, 164, 176
difference principle, 124
dignity, 44, 61, 115, 119, 147, 151
discipleship, 112, 141
discursive engagement, 87, 129, 130
dissonance, 141

distributive justice, 98, 120, 121, 124, 125, 128, 130
divine illumination, 71–72
divine wisdom, 53
DNA, 55
doing, 45, 76, 101, 138, 170
doubt, 14, 83, 91, 165
dread. See "angst"
duty, 12, 16, 104, 111, 137, 150

early church fathers, 2, 17, 55, 115, 122, 151
education, xi, 121, 123, 125, 128, 149
efficient causes, 65–66, 79, 81, 104
eidetic reduction, 29, 165
eliminativism, 36
emotions, 20, 85, 88, 103, 104, 149, 165
emotivism, 103, 113, 119, 125, 128, 132
empirical truth claims, 96
empiricism, 21, 24, 68, 97, 135, 136
emptiness, 141
ends, 108, 118, 132
Enlightenment, 5, 8, 17, 19, 20–22, 24, 32, 33, 36, 37, 40, 45, 63, 67, 69, 70, 72–73, 74, 76, 83–86, 90, 91, 93, 100, 103, 104, 107, 110, 111, 118, 122, 130, 133, 135, 136, 147, 167
ens, 41, 42, 46, 52
entitative existence, 145
entities, 15, 34, 47, 69, 107, 169–70
epicureanism, 14, 16, 18
episteme, 76
epistemology, xi, xii, 1, 2, 4, 6, 11, 13, 15, 16, 21, 25–26, 33, 41, 67–97, 110, 129, 133, 137, 144–45, 147, 151
epoche, 29
equality, 115, 123, 124
equivocations, 165
eristic arguments, 14
esse, 41–43, 88
esse commune, 42
essence, xii, 9, 19, 27, 33, 34, 41–42, 44–45, 49, 50, 52, 53, 55, 56–58, 61, 65, 69, 74, 75, 79, 87–88, 96, 97, 105, 106, 107, 139, 141–43, 148, 165

ethics, xi, xii, xiv, 1, 2, 4, 6, 11, 12–13, 19, 24, 31, 68, 97, 98–132, 137, 145–46, 147, 150, 163, 172
eudaimonia. See "happiness"
event, 11, 30, 38, 40, 47, 80–82, 87, 104, 165, 166–67, 169
evidence, 12, 68, 80, 81, 84, 86–91, 92, 160, 162
evil, 19, 108, 148
exegesis, 22, 105
exemplification. See "instantiation"
existence, 1, 4–5, 9, 15, 18, 19, 22, 23, 29, 33, 34, 37, 38, 40–43, 44–45, 46, 47, 48, 50, 51, 53–55, 56, 57, 58, 62, 63, 64–65, 70, 75, 80, 82, 83, 84–85, 86, 88, 91, 92, 99, 109, 117, 119, 137, 139–40, 141–43, 145, 170, 173–74
existential recollection, 165
existential Thomism, 6, 138–43
existentialism, xiv, 22, 25, 29–130, 31, 67, 136, 138–43, 144
existents, 41, 48, 56, 61, 72, 76
experimentation, 85, 91, 174
explanations, 11, 84, 167
expressive truth claims, 96–97
extension, 43, 45, 79
extra-mentality, 48

facticity, 85, 139
faith, xii–xiii, 2, 3, 4, 7, 8, 10, 11, 19, 25, 29, 51, 70–71, 82, 88, 909, 105, 110, 114, 116
fall of Rome, 6, 17, 18
false dilemmas, 165
falsifiability, 27
fascism, 23
faulty cause-and-effect arguments, 165
felicity, 149
feudalism, 102
fictions, 47
fideism, 3, 102, 105, 117, 161
final causes, 65–66, 106
First Vatican Council, 8
First World War, 10, 23
flourishing. See "happiness"
for-itself, 139
formal causes, 65–66

formation, xi–xii, xiv–xv, 101, 112, 119, 121, 150
forms, 5, 13, 15, 36, 47, 48, 52, 53–55, 58, 63, 72, 76, 78, 90, 106, 110, 160, 161, 164
fortitude, 17, 103, 108, 110, 114, 131, 150
foundationalism, 81, 84, 146
Frankfort School, 24, 96
free will, 18, 19, 46, 48, 60, 100, 103, 104, 105, 112, 131, 148, 170
freedom, 44, 89, 103, 124, 128, 129, 130, 142
French Revolution, 18, 102
friendship, 104, 120–21, 149
fulfillment. See "happiness"
fusion of horizons, 30
future, 25, 30, 45, 94, 139, 140, 142, 166

geist. See "absolute mind"
general will, 123
generation. See "creation"
global warming, 126
God, 2, 3, 4, 8, 9, 10, 16, 17, 18, 19, 20, 25, 30, 34–35, 36, 38, 39, 40, 42, 44, 45, 48, 53, 55, 62–63, 66, 71, 82, 86, 89, 92, 105, 106, 109, 112, 116, 117, 118, 120, 123, 125, 137, 139, 141, 142, 143, 148, 151, 161, 166, 169, 173–74
golden age of Greek philosophy, 14–17
good life. See "good"
good (the good), xiv, 12, 15, 17, 18, 62, 98, 99, 102, 106, 108–12, 113, 116, 122, 129, 130, 131
goodness, 39, 46, 61, 74, 96–97, 174
government regulation, 127
grace, 3, 4, 71, 100, 104, 111, 112, 116, 142, 149
guilt by association, 165

habit, 60, 95, 100, 101, 108, 109, 114, 117, 119
habitus. See "habit"
haecceitas. See "essence"
happiness, 3, 10, 20, 100, 108, 109, 114, 124, 149, 151
Hasidic Judaism, 30

SUBJECT INDEX

hedonism, 16, 23, 72, 110, 126
hermeneutic circle, 30
hermeneutics, xiv, 18, 26, 30, 69, 134, 138, 141, 144, 164, 166
heuristic, 166
higher criticism, 89
history, xi, xiv, 11–13, 14, 25, 27, 36, 102, 130, 161, 164, 165, 169, 170, 172, 174
holocaust, 23
hope, 104, 110, 114, 116
hubris, 23, 85
human excellence, 114
humanism, 20
humility, 110, 114
hylomorphic theory, 54–55, 147
hypostasis. See "suppositum"
hypothesis, 84, 86, 93, 166, 170

ideal speech situation, 129
idealism, 5, 15, 16, 21, 22–23, 24, 25, 34, 35, 36, 37, 38, 76, 136, 144
ideas, 15, 36, 40, 47, 53, 55, 72, 76, 84, 86, 87, 90–91, 93
identity, 13, 25, 33, 45, 63, 64, 89, 96, 133, 140, 149
idolatry, 122
illusion, 5, 84
imagined order. See "social imaginaries"
immediatism, 69
immigration, 123
impressions, 78, 89, 91
in fieri. See "becoming"
Incarnation, 35
incomplete substance, 64
indifference. See "apathy"
induction, 73, 81, 92, 93, 94, 166, 170
industrial revolution, 22
inference, 51, 59, 64, 73, 88, 92, 93–94, 167, 172
infinite regress, 79–82, 83
infinitism, 80, 83
inherence, 51–52, 55, 56, 59, 61, 64, 66, 74, 95
in-itself, 139
innate structures, 21, 36, 38, 137
inner light, 117

inner sense, 167
inquiry, 35, 36, 40, 105, 138, 169, 170
instantiation, 42, 43, 53, 141
intellect, 42, 48, 62, 63, 69–70, 71, 87–88, 102, 104, 137
intelligence, 2, 4, 131, 138, 169
intelligibility, 7, 48, 61, 62, 63, 145
interpersonal communications, 47, 120
interpretation. See "hermeneutics"
intersubjective agreement, 81–82, 84, 96
intuition, 26, 91, 146, 167
investigation, 2, 19, 27, 33, 49, 67, 75, 76, 95, 134, 138, 166, 171
Israel, 11, 127

Jansenism, 112
judgment, 71, 74, 76, 87, 88, 114, 126, 130, 151, 164, 166, 167, 171
just (the just), xiv, 98, 100, 103, 105, 106, 112, 120–32
justification, 1, 68, 79–86, 96, 146

knowability. See "intelligibility"
knowledge, xv, 1, 4–5, 8, 15, 17, 21, 28, 29, 31, 32, 33, 34, 36, 38, 48–49, 67–97, 104, 105, 110, 129, 138, 146, 149, 161, 162, 164

language, 9, 25, 26–27, 28, 29, 32, 36, 37, 95, 96, 103, 107, 129, 133, 144, 147, 161, 167–68, 172
Language games, 127, 128, 134
latin fathers, 67
law and order, 123, 131
leap of faith, 25
lebenswelt. See "life world"
legal reasoning, 168
lex orandi, lex credenda, 88
liberalism, 30, 111, 127, 130
libertarianism, 30–31, 111, 123, 127–28, 130–31
liberty. See "freedom"
life world, 29
lifestyle, 16
linguistic behavioralism, 26
linguistic turn, 19, 26, 28, 171

logic, xi, 6, 18, 27, 28, 32, 67, 68, 69, 167, 168, 171
logical being. See "mind-dependent being"
logical positivism, 25, 26, 36, 144
logos, 16
loyalty, 104
Lutheran Tradition, 111
Lyceum, 6

major logic, 67
materia primus. See "undesignated matter"
materia secunda. See "designated matter"
material causes, 65
materialism, 15, 22, 37, 45, 69, 141
matter, 16, 36, 37, 42, 49, 50, 51, 52–55, 56, 58, 65, 83, 147
maximization, 127, 131
mean, 15, 115–16
meaning, 2, 4, 9, 11, 25, 29, 30, 32, 36, 37, 38, 44, 47, 48, 62, 66, 85, 106, 107, 108, 111, 121, 123, 133, 134, 139–46, 148, 165, 167, 172, 173
mediated realism, 69
meekness, 110
memory, 11, 64, 86, 88–89, 90
mercy, 17
meta-ethics, 26, 146
metalinguistic nominalism, 37
metaphysics, xi, xii, xiii, 1, 2, 4, 5, 6–7, 11, 12–13, 15, 16, 17, 18, 19, 20, 21, 22, 23, 27, 32–66, 67, 68, 73, 85, 104, 105, 109, 111, 129, 133, 134, 136, 137, 145, 147
methods, xi, 11, 14, 19, 21, 27, 68, 92, 94, 144, 160–74
mind, 5, 8, 15, 21, 22, 23–33, 34, 36, 37, 39, 41, 43, 47–49, 53, 57, 58, 61, 62, 71, 73, 74, 75–76, 78, 79, 80, 83, 84, 86, 87, 88, 90, 91, 95, 96, 107, 137–38, 145, 149, 166, 167
mind–body problem, 86, 147
mind-dependent beings, 33, 41, 43, 47, 161
mind in a vat, 83, 84, 92, 161

minority rights, 126–27
models, 53, 76, 168
modernism, 31
monads, 37
monasticism, 18, 70
monetary policy, 127
monism, 35, 38–39
moral efficacy, 100, 116
moral (the moral), xiv, 4, 12, 17, 19, 21, 25, 35, 61, 71, 85, 98–132, 133, 137, 143, 146, 147, 149, 150, 163, 164, 168, 171, 174, 176
morality. See "moral"
motivation, 129, 131
movement, 44, 45, 56, 60, 66, 95, 116
mythology, 10–11

narrative, 31, 47, 48, 133, 172
natural law, 100, 103, 105, 116–18, 122, 143, 150, 163, 168
nature philosophy, 13, 63
necessity, 27, 74, 79, 92, 109
negations, 47
negative rights, 127
neighbors, 149
neoplatonism, 14, 17, 25
neo-Thomism, 6, 135–36
neurosciences, 2
Newtonian physics, 12
nobility, 109
nominalism, 12, 18–19, 34, 35, 37, 42, 61, 105
non-being, 65
non-sequiturs, 166
normative truth claims, 96–97
noumena, 21, 74, 86, 91, 94, 136–37
numbers, 5, 13, 40, 47, 167

obedience, 113
obligations, 123, 163, 168
observations, 92
Ockham's razor. See "principle of parsimony"
ontology, 98, 106, 111, 139, 147, 169
operativity, 148
opinion, 80, 82, 105, 162
optimism, 10, 22, 25, 73, 116, 128, 130
optimization, 127

original position, 124
original sin, 71, 166
Ottomans, 6
ousia. See "substance"
outcomes, 118, 122–23, 125, 126, 164, 172
overman, 25

pain, 16, 24, 104, 107, 110, 118, 125, 126, 130–31, 150
pantheism, 38
paradigm shifts, 12
participation. See "instantiation"
patriotism, 126
perception, 11, 21, 36, 71, 72, 73–74, 77, 81, 86, 87, 89, 91, 117, 137, 162, 167
perdurantism, 45
perennial tradition. See "Aristotelian-Thomas Tradition"
perfection, 61, 62, 71, 101, 109, 173
person, 9, 20, 22, 26, 29, 32, 44, 55, 57, 60, 64, 66, 82, 86, 95, 98, 108, 109, 111, 113, 121, 124, 127–28, 130–31, 133, 138, 139, 140, 141, 142, 147, 148–49, 151, 165
personal preferences. See "emotivism"
personalism, 9, 31, 102, 131, 139, 146–50
pessimism, 116
phenomena, 21, 70, 74, 76–77, 86, 91, 94, 137–38, 161, 167, 170
phenomenalism, 9, 29, 67, 138, 140, 146, 147, 148, 162, 165
philosophy of language, 32
philosophy of religion, 32
philosophy of science, 32
phronesis. See "practical knowledge"
Pietism, 119
place, 60, 95
pleasure, 16, 24, 66, 104, 110, 110, 118, 120, 125–26, 130–31, 150
pluralism, 35, 38–39
poisoning the well, 166
politics, 6, 9, 20, 21, 24, 26, 111, 123
positive law, 150
positive rights, 123
positivism, 22, 24–25

possible worlds, 169, 174
possibles. See "potential real being"
postmodernism, 12, 26, 31, 38, 67, 103, 107, 111, 133, 134, 144, 149, 150, 163, 167–68
posture, 50, 95
potency, 43–44, 46, 65, 75, 137
potential being, 39, 43–46, 57, 137
potential real being, 43–44, 58, 61, 65, 95, 96
power, 20, 25, 31, 46, 70, 87, 88, 89, 91, 101, 103, 104, 107, 111, 133, 149, 150
Power structures, 168
practical knowledge, 76, 114
pragmatism, 26, 31, 67, 123, 128–31
prayer, 2–3, 24, 62, 88, 117, 161
predestination, 105, 112
predicamentals, 59–60, 61, 95–96, 160
predication, 59–60
preexistent knowledge. See "recollection"
preference utilitarians, 126
preferential option for the poor, 151
premises, 92–93, 162, 163, 172–73
prescriptivism, 132
presence, 51, 139, 161
presocratics, 1, 13–14
pride, 141
primary substances, 13
principle of parsimony, 37, 168–69
prison reform, 124
privatization, 127
probability, 85, 93, 94, 160
procedural justice, 98, 123–24
progress, 22, 23, 31, 85, 101, 130, 148
prohaireses. See "purposive choices"
project, 143
proofs of God's existence, 18–19, 82, 92, 173–74
properties. See "accidents"
property rights, 107, 123, 127, 128, 131, 151
propositions, 27–28, 40, 47, 49, 72, 78, 87, 94–97, 144, 161, 162, 164, 165, 167, 168, 172, 174
prosperity, 121
proto-metaphysicians, 13–14

providence, 62, 116
prudence, 100, 103, 108, 110, 114, 119, 131, 150
psychology, 1, 29, 32, 139, 169
puritan ethic, 132
purpose. See "meaning"
purposive choices, 104, 148
Pythagoreans, 13, 25

quaestio disputatae, 19
quality, 60, 95
quantity, 60, 95
quiddity. See "essence"
quodlibetical disputation. See "scholastic method"

ratiocination, 169
rationalism, 14, 19, 21, 63, 67, 68, 69, 70, 72–73, 76, 78, 80, 83–84, 85, 89, 90–91, 92, 93, 107, 110, 136, 149, 162, 163, 166
realism, xi, xii, 3, 4–5, 7, 8, 10, 13, 15, 16, 19, 33–35, 38, 39–40, 41, 50, 52, 58, 61, 63, 68–70, 74–76, 78, 79–82, 83, 86–90, 92–93, 99–102, 105, 106, 110, 130, 131, 133, 134, 144, 145, 163
realpolitik, 10
reason, 4, 5, 8, 11, 19, 41, 43, 45, 46, 47, 49, 57, 61, 62, 69, 70–72, 73, 75, 76, 79, 87, 88, 90, 104, 105, 106, 108, 115, 116–17, 118, 168, 170
recollection, 72, 78, 86, 90, 93, 161, 165
red herrings, 166
reduction, 27, 28, 29, 149, 169–70
reflection, 40, 42, 68, 69, 78, 79, 82, 83, 93, 94, 133, 148, 151, 165, 171
Reformation, 8, 18, 71, 100, 101, 102, 122
Reformed Tradition, 22, 111–12
regressive argumentation, 170
relations, 60, 95
relativism, 2, 5, 12, 61, 99, 102–3, 118, 149
religion, 16, 30, 32, 73, 111–12, 113, 124, 126, 130
Religion of Humanity, 24
Renaissance, 8, 9, 20

reparations, 128
ressourcement, 151
results. See "outcomes"
retributive justice, 98
revelation, 2, 4, 19, 72, 169
rhetoric, 14, 170
right to vote, 125
risk aversion, 125, 131
romanticism, 112
root sin, 141
Rule of St. Benedict, 18, 68
Russian Revolution, 24

sanctification, 112
scholastic method, 19, 164
scholasticism, 112
science, 1, 2, 3, 7, 8, 20, 21, 22, 26, 27, 29, 30, 31, 32, 36, 54, 55, 67, 74, 81, 89, 93, 110, 114, 129, 144, 169, 170, 172
scientific method, 73, 94, 128, 170
scientism, 35, 38, 85, 170
Scripture, 18, 89, 105, 122, 142, 151, 161
Second Vatican Council, 82, 146, 148, 151, 171
see-judge-act, 151, 171
self. See "person"
self-ownership, 107, 127–28
seminaries, 101, 133
semiotics, 171
sense data, 21, 70–71, 73, 83, 86–89, 91, 93
sense impressions, 78, 88, 89, 91
sense of the faithful, 82
sense-making, 11, 34, 73, 82, 85
senses, 5, 39, 46, 51, 59, 70, 71, 72, 73, 78, 87–88, 91, 137, 167
sensible world, 5, 7, 12, 13, 14, 15, 16, 18, 21, 33–34, 35, 36, 38, 40, 41, 44, 45–46, 48–49, 50, 51, 53, 54–55, 57, 58, 59, 61–62, 63, 69, 71, 72–74, 76–77, 78–79, 80, 82, 85, 86, 87, 91, 92, 94, 107, 137, 138, 145, 147, 163
sensuality, 141
sensus fidelium. See "sense of the faithful"
sentences, 94
Sermon on the Mount, 112

servant leadership, 141
set theory, 26, 171
signs and symbols, 134
sin, 3, 71, 100, 101, 116, 117, 125
situational sensitivity, 119
skepticism, 14, 21, 37, 68–69, 70, 73,
    80, 83–84, 86, 93, 135, 149
slavery, 127, 128
slippery slope, 171
social conventions, 16
social imaginaries, 10, 48
social justice, 33, 26, 151
social stratification, 102
socialism, 132, 146
sola gratia, 111
solidarity, 151
solipsism, 5, 149
sophistry, 13–14, 103
soul, 2, 9, 46, 55, 87, 89
space and time, 12, 33, 38, 40, 43, 45,
    47, 50, 53, 56, 166, 169
special pleadings, 166
species and genera, 40, 44, 53
speech acts, 29
spirituality, 8, 12, 18, 71
Stalinism, 23
standards of behavior, 4, 103, 119
statements, 72, 94
states of affairs, 28, 40, 47
straw man arguments, 166
stochastic processes, 172
stoicism, 3, 10, 16, 19
story-telling, 11, 172
subject, 30, 36, 47, 50, 51, 59, 64, 75, 94,
    131, 138, 172
subjective experience, 29
subjectivism, 5, 99, 102, 149, 150
subsistence, 41, 42–43, 47, 145
subsistents, 41, 56
substance, 13, 33, 34, 37, 38, 41, 42–43,
    45–46, 49, 52, 54–55, 56, 58–60,
    61–64, 66, 74, 78, 88, 95, 105,
    137, 143, 147
substantia prima, 52
substantia secunda, 52
substantial change, 55, 63–65
substratum, 49–50
suffering, 23, 105, 140, 148

supererogatory, 101–2, 112
suppositum, 52, 54
syllogisms, 92–93, 166, 172–73
synthesis, 24, 164
synthetic a priori knowledge, 77, 79, 137

tabula rasa. See "blank slate"
tautologies, 72, 78, 167, 174
taxation, 127, 128
techne, 76
teleology, 35, 38, 56, 65, 106, 109
telos, 44, 62, 98, 108, 110, 121, 172
temperance, 100, 103, 108, 110, 114,
    131, 150
Ten Commandments, 101, 103, 112,
    117, 133
testimony, 86–87, 89–90, 174
text, 26, 30
theodicy, 19, 32
theological reflection, 151, 171
theology, xi, xiii, 3, 6, 8, 12, 18, 19, 33, 53,
    100, 101, 107, 110, 147, 161, 176
Theology of the body, 29, 147
theory of relativity, 12
thesis, 24, 164
things. See "entities"
thisness. See "essence"
Thomism, xiv, 6, 9, 29–30, 133–51
thought experiments, 83, 124, 169, 174
three hierarchs, 17
thrownness, 25
timeframe problem, 126
transcendence, 63, 148–49
transcendental idealism, 21, 36, 37, 68,
    76, 136
transcendental properties, 61–63, 74
transcendental reflection, 94
transcendental Thomism, 6, 136–38
transubstantiation, 51–52
trope theory, 37
truth, 2, 4, 5, 11, 14, 21, 27, 30, 31, 47,
    55, 61–62, 63, 67, 68, 71, 72, 73,
    74, 77, 78, 79, 83, 84, 84, 86, 87,
    90, 92, 94–95, 96–97, 103, 105,
    108, 109, 115, 117, 128, 129,
    144, 147, 149, 160, 162, 163,
    164, 165, 166, 167, 168, 169,
    173, 174

truth claims, 11, 30, 47, 73, 78, 82, 92, 94, 96–97, 128, 144, 167
turn to the self, 26, 29
turn to the text, 30

übermensch. See "overman"
uniformity of nature, 92
unity, 17, 34, 38, 53, 57, 61, 69, 74, 137, 140
Universal Declaration of Human Rights, 118
universals, 5, 12, 18, 19, 34, 37–38, 47–49, 59, 171
universities, 1, 10, 19, 136
unmoved mover, 35, 80, 143
utiles, 24, 126–27
utilitarianism, 16, 22, 23, 31, 112, 118, 133, 126–27, 130, 131

vanity, 141

verification, 28, 73, 127
verisimilitude, 108, 116, 174
vice, 104, 108, 115–16
Vienna Circle, 25–26, 144
virtue ethics, xiv, 6, 12, 24, 31, 101, 112, 118, 137, 146, 150
virtues, 100, 101, 102, 103, 108, 109–10, 111–12, 113–18, 119, 120–21, 122, 132, 133, 141, 149, 150

warrants. See "evidence"
way of the cross, 141
wealth, 102, 124, 127, 128
whatness. See "essence"
will to power, 25, 103, 107, 149
witness, 63, 80, 82, 83, 89–90, 141
workers's rights, 151
world mind. See absolute mind

www.ingramcontent.com/pod-product-compliance
Lightning Source LLC
Chambersburg PA
CBHW071439150426
43191CB00008B/1176